DATE DUE

AP 29 '91			

DEMCO 38-296

FROM SAVAGE TO NOBLEMAN
Images of Native Americans in Film

by
MICHAEL HILGER

The Scarecrow Press, Inc.
Lanham, Md., & London

4 Pleydell Gardens, Folkestone
Kent CT20 2DN, England

British Cataloging in Publication Information Available

Library of Congress Cataloging-in-Publication Data

Hilger, Michael, 1940–
From savage to nobleman : images of Native Americans
in film / Michael Hilger.
p.   cm.
Includes bibliographical references and indexes.
1. Indians in motion pictures.   I. Title.
PN1995.9.I48H55   1995   791.43'6520397—dc20   94–42057

ISBN 0–8108–2978–9 (cloth : alk. paper)

Printed in the United States of America

 The paper used in this publication meets the minimum requirements of
American National Standard for Information Sciences—Permanence
of Paper for Printed Library Materials, ANSI Z39.48–1984.

To my wife, Melinda

ACKNOWLEDGMENTS

Thanks to Veda Stone, who encouraged me to apply for the grant that started this project; to Steve Swords, Roger Anderson and Marek Labinsky who assisted me with the initial research; to Nick Hilger and John Hoogesteger, who continue to help me understand the problems of urban Native Americans; to my students in English 242—(The American Indian in Literature and Film), at UW-Eau Claire, who always give me new insights; to Judith Bien of Video Vistas, who helped me find obscure videos; and to my wife, Melinda Smith, who edited the manuscript.

CONTENTS

CHAPTER ONE

FROM SAVAGE TO NOBLEMAN: TRADITIONAL IMAGES OF NATIVE AMERICANS

An incident from John Ford's *Cheyenne Autumn* (1964) dramatizes the two prevailing images of the fictional Native Americans in narrative film. A newspaper editor repeats the typical headlines about the Cheyenne in all the major papers, "Bloodthirsty Savages on the Loose, Burning, Killing, Violating Beautiful White Women," and concludes, "It's not news anymore." He then says, "We're going to take a different tack. We're going to 'Grieve of the Noble Red Man.' We'll sell more newspapers that way." With a disregard for historical accuracy similar to that of the editor, directors of the Westerns have used the images of the Savage or the Noble Red Man to show the superiority of their heroes, or to comment on political, social and moral issues of their day. These images force the Native American characters into a circle where they are ultimately too bad or too good to be believable fictional characters—a circle in which they also are only vehicles for contrast to white heroes of the Westerns and the values of white culture.

Behind this portrayal of Native American characters is also a movement of racial attitudes. At one extreme is the unconscious or overt racism of the Savage image; at the other extreme is liberal sympathy or pity for the mistreated, and often doomed, Noble Red Man. Somewhere between the extremes is empathy, a sense of understanding and respect for the uniqueness of Native American cultures, an attitude reflected primarily in recent films. As this study traces the images of the Savage and Noble Red Man through the historical periods of the cinema, it will reveal little about Native American people of the past or present, but a lot about the evolution of white American attitudes and values.

The image of the Savage, along with the racism it reflects and promotes, has been part of the Western from the beginning. In D. W. Griffith's *The Battle of Elderbush Gulch* (1913), a Native American tribe attacks a group of settlers who have killed the son of their chief. After the warriors sack a town, kill men, women and a baby, and are about to massacre some people in a ranch house, the Cavalry routs them. In Griffith's later film, *America* (1924), savage Mohawks fight with the British against the colonists and attack a fort, only to be driven off by the hero and his men. With seemingly endless minor variations, this plot formula, in which the Native Americans are wild, unpredictable Savages, motivated by vengeance and bent on raping and killing, became a staple of the Westerns. This image of the Savage persists through most of the history of the Western, and even though more recent films such as *Little Big Man* (1970), *The Outlaw Josey Wales* (1976) or *Dances with Wolves* (1990) seem to reject this image, they really just transfer it to evil white soldiers or politicians.

The opposing image of the Noble Red Man, and the associated guilt and pity for the vanishing Native American, also has been part of the Western from the beginning. In D. W. Griffith's *The Redman's View* (1909), white settlers displace a band of Kiowa from their land and finally allow the noble young Minnewanna, the chief's daughter, and her lover, Silver Eagle, to rejoin their banished tribe and visit the grave of her father. *The Biograph Bulletin* notes that the film beautifully depicts the suffering of Native Americans who were made "to trek from place to place by the march of progress which was ever forging its way into the West" (Bowser 149). Another Griffith film, *Iola's Promise* (1912), subtitled "How the Little Indian Maiden Paid her Debt of Gratitude," also follows the pattern of the Noble Red Man. After a white miner helps Iola, she repays him by rescuing his beloved just as she is about to be burned at the stake. Though Iola is fatally wounded in the rescue, she also shows her gratitude by locating gold for the man before she dies. Such stories of tribes being pushed out of existence by the settlers and soldiers, or of Native Americans good enough to be friendly to whites whatever the sacrifice, also became formulas. That the image of the Noble Red Man exists side by side with the image of the Savage in *Iola's Promise* and in other Griffith Westerns is not unusual. In fact, they are often juxtaposed to emphasize the nobleness of positive Native American characters like Iola. Throughout the history of the Western, these images continue to be unpredictably mixed until the Noble Red Man becomes the predominant image in recent Westerns such as *Little Big Man* (1970), *The Outlaw Josey Wales* (1976), *Dances with Wolves* (1990) and *Geronimo, An American Legend* (1993).

The Western always measures the goodness of the Noble Red Man and the badness of the Savage by the way these character types react to the superior white characters, never by their intrinsic nature as Native Americans or as members of different tribes and bands. The noble characters are good because they are friends to the whites and realize they must adapt to white culture or face extinction. On the other side of this equation, the savage characters are bad because they are enemies to the whites and obstacles to westward expansion. The profiles of typical female and male characters reveal this bias.

The noble female characters are usually darkly beautiful and sensual "princesses" who show a special willingness to love and be loyal to white men, even though they must often suffer for their devotion. Some of the most extreme examples of this type appear in the silent films. For instance, in *The Indian Squaw's Sacrifice* (1910), the title character, Noweeta, nurses a wounded white man back to health and then marries him. After they have a child, her husband meets a white woman he had loved before. When Noweeta realizes that her husband still loves the woman, she goes off to the woods and kills herself so that her husband can be free to marry the white woman. This same pattern, with minor variations, occurs in *The Kentuckian* (1908) and De Mille's *The Squaw Man* (1914), a film so popular that it was remade several times.

A similar character type is the noble young woman who decides to leave her beloved white man even though she still loves him deeply. For example, in *The Far Horizons* (1955) Sacajawea leaves Captain Clark at the end because she doesn't fit into his civilized life, and in *Captain John Smith and Pocahontas* (1953), the title character stays behind to keep the peace (and marry another white man) when John Smith returns to England. Like Pocahontas, the typical noble young woman will almost always choose to marry a white man rather than a man of her race.

However, the romances and marriages between Native American women and white men usually have a sad ending. For example, in *Broken Arrow* (1950), the beautiful Sonseeahray rejects the Apache she is promised to and marries the white hero, only to be gunned down at the end. In *A Man Called Horse* (1970), the lovely Running Deer refuses the offer of Black Eagle and weds the white hero, only to be killed during a battle with the Shoshone. This taboo against mixed romances and marriages in the plots of the Westerns persists even to *Dances with Wolves*, in which the "Lakota" woman who falls in love with the hero is really a white woman. When the characters involved in a mixed marriage or romance do survive, in films like *The Red Woman* (1917), *The Big Sky* (1952), or *Black Robe* (1991), they do so only in the wilderness, far away from white society. So, even though the good and beautiful Native American woman of the Westerns has a special ability to recognize the superiority of the white heroes, she is punished if her love or loyalty goes too far.

The opposing image is the savage female or "squaw" who is frequently hostile to whites and often a physically unattractive character. For example, in *The Last of the Mohicans* (1936) a crowd of ugly and mean-looking Huron women harass two white female captives and then, with diabolical looks on their faces, torture the hero by jabbing him with sharp sticks. In *A Man Called Horse* (1970), an old woman, Buffalo Cow Head, treats the hero very harshly at first, hitting him with a heavy stick. Though they adopt each other at the end, at one point the hero refers to her as "a horrible old hag." Even more sympathetic female characters become objects of derision if they are not beautiful. In *The Searchers* (1956), the young friend of the hero unwittingly acquires a plump Cheyenne "wife" whom he calls "Look." Immediately, she becomes the butt of humor when the snide hero ridicules their "marriage," and later when the young man kicks her away from his bedroll and she rolls down a hill. After she leaves their camp, they later find her body in a tepee of a village raided by soldiers. Even in this unrequited "romance," the female character dies. Ultimately, then, Native American female characters, whether they are beautiful or not, can seldom survive a companionship with a white man.

The companionship between the white hero and his Native American friend, on the other hand, is always positive and a key to the noble male. Some notable examples are Hawkeye and Chingachgook (*The Last of the Mohicans*) (1936), Tom Jeffords and Cochise (*Broken Arrow*) (1950), Josey Wales and Lone Watie (*The Outlaw Josey Wales*) (1976), John Dunbar and Kicking Bird (*Dances with Wolves*) (1990) and, of course, the Lone Ranger and Tonto. Because he is the hero, the white man is dominant in these companionships, but, especially in the more recent films, the Native American characters are somewhat more equal in knowledge and intelligence.

The most typical and well-known example of such a relationship is the story of the Lone Ranger and Tonto as portrayed on TV during the late '40s and early '50s. That legendary duo comes together when Tonto (Jay Silverheels), a member of a tribe which had been massacred, finds the Lone Ranger (a member of the Texas Rangers), who had been left for dead by the villains. Tonto recognizes the wounded man as "Kimosabe" (the bright scout) who had saved his life when they were boys. With typical gratitude, the noble Tonto uses traditional medicines to nurse the Ranger back to health. Then Tonto helps the Lone Ranger find and heal the white stallion, Silver, who had been wounded by a buffalo. Finally, Tonto gives the masked man the idea of using silver bullets to represent a new kind of justice not based on killing, and the two loners become friends who devote their lives to the cause of law and order in the old West. Because Tonto and his friend are caught up in a noble cause, especially given the concern for law and order and social responsibility in the 1950s, he is an admirable character, though one decidedly inferior to his white companion in his ability to speak English and think out problems. Not surprisingly, in a newer version of the story, *The Legend of the Lone Ranger* (1981), Tonto (Michael Horse) is less inferior to his white friend and not only speaks well, but is outspoken on Native American rights.

An episode from the 1950s Lone Ranger TV series, in which the masked man and Tonto help a starving tribe, epitomizes the basis for the images of the typical noble and savage male Native American characters. The Noble Red Men of this episode are a chief named White Hawk, his son, Little Hawk, and a boy called Arrow Foot. The Savage is White Hawk's other son, Fleet Horse, the pawn of white villains who are after silver on the tribe's land. The story begins as the Lone Ranger and Tonto rescue a stagecoach from an attack by the villains and find that one of the passengers is Little Hawk, a young man they know who is on his way back to his tribe after graduating from college. The heroes take Little Hawk, dressed in a suit and wearing a narrow headband over his short cropped hair, to his village. As he greets his father, his brother, Fleet Horse, appears, wearing an Apache tunic and sash and a headband over his long hair, and spouting anti-white rhetoric. In quick succession, the Lone Ranger defeats the evil brother in a traditional fight, and Little Hawk persuades his people to work to cultivate fields rather than follow his rebellious brother in a war with the whites. When the tribe agrees to work, the Lone Ranger promises to bring supplies which have been donated by the white settlers. Then he and Tonto capture the villains who have been inciting Fleet Horse to violence. At the end, with the tribe working diligently in nearby fields, White Hawk kills his son Fleet Horse. He then says to his noble son, "The bad part of me died with your brother; the good part will be reborn tomorrow when you become chief." Before the heroes leave, Tonto says to the Lone Ranger, "Them happy now, Kimosabe." Then, as they ride away, Little Hawk says to young Arrow Foot, who has learned his lesson about being a good Native American, "We should all give thanks to the men who made it possible to hold our heads up and walk with pride."

By contemporary standards the messages of this episode are, of course, too extreme and obvious. However, the paternalism of the hero, the sneering exploitation of the white villains, the portrayal of the Native Americans according to their acceptance of, or rebellion against, white values are part of most Westerns, in varying degrees of subtlety. This Lone Ranger episode also reveals one other typical kind of noble Native American, the wise older chief. The basis of White Hawk's wisdom (and his rejection of his rebellious son) is his belief that his tribe must adopt the new ways of the more educated whites if they are to survive. Other peace-loving chiefs, like Old Lodge Skins in *Little Big Man* (1970), have a similar belief that their tribes cannot escape the domination of the whites and thus must face extinction or learn to accommodate their way of life to that of the whites. Once again a typical noble character is portrayed according to his acceptance of white superiority.

Another measure of the noble or savage Native American male of the Westerns is his attitude toward white women. Just as the noble female characters are drawn to white males, so also are the noble males attracted to white women. And their romances often come to the same sad endings as those of the females, again because of a taboo against miscegenation. For example, in *A Red Man's Love* (1910) the Native American abandons the woman from his tribe he has promised to marry after he falls in love with a white woman whom his tribe has captured. Motivated by his love, he rejects his tribe, rescues the woman, and brings her to the home of her father. However, when he asks the white woman to marry him, she and her family cruelly reject him. Another classic example is the romance between Nophaie and Marion, the white school teacher, in *The Vanishing American* (1925). The noble Nophaie's love, which can never be truly requited, pushes him to numerous grand and selfless actions, including his death as he tries to restore peace between his tribe and the whites.

On the other hand, the savage characters, driven by their

hostility, capture and rape white women. For instance, in *The Stalking Moon* (1968), a renegade Apache kills many whites as he tries to recapture his white wife and son. The woman deeply fears the savage warrior who had captured her and given her only the choice of death or marriage. She is safe and happy only when the hero finally kills her savage husband. Another example of the way savage characters treat captured white females occurs in *The Searchers* (1956). The Comanches first rape and kill a mother and then kidnap her daughters, one of whom they also rape and kill later. As the heroes search for the other daughter, they observe at an army post the bodies of captured women and the survivors who have been driven to pathetic states of insanity by their Comanche captors. Near the end of the film, when the hateful hero finds the surviving daughter, he tries to kill her because she has lived with the Chief Scar of the Comanches. Later he rescues her only after achieving a catharsis of his hate by scalping the dead body of Scar. *The Searchers*, one of the great Westerns, is sadly also a prime example of the racism behind the portrayal of the savage Native American as defiler of white women.

The savage, hostile characters, like the Comanche, Scar, or Fleet Horse of the Lone Ranger episode, are the fierce, unscrupulous adversaries of the white hero and thus the antagonists in typical plots of the Westerns. Often they are rebellious young braves like Fleet Horse who reject their peace-loving old chiefs and join the white villains to accomplish their evil ends. Or they are hostile bands who ambush stagecoaches and attack everything from remote farms to pony express riders. In the older films, the stock savage characters are often neither identified by tribe, nor given adequate motivation for their vengeance; they are simply the melodramatic villains who complicate the plot and allow the heroes to triumph over them. In the later films, especially those of the '50s. and '60s, the hostile characters have clearer motivation. Even in *The Searchers* (1956), the Comanche chief, Scar, attacks the farm of the hero's relatives and kidnaps the two girls because whites have killed two of his sons. In fact, the sympathy towards Native Americans in films like *Apache* (1954) or *Geronimo* (1962) can often be measured by the degree of motivation given to the main characters. Whatever the motivation, however, the savage Native Americans of the Western must be vanquished by the hero and the degree of ignominy or honor in their inevitable defeat is another measure of sympathy.

Generally, then, whether the Native American characters are friendly or hostile, they have a poor survival rate in the plots of the Westerns. These stereotyped film characters are victims of their primitive emotions: if treated well, they are capable of love, loyalty or gratitude so powerful that it can become destructive; if treated badly, they are capable of vengeance so tenacious and fierce that it surely will lead to their destruction. And, of course, such characters emphasize the superiority of white society and the male hero, which is the primary wish fulfillment that drives the genre of the Western. With only minor variations, from the beginnings of the Western to *Dances with Wolves,* all Native American characters have been reduced to the extremes of Noble Red Man or the Savage. The repetition of these images encodes or programs audiences, depending on their individual backgrounds, to believe they really know Native Americans as mistreated noblemen or dangerous enemies. As Frederic Jameson notes, "movies are a physical experience, and are remembered as such, stored up in bodily synapses that evade the thinking mind" (1). Audiences of the Westerns "remember" Native Americans according to the repeated content of the images. They feel they own these characters who exist as pictures in their memories, pictures which never talk back and which behave in wonderfully predictable ways. However, if audiences can learn to recognize the content of the images and see that they have been a consistent and fairly obvious part of the Westerns, they can begin to reduce this level of encoding rather quickly .

A more complicated encoding, however, involves the form of the movies, the film techniques used to color attitudes towards the Native American characters in individual films. From the beginning, the directors of Westerns have played upon certain basic film techniques in their portrayal of Native Americans. Long, medium and close-up shots, camera angles, composition, editing and acting are key to what the film "language" says about Native American characters. The repetition of these techniques throughout the history of the Western deeply encodes attitudes towards Native Americans in audiences. A discussion of the portrayal of Native Americans in narrative film, therefore, must not only consider the content of the images but also how attitudes towards Native American characters are expressed by film techniques.

The distance and angle from which audiences see characters and settings are basic techniques filmmakers use to shape responses. The long shot, which gives a view of the whole scene, emphasizes the setting or environment. In the Western, the landscape is central and thus long shots are common and often the first perspective from which the audience sees hostile tribes about to attack. A classic example occurs in John Ford's *Stagecoach* (1939), a film in which the threat of an attack by Apaches is a major source of tension. Just before the attack, Ford cuts to a long shot of the stagecoach from a bluff high above (a high-angle shot), to a long shot of the Apaches on the bluff from the perspective of the stagecoach (a low-angle shot), and then to a medium shot of the Apaches, and finally to a close-up shot of their leader, Geronimo (both low-angle shots). The long shot starts this scene; then the camera angles, medium and close-up shots, and editing all work together to manipulate the reaction of the audience to the attack. As we shall see when we look at the other techniques Ford uses in this scene (camera angles and editing), the form of the shots emphasizes the basic image of the savage Apaches. The long shot also can be used to portray the noble but doomed Red Man. For example, at the end of *The Vanishing American* (1925), in an extreme long shot of considerable duration, a funeral procession for the dead warrior, Nophaie, starts to fade away into the landscape (and sunset). This long shot gives the audience the illusion that the hero and his tribe are literally vanishing.

The medium shot, which focuses on a character from the knees to the head, is a more neutral perspective than the long shot and often is as close as the audience gets to Native American characters in the Western. The close-up shot, however, focuses attention on a character's face or a significant object in the setting. A pattern of such shots of the hero, for example, will cause the audience to identify with and respect the character. On the other hand, a close-up of a character whom the audience has seen only in long shots or not at all, such as Geronimo in *Stagecoach*, will cause fear or a sense of threat. A prime example is the first view of Scar, the savage Comanche chief, in John Ford's *The Searchers* (1956). Ford's camera follows a little girl who runs from her home, which is about to be attacked by the Comanche, and tries to hide. Then he cuts to a close high-angle shot of the girl as she cowers to the ground while a shadow moves over her. Finally, he cuts to a close-up of Scar's face from the low-angle perspective of the girl. The shot, angle and lighting (Scar's face is lit from below) make the savage character deeply threatening and memorable.

In the above examples from the two John Ford Westerns, camera angles were a key part of the shot's effect. In the low-angle shot, the camera looks up at the subject and makes it appear imposing, strong or threatening, as in the above-mentioned close-ups of Geronimo and Scar. In the high-angle shot, the camera looks down on the subject and makes it appear dominated, powerless or threatened, as in the long shot of the stagecoach. These camera angles have characteristic patterns in the Westerns: the white hero is often "looked up to" in a series of low-angle shots, whereas victims of hostile tribes or warriors defeated by the heroes frequently are seen from a high-angle. In some of the newer Westerns like *Broken Arrow* (1950) or *Little Big Man* (1970), the low-angle shot is used to portray noble Native American characters like Cochise, who is usually seen in medium and close-up low-angle shots, or Old Lodge Skins, who is frequently seen in warmly lit low-angle close-ups.

In Westerns, techniques of composition, especially placement of characters in the frame, often favor the white hero by placing him more in the foreground and higher in the frame than the other characters. Such placement is typical in films with Native Americans who are companions of the hero. For instance, in the Lone Ranger series the hero is often placed in a more emphatic position than his friend,

Tonto. In *The Last of the Mohicans* (1936), Chingachgook and Uncas usually appear on either side of and slightly behind Hawkeye. A more recent film, *The Outlaw Josey Wales* (1976), breaks from this pattern when Wales and Ten Bears, the Comanche chief who is very much his equal, are placed in close to the same plane in the frame. In each of these examples, the way the placement directs the attention of audiences has a subtle, and maybe unconscious, effect on whether they remember the Native Americans as positive or negative characters.

Editing also controls the attention and feelings of the audience. In the Westerns some of the most powerful examples occur in the depiction of attacks by hostile tribes. In the above example from *Stagecoach* (1939), Ford's slow pace of cutting between the shots leading up to the attack of the Apaches (for the purpose of suspense) changes to a more rapid cross-cutting between the two lines of action, the attacking warriors and the whites defending themselves in the stagecoach. The cross-cutting from the tracking shots (the camera moving at the speed of the horses) of the Apaches gaining on the stagecoach to the reactions of those riding inside lets the audience identify with the whites as victims. This cross-cutting builds to the point where the pregnant woman in the stagecoach is about to shoot herself to avoid being captured. Then the sound of the bugle signals a cut to the cavalry routing the Apaches. In *The Searchers* (1956) Ford intensifies the horror of an impending attack by cross-cutting between the men who learn they have been tricked by the Comanches into leaving the farm and the helpless people on the farm as they realize the Comanche are about to attack. In each line of action, Ford focuses on the reactions of anxiety and terror among the white characters. In fact, he never shows the attack itself, but only the reactions of the men who return to find the bodies. This classic example of manipulation, in which what is not shown is more terrifying and involving than what is shown, leaves the audience with an intense feeling that the whites have been terribly victimized by the savage Comanche.

In more recent films, editing, especially cross-cutting and

rapid cutting, also has been used to influence the audience's attitude toward sympathetic, noble Native American characters who are attacked by evil soldiers. In *Little Big Man* (1970) the editing of Custer's attack on the Cheyenne camped at the Washita River is a striking example. The cross-cutting between the hero's somewhat humorous rescue of Old Lodge Skins, who thinks he's invisible, and rapid successions of shots of Cheyenne women and children being brutally murdered by the soldiers emphasizes the horrible victimization of the tribe. This feeling is punctuated at the end of the sequence by a cut from a slow-motion shot of the hero's Cheyenne wife and their baby being killed to a shot of the hero watching helplessly, during which the harsh sounds of the attack drop out, and the silence lets the horror of the massacre impact on the audience.

Another example of such editing occurs in *Windwalker* (1980), in which a Cheyenne family are the good characters and a group of Crow warriors pursuing them are the villains. Because this film has only a small amount of dialogue, the action sequences become crucial for engaging the audience. In one scene, the director depicts the movement of the hero and his family through the woods in a tracking shot (the camera and audience move with the characters) from a slightly high-angle perspective that suggests their vulnerability. Then he cross-cuts to low-angle close shots of the Crow in their warpaint, positioning themselves for the attack on snow-covered ridges above the family. The contrast of their war paint with the snow seen in close up shots makes them appear especially threatening. Thus cross-cutting not only builds suspense but also draws the sympathy of the audience to the noble Cheyenne

As the above example from *Little Big Man* indicates, the use of sound complements the impressions of Native American characters. For the savage characters, especially during war dances and attacks on whites, their almost otherworldly whooping and yelping is the most common sign of their terrible fury. In addition, music, whether in the background or as part of the synchronous sound, sends somewhat more subtle messages about such characters. The rhythmic imitation of war drums, with its descending parallel tones, signals the presence of hostile tribes and builds suspense about when they will attack. Also, of course, the sound of the bugle signifies the rescue of the white victims by the cavalry and the impending defeat of the hostiles. Such synchronous music also can create sympathy for noble Native American characters. In *Little Big Man*, the drum rolls and the melody of "Gerry Owen," played by Custer's band, strengthen the feeling of pity for the Cheyenne in the Washita massacre sequence discussed above. Finally, in addition to synchronous sound and the musical score, another technique, the voice-over (the use of narration in which the words are not spoken by anyone on the screen), conditions the response of the audience to the Native American characters. In such films as *Broken Arrow* (1950), *Dances with Wolves* (1990), *Son of the Morning Star* (1990), and *Geronimo, An American Legend* (1993), voice-overs by the hero or heroine reinforce the already positive images of the noble characters and tribes.

All of the above film techniques encode the images of the Savage and Noble Red Man. Another key element in this process is acting, especially in the sense of the actor as a presence on the screen. The non-Native American actors who played most of the major Native American characters in the Westerns often acted their parts well, but they were not believable as screen presences, especially when Native American actors played minor characters in the film. Long after the powers of Hollywood decided that white actors could no longer play Black or Asian characters, they still chose them for Native Americans in the Westerns. This practice began to change, though very slowly, when actors like Chief Dan George in *Little Big Man* (1970) and *The Outlaw Josey Wales* (1976), and Jay Silverheels as Tonto before him, illustrated the importance of having Native American actors play Native characters. The screen presence of Jay Silverheels gave the character of Tonto a dignity that could not be destroyed by all its other negative elements, and the presence of Chief Dan George as Old Lodge Skins and Lone Watie dramatized conclusively the believability that a Native American actor could infuse into a major character. The recognition of what Native Americans could

bring to the screen led to the selection of actors like Will
Sampson, Graham Greene, and Rodney Grant to play major
characters in Hollywood films. The use of Native American
actors, which is becoming more and more a given in
significant independent and Hollywood films, is the major
step towards a more empathetic portrayal of Native American characters. This, in turn, will encode more positive and
realistic images of Native Americans.

Like acting, all of the above film techniques are part of a
film "language" that repeats itself and changes throughout
and beyond the history of the Western. This book will trace
the images of the Savage and Noble Red Man, and the film
language used to express them, throughout the history of
film. Each chapter will begin with a discussion of representative films of that historical period, with attention to both
the content of their images of Native Americans and their
use of film technique. These interpretations of representative films will provide a context for the plot summaries that
make up the remainder of the chapters.

The summaries of the films for each period will be
arranged under the images of the Savage and the Noble Red
Man, with the appropriate narrative and thematic subhead-
ings for each category. Whenever possible the summaries
are based on a viewing of the film, but some are drawn from
plot summaries and reviews. Comments from contemporary reviews, which accompany some of the plot summaries, will suggest, at least to a limited degree, the encoding
of stereotypes for each period.*

The summaries will focus on the role of the Native
American characters in the plot and thus pass over, in some
cases, major elements of the plot as a whole. Their purpose,
and that of their organization, is to provide an overall
context from which the reader can evaluate the content and
film technique of individual films. Because of their brevity,
they will, of course, never catch the nuances, and are always
meant to be just a preface to a careful viewing of the film. As
an example, the summary of *Dances with Wolves* is quite
similar to those of other modern Westerns with a sympathetic view of the Native American. Within the overall
context, that touted film is only a little different, but those

differences—the careful integration of the Lakota language
and the casting of just the right Native American actors to
play all the Native characters—are truly unique. This book
emphasizes similarities among the films, whereas a careful
viewing of individual films will always reveal a fascinating
series of variations.

NOTE

*References to film reviews are parenthetical in the text, and the
year of the review is the same as that of the film unless otherwise
noted. Most quotes from *Variety* and the *New York Times (NYT)*
are taken from *The Variety Film Reviews* and *The New York Times
Film Reviews,* both of which arrange the reviews by year, month
and day. Hence the references to these sources will not contain
page numbers.

For other discussions of Native Americans in media, see
O'Connor's *The Hollywood Indian* and Stedman's *Shadows of the
Indian.* See also Spears' "The Indian on the Screen," Price's "The
Stereotyping of North American Indians in Motion Pictures,"
Marsden and Nachbar's "Images of Native Americans in Popular
Film," Calder's "Taming the Natives" in Calder's *There Must Be a
Lone Ranger,* Tuska's "Images of Indians" in his *The American
Western in Film,* and the entry, "Indians/Native Americans" in
Buscombe's *The BFI Companion to the Western.*

CHAPTER TWO

THE SILENT FILMS

Especially in the early part of the Silent era, which began less than twenty years after Wounded Knee, Native Americans are a very popular subject for narrative films. Among the films of the first star of the Westerns, Bronco Billy, are *The Cowboy and the Squaw*, *The Dumb Half-breed's Defense*, *An Indian Girl's Love*, *The Faithful Indian* and *The Tribe's Penalty* (Weaver, 30–31); and among the films of the first movie studios in New Jersey are *His Indian Bride*, *How the Boys Fought the Indians*, *The Indian Land Grab*, *The Redman and the Child*, *An Up-to-Date Squaw* and *The True Heart of the Indian* (from listings in Spehr). Although many of the early films are no longer extant, the ones that remain and contemporary film reviews suggest that a considerable number of films had a sympathetic view of Native American characters as Noble Red Men. However, the image of the Savage also found its way into many films, especially towards the end of the Silent period when the Western became a more defined genre. Two early films by D. W. Griffith, *Iola's Promise* (1912) and *The Battle at Elderbush Gulch* (1913), represent well these opposing images in the first part of this era. Later in the period, *The Vanishing American* (1925) not only develops a more complicated image of the Noble but doomed Red Man, but also depicts the central Native American character as a victim of white prejudice. And, finally, *The Silent Enemy* (1930) uses native actors to portray the culture of Native Americans before contact with whites. These films mark continuing patterns in the history of the Western.

Contemporary film reviews reveal the controversy over

the portrayal of Native American characters. In a 1912 review of the Bison 101 Headliners, Louis R. Harrison rejects the portrayal of Native Americans as victims and argues that it was historically appropriate for whites, "the representatives of progress," to overcome "the representatives of degeneration." Harrison sees the Native American as a person who uses only "that part of his brain which enabled him to be crafty in the hunt for food." On the other hand, the white man "cultivated brain along with brawn," and was able to conquer the inferior native tribes because the settler was "a man, every inch of him, and the iron in his blood has descended to those who promulgated the Monroe doctrine" (*Moving Picture World*, 27 Apr., 320–22). Harrison's view of Native Americans in this and other reviews represents the attitudes of white supremacy and racism that demanded the image of the Savage.

Harrison's need to write such reviews, however, suggests that the opposing image of the Noble Red Man, and the associated liberal belief that Native Americans were being mistreated by whites, is prominent in the early Westerns. Another writer for *Moving Picture World* represents this view. In a 1911 review, he argues that the public is aware that Native Americans have been "misjudged and slandered in the past" because the new movies are "helping to set the Red Man right in history and in his position before the American people." He points out that the best Western films hold up the nobility of the Indian way of life to "the belated admiration" of the white audience, and concludes that "this tendency to do the Indian justice runs through all the pictures" and accounts "for the continued popularity of Indian films" (5 Aug., 271). Films such as *Lo, the Poor Indian* (1910), in which the character is punished by laws he doesn't understand, or Griffith's *Ramona* (1910), based on a popular Helen Hunt Jackson novel about the plight of Native Americans, are examples of early attempts to raise social consciousness.

D. W. Griffith's *Iola's Promise* (1912) highlights the image of the Noble Red Man, but also uses the opposing Savage image. At the beginning, Iola (Mary Pickford), a maiden who has been captured by cutthroat villains, is rescued by a

Yankee prospector, who takes her to his cabin, treats her wounds and feeds her. The note between the scenes describes her reaction: "And the simple savage touched by the goodness of her benefactor gave him her heart in a sudden ecstasy of gratitude." This beautiful woman, draped in a blanket and wearing her dark hair in a head band, promises to help the miner to find gold. When he asks her to cross her heart on the promise, she calls the whites "cross heart people" and devotes herself to them. Because the prospector she loves has told her to do so, she reluctantly returns to her village, described as "The camp of Iola's savage and turbulent tribe." Though Griffith paints Iola as a noble character, he depicts the other members of her tribe, especially the warriors, as typical Savages.

When a wagon train comes near their camp, the warriors ride out and stage a fierce attack, during which they are seen from a high angle as they ride around the wagons in "the circle of death." During the attack, the warriors drag away the prospector's sweetheart and her father, roughly tie them to a tree and pile up branches for "the terrible death at the stake." At this point Iola tells them not to hurt the cross heart people, but they push her away. Iola, however, rescues the whites by taking the woman's hat and cloak so that the braves chase and shoot her while the others escape. After the miners drive off the hostile warriors, the prospector's girl tells him that Iola "let them shoot her to save us." He rushes to find her, and, fatally wounded, she staggers towards him and shows the gold she has found for him. He reaches to shake her hand and says, "Put her there. Girl, you sure done noble!" She tells him that she kept her promise and that he shouldn't feel bad because she won't suffer anymore. Then she dies in his arms (with his girl friend's arms around him), to end the story of "the Indian maid's supreme sacrifice." Iola is a prime example of the grateful, loyal and noble character who is willing to give even her life for the white man. As such, she is a perfect foil to the savagery of her tribe.

Similar noble Native American characters, many of whom are in love with a white person even though they are from tribes hostile to whites, persist throughout the Silent period. A notable example of this type is the character of Nophaie (Richard Dix) in *The Vanishing American* (1925). Although this film is sympathetic to the Native American, it uses the image of the Noble but doomed Red Man to stress the superiority of white society in general and the Christian religion in particular. At the beginning, the filmmakers use a note between the scenes, the parallel of the voice-over for silent films, to quote Herbert Spencer's idea that in history, as in nature, the fittest survive. As the film progresses, the story of a Noble but doomed Red Man, Nophaie, the Warrior, shows how the Native Americans lose the Darwinian battle for survival to the whites.

In a long prologue depicting the history of native people in North America, Nophaie first appears as the "Indian" conqueror of the Cliff Dwellers, one of whom prophesies that a stronger race will eventually conquer the Native Americans. In the next episode, the Spaniards appear and challenge the Warrior. Nophaie, seen in an extreme long shot from the low-angle perspective of the Spaniards, rides his white horse back and forth on the high bluff and seems invincible. However, one shot from a Spanish gun kills him, and his death moves large numbers of Native Americans, already weakened by Spanish wine, to bow in homage to a few Spanish soldiers. In the final episode of the prologue, set in the early days of the United States, Kit Carson and the cavalry challenge Nophaie and his tribe. Again Nophaie rides his white horse on a high bluff, and this time he is killed by a shot from a cannon positioned far below him. The members of his tribe end up, contrary to the promises of Kit Carson, dominated by an evil Indian agent on a reservation. In this setting, Nophaie appears as the main character of the film.

On the reservation, Nophaie, the Warrior, meets the forces that will ultimately destroy him as the symbolic leader of his tribe. His first mistake is falling in love with Marion, the white school teacher on the reservation, and accepting her Christian religion. In one scene, Marion reads her Bible to Nophaie, who is seen from a slight high angle sitting on the floor at her feet, as she teaches him about self-denial and martyrdom. This perspective suggests the

Warrior is less powerful than the white woman and is already being controlled by her religion. This control becomes apparent later in a scene during World War One when a little Bible given to him by Marion prompts Nophaie to save the life of his white rival for her affections. After the war, as Nophaie tries to worship the gods of his tribe, he looks at the Bible and decides to invoke instead the Christian god. Finally, near the end of the film, as he tries to stop the attack of his people on the whites, he is fatally shot in the chest through the little Bible.

The attack of his tribe on the evil Indian agent, Booker, is fully justified. While the men of the tribe have been away fighting for their country, Booker (who dies from an arrow through his throat) had taken their land and caused the death of a young woman from the tribe. In spite of this, Nophaie, motivated by the Christian spirit, tries to stop the fighting, only to be fatally wounded by one of his own people. While lying on the ground with Marion holding him in her arms and a member of his tribe on either side, he says, in his last words, that he finally understands the idea that losing one's life means gaining everlasting life. The Warrior has literally become a saint, a martyr whose death brings peace between his people and the whites. However, this act marks the ultimate end of the warrior spirit because it has been transformed into a Christian spirit.

The film ends with an extreme long shot of a lengthy procession of the tribe vanishing into the horizon as they carry the body of Nophaie away for burial. This procession makes a striking image of the Noble but doomed Red Man slowly but steadily being moved out of the picture by the stronger society and religion of the whites. Such an image fills the audience with sympathy, but the film as a whole frees them from any direct sense of responsibility because it suggests that the destruction of Native American culture is just the natural result of social evolution.

Another notable film of the late part of the era, *The Silent Enemy* (1930), also uses the Noble but doomed Red Man image, but counteracts it with the outcome of its plot. The film deals exclusively with Native American life before contact with the white man, as did a considerable number of silent films with titles such as *The Squaw's Love* (1911), *The Legend of Scarface* (1910), *A Sioux Spy* (1911), *An Indian Idyll* (1912) and, of course, *Hiawatha* (1913). The film also has an all-Native cast, with a Sioux actor (Chief Yellow Robe) playing Chief Chetoga; a Blackfeet (Chief Long Lance) as the hero, Bulak; a Penobscot (Spotted Elk), as Newa, the woman who loves him; and an Ojibway (Chief Akawanush) as Dagwan. After noting the tribal heritage of the actors, the filmmakers explain that the film was "produced with a full awareness that the Indian and the wilderness were both rapidly vanishing." The opening monologue of Chetoga, seen in a full shot from a low angle which underscores his power as a spokesman, reinforces this attitude: "How! This picture is the story of my people. I speak for them because I know your language. Soon we will be gone. Your civilization will have destroyed us, but by your magic we will live forever. We thank the white man who helped us make this picture."

The plot of *The Silent Enemy*, said to be based on the journals of the Jesuit missionaries, is, however, clearly fictitious. The opening shots establish the Ojibway as children of nature, happily working together in their camp. However, the tribe faces a problem: the game in their area has disappeared and the hero, Bulak, the great hunter, and the villain, Dagwan, the medicine man, are in conflict over the best solution. They also both want to marry the beautiful Newa, who has been promised to Dagwan but loves Bulak. After Bulak leads a hunting party down river, winter arrives and Dagwan misuses his magic to find food for the tribe, who are becoming victims of the "silent enemy," hunger. When Bulak returns empty-handed, the chief calls a council and finally decides to reject the plan of Dagwan and take Bulak's advice to travel north and find the caribou herds. After much suffering, and other devious activities of Dagwan, the tribe arrives at the land of the caribou. However, the herd is nowhere to be seen, and Dagwan convinces the tribe that Bulak, who was named the new chief by the dying Chetoga, must die. Just as Bulak is about to be killed, the caribou appear and he is vindicated. At the end, the treacherous Dagwan walks into the wilderness to face a death from hunger, and Chief Bulak, with his wife, Newa, looks forward to sharing years of abundance with his tribe. Although this melodramatic plot shows the Native Americans' ability to survive before the arrival of white men, the film as a whole accepts the image of the Noble but doomed Red Man.

The opposing image of the Savage also appears in the silent melodramas. Iron Eyes Cody, an actor whose career has spanned the history of cinema, explains the need for this kind of film: "There had been bloody wars fought out on the plains, at this time just 40 years ago. The people wanted blood and sentiment and nobody in the movie business was about to deprive them of it . . ." (33–34). One of the earliest silent films on record, *The Pioneers* (1903), portrays the image of the bloodthirsty Savage by showing warriors attacking a family of settlers living in a remote cabin, killing the parents, and kidnapping a young daughter.

Even D. W. Griffith, who made numerous films sympathetic to Native Americans, emphasizes the Savage image in his *The Battle at Elderbush Gulch* (1913). The tribe in this film are Savages, who first appear during a ritual described as "The Dog Feast-Sunka Alawan—May you eat dog and live long." In the next scene, members of the tribe, some with war bonnets, dance wildly and then are seen asleep when the chief's son returns. Because this young man and his friend have missed the feast and still have a hunger for dog meat, they move out and find two little dogs that belong to the young heroine. Just as they are about to kill the dogs, a rancher shoots the chief's son. This provokes a savage response, as a note between the scenes indicates: "The death of the chieftain's son fans the ever ready spark of hatred and revenge [in the tribe]." The warriors ride out of camp, to start "The Attack," which involves all of the second reel.

They first attack and overrun the town. Griffith emphasizes the savagery of the attack in several distinctive shots. In one of them, at the edge of the frame, a warrior scalps a woman, and, though the actual scalping occurs outside the frame, the audience sees the movement of his arm and the woman's feet twitching. Then he grabs her baby and starts the movement of dashing it to the ground as Griffith cuts to the next shot. In another shot, a brave reaches down and grabs the hair of a wounded settler and then is seen raising up with his knife after the scalping. Though Griffith couldn't show these acts of violence because of the movie codes of his time, his editing and attention to detail make them seem more grim than a graphic depiction.

In the last part of the attack, which is on the ranch house, Griffith uses cross-cutting between the actions of the tribe, the people in the house, and a cavalry troop to build suspense about the outcome. After rapid cuts from the warriors, who move ever closer to the house and burn one of the out-buildings, to the beleaguered people in the house, several of whom are women, Griffith cuts to an extreme high-angle shot of the warriors circling the house, a perspective that emphasizes the hopelessness of the settlers. However, just as the men in the house are running out of ammunition and the warriors are ready to break in, the cavalry comes to the rescue and routs the savage tribe.

This pattern of Savages as a threat to white settlers repeats itself in numerous films, a few examples of which are *Riders of Vengeance* (1919), with marauding Apaches, *In the Days of Buffalo Bill* (1922), a serial with chapters such as "Prisoners of the Sioux" and "The Scarlet Doom"; and *The Pony Express* (1925), with hostile Sioux attacking a town. This image of the Savage complements that of the Noble but doomed Red Man. Just as audiences could accept destruction of noble Native American tribes as inevitable social evolution, so they could also feel good about the killing of bloodthirsty Savages. Both scenarios allowed them to walk out of the theatre feeling that justice had been served in the settling of North America.

The following summaries, which provide many other examples of the Savage and Noble Red Man images, are representative but not exhaustive. From 1910 to 1913 alone, 100 or more films with Native American themes and characters appeared each year. Throughout the Silent period, Native Americans remained popular subjects for film. Also, the 1930 cut-off date for the Silent films is arbitrary because some films before this date have music, sound effects and recorded dialogue.

NOTE

Ralph and Natasha Friar give extensive lists of silent films (the early chapters on silent film and 287–323). The best primary source for plot summaries of films is *Moving Picture World* (*MPW*), the first film magazine. Published from 1907 to 1927, this periodical describes many of the films dealing with Native Americans. Finally, *The Biograph Bulletin* (1908–1912) provides detailed plot summaries of the early D. W. Griffith films.

IMAGES OF THE SAVAGE

A staple of the Western is, of course, the excitement and cruelty of an attack by hostile warriors. Often a minor part of the whole plot, the attack is central to the portrayal of the Savage, and the theme of the Native American as threat to progress or western expansion. The following are the major types of attacks in the silent films. As the comments of contemporary film critics indicate, some of them became over-used formulas relatively early in the period.

Attacks on Covered Wagons

Pioneers Crossing the Plains in '49 (Pathé, 1908)
Warriors attack covered wagons and capture a white girl and her lover. Later the girl escapes and rescues her lover whom they had tied to a wild horse.

Under the Star Spangled Banner (Kalem, 1908)
A tribe attacks an immigrant family in a covered wagon, but are driven off by the U. S. Cavalry carrying the American flag.

Early Days in the West (Bison, 1912)
A white woman rejects the love of her guide, Mahomena.

When her white lover ridicules him, he gains his revenge by helping hostile Sioux attack their wagon train. Two other examples of Native Americans rejected by a white woman and thus driven to vengeance are *Indian Blood* (1913) and *Burning Brand* (1913).

The Massacre (Biograph, 1912)
Warriors who are avenging an attack on their village circle a wagon train and kill everyone but a woman and her child before the U. S. Cavalry comes to their rescue. The *Biograph Bulletin* notes that the "film depicts the struggles of the early pioneers in the Northwest in their conflict with the fierce Indian tribes of that time." (*MPW*,14 Feb., 1914)

Call of the Blood (Cinecolor, 1913)
Native Americans attack a covered wagon and kidnap a pregnant woman who later dies in captivity after she gives birth to a daughter. The girl grows up with the tribe and eventually is courted by a member of the tribe and a white officer who finally discovers that she is his long-lost sister.

The Aryan (Triangle, 1916)
After a woman convinces the misogynist hero that white men must protect women of their race from the hostile tribes, he rescues a wagon train from his own gang of Native Americans and mixed-bloods.

Wagon Tracks (Artcraft, 1919). Lambert Hillyer
Hostile warriors threaten a wagon train. A *Variety* reviewer comments on such a standard use of an attack: "to form a climax, the Indians are dragged in." (15 Aug.)

White Oak (Paramount, 1921). Lambert Hillyer
The villain plots with Chief Long Knife (Chief Standing Bear) and his tribe attacks a circled wagon train. At the end, the hero comes to the rescue, and Chief Long Knife kills the villain who had betrayed him.

The Covered Wagon (Paramount, 1923). James Cruze
In this big-budget Western, hordes of hostile braves

attack the wagon train. Tim McCoy, the technical adviser for the film, used 750 members of various western tribes for the attack sequences. The hero, Jim Bridger, has two Native American wives, played by Native actors.

The Rainbow Trail (Fox, 1925). Lynn Reynolds
The hero comes to the rescue of a lone covered wagon under attack. A *Variety* reviewer points out a typical pattern: "The picture starts with an Indian attack . . . with Mix (the hero) riding to the rescue and the routing of the redskins." (3 June)

The Thundering Herd (Paramount, 1925). William Howard
Warriors surround a wagon train and are finally routed. A *Variety* reviewer notes that the film "finished with some of the best Indian battle stuff that has been shown in a long, long while . . ." (25 Feb.)

The Devil Horse (Pathé, 1926). Fred Jackman
After the tribe of Prowling Wolf (Robert Kortman) attacks a wagon train, the only survivors, the hero and a colt named Devil Horse pursue their adversaries. When Prowling Wolf, who has captured a white woman, incites his tribe to attack a fort, the hero, riding Devil Horse (which can recognize Native Americans by their smell), comes to the rescue and gains revenge.

The Last Frontier (Producers Dist., 1926). George Seitz
Pawnee Killer (Frank Lackteen), a Sioux chief, attacks a wagon train, stampedes buffalo through a town and eventually battles with General Custer.

Men of Daring (Universal, 1927). Albert Rogell
A villain incites Blackfeet, Sioux and Cheyenne led by Lone Wolf (Bert Apling) to attack a wagon train.

The Glorious Trail (First National Pics., 1928). Albert Rogell
Stirred up by a villain, the tribe of Chief High Wolf (Chief Yowlachie) attacks settlers, work crews, and wagon trains.

The Big Trail (Fox, 1930). Raoul Walsh

A hostile tribe once again attacks a wagon train. A *Variety* reviewer comments that "the silly melodrama commences to weary, for it's the same thing over and over again, including the Indian attack on the wagon trains made corral." (29 Oct.)

Attacks on the Cavalry or Soldiers in Forts

On the Little Big Horn (Selig, 1909)

Rain in the Face, a warrior arrested earlier by Custer's brother, takes revenge by leading General Custer and his soldiers to the river near which they are killed.

The Last of the Mohicans (Thanhouser, 1911)

Chingachgook and Uncas are the noble friends of the hero. Magua, the savage Huron, leads a vicious attack on Fort Henry.

Custer's Last Fight (Bison, 1912). Thomas Ince

This version of Custer's final battle with the Plains tribes provokes a racist comment from an *MPW* critic who believes that filmmakers who created the "Noble Redman" should be made to live with real Indians who are "merciless to the weak, inhuman in their outrages on white women and children . . . and incapable of gratitude . . ." (22 June, 1118)

The Indian Wars (Col. William F. Cody Historical Pictures, 1914)

This famous film chronicles the major battles, including Little Big Horn (Brownlow, 224–35). An *MPW* reviewer advises his readers to take children to the film "for an afternoon with the great leaders of our army, with great chiefs of our Indian tribes and two hours in the open world that has been made sacred by heroic blood of the nation's fighting heroes." (12 Sept.,1500)

The Bugle Call (Triangle, 1916). Reginald Baker

By a clever deception, warriors divert the main body of troops and then attack the undermanned fort. However, they are, in turn, tricked into thinking the troops are returning by a boy who plays the bugle call.

The Last of the Mohicans (Associated Producers, 1920). Maurice Tourneur

In this version of Cooper's novel, the hero and his friends, Chingachgook (Theodore Lerch) and Uncas (Albert Roscoe), struggle with the evil Magua (Wallace Berry), who leads an attack on the fort. A *Variety* reviewer comments on the violence of the attack: "Someone gets firewater to the redskins and they take part in an orgy of blood and suggested rapine that was terrible enough in print, but unspeakable in a picture." (7 Jan.)

Warrior Gap (Vital, 1925). Alvin Neitz

Based on Charles King's *Warrior Gap*, this film tell the story of Sioux Chief Red Cloud's (Len Haynes) attacks on the U. S. Cavalry.

The Flaming Frontier (Universal, 1926). Edward Sedgwick

Corrupt politicians, a crooked Indian agent and unscrupulous buffalo hunters cause the Sioux to retaliate. Led by Sitting Bull (Noble Johnson) and Rain in His Face (Joe Bonomo), they defeat Custer in the Battle of Little Big Horn. A *Variety* critic notes that the hostility of the Sioux is well motivated: "The theme deals with the swindling of the Indians out of their lands . . . that culminated in the massacre of Custer . . . and the Indian War that follows." (7 April)

General Custer at Little Big Horn (Sunset, 1926). Harry Fraser

Once again Custer fights the Sioux and Cheyenne in the most famous battle of the Indian wars. A *Variety* reviewer comments: "Aside from showing in as much detail as possible how the Indians got together for the clash that killed Custer, it has no moral lesson; mainly historical, a stark tragedy of the plains, showing bodies strewn all over 40 acres or so of land." (2 Nov., 1927)

War Paint (MGM, 1926). W. S. Van Dyke
Whites capture Iron Eyes (Chief Yowlachie), an Arapahoe medicine man. When he escapes and attacks the fort in revenge, Chief Fearless Eagle (Chief White Horse) helps the hero come to the rescue. A *Variety* critic comments on the motivation for the attack: "Back in the days of the Indian extermination all of their uprisings were not wholly the fault of the red man. Perhaps the moving pictures some day will tell all the truth about the American Indian and his decline." (20 Oct.)

The Frontiersman (MGM, 1927). Reginald Barker
After the Creek tribe, led by White Snake (Frank Hagney) and Gray Eagle (Chief Big Tree), massacres an entire fort and captures a white woman, the hero and his soldiers rescue her and stop the uprising.

The Red Raiders (First National Pics., 1927). Albert Rogell
Scar Face Charlie (Chief Yowlachie), an evil spy, incites the Sioux tribe to attack a fort, but the hero comes to the rescue.

Attacks on Trains (and railroad workers) and Stagecoaches

Riders of Vengeance (Universal, 1919). John Ford
The hero rescues a school teacher from a stagecoach being attacked by Apaches, and later saves a wounded man during another Apache attack.

The Orphan (Fox, 1920). J. Gordon Edwards
The hero fights off a hostile tribe as they attack a stage-coach. A *Variety* critic notes that such Westerns "hand out film food to a grown-up audience, consisting of a fast riding horseman picking off Indian braves after 'white squaws' in

a stagecoach, or else on the warpath, picking them off as an expert would demolish clay pipes at a shooting gallery." (30 April)

The Iron Horse (Fox, 1924). John Ford
This film portrays the building of the western railroad lines. Hordes of warriors led by a Cheyenne chief (Chief Big Tree) and a Sioux chief (Chief White Tree) attack railroad workers and trains because they see the railroad lines as a threat to their way of life. A *Variety* reviewer notes that the film is a fine example of "the great theme of Indians and soldiers." (3 Sept.)

Buffalo Bill on the U.P. Trail (Sunset, 1926). Frank Mattison
When the chief's hostile son, White Spear (Felix Whitefeather), starts a buffalo stampede to cover his attack, the hero comes to the rescue.

Attacks on Settlers and Other Representatives of Progress

Days of the Early West (Champion, 1910)
Two religious pioneer families build a cabin in the wilderness. A short time later marauding braves attack and set the cabin on fire, but the townspeople arrive and, at the last moment, rescue the families.

A Frontier Hero (Edison, 1910)
A warlike tribe attacks pioneer families as they try to settle the frontier in the 1840s. An *MPW* reviewer comments that such attacks were "a menace" to the settlers that this film "illustrates graphically." (6 Aug., 296)

Kit Carson (Bison, 1910)
The hero rescues settlers from an attack. An *MPW* reviewer notes that the film has all the "features of the old time frontier story" including "a surrounding band of whooping redskins, showering arrows into the stockade." (10 Sept., 575)

Flaming Arrows (Pathé, 1911)

Native Americans on the warpath trap some settlers in a cabin and shoot flaming arrows to smoke them out.

Forest Rose (Thanhouser, 1912)

This film, in which a hostile tribe attacks a pioneer and kidnaps his daughter, provokes another racist comment from Louis Harrison: "There is very little that can be truthfully represented as ideal in the character of a people gloating over the hideous torture of innocent women and children. They represent a hindering and utterly useless element in the civilization of mankind." (*MPW*, 30 Nov., 861)

The Battle of Elderbush Gulch (Biograph, 1913). D. W. Griffith

Discussed in the introduction (23–24), this film tells the story of a hostile tribe that attacks a group of settlers and is about to kill them when the cavalry comes to the rescue.

The Virginian (Lasky, 1914)

Hostile warriors stage bloody attacks on the colonists. A *Variety* critic comments on the unbelievable ways in which Indians are killed during these attacks. The hero, who is badly wounded, "spies an Indian several hundred feet away and shoots left-handed from his hip with fatal effect." (11 Sept.)

America (UA, 1924). D. W. Griffith

In this film about the revolutionary period, Mohawks led by Chief Joseph Brant (Riley Hatch) and other tribes of the Six Nations fight with the British against the American colonists. In some of the battles British soldiers disguise themselves as Mohawks. In the final climactic battle, the hostile tribes attack a fort and, as they break the gates and are about to kill the women inside, the hero and his men come to the rescue.

Kidnapping and Torturing

As can be seen from the above summaries, Native Americans portrayed as Savages sometimes take whites, especially females, as prisoners during their attacks. Such kidnapping, and also torture and the use of fire, are typical evil deeds of the Savage.

Daniel Boone (Edison, 1907)

A warlike tribe kidnaps Boone's daughters, and then captures and tortures him. Aided by a girl from the tribe who had been treated well by the daughters earlier, Boone escapes and saves his children. Then he gets his revenge by killing the chief of the tribe.

A Trapper and The Redskins (Kalem, 1910)

After a hostile tribe kidnaps a girl and then captures her father, the girl's mother and some neighbors rescue them and take revenge on the tribe. A *Variety* reviewer writes: "The band is killed off in fine stockyard order and everything ends happily except for the Indians." (26 Feb.)

In the Days of the Six Nations (Republic, 1911)

After a treacherous Native American guide leads a lieutenant and two women into a trap, the hero rescues them. Later, however, warriors capture the same women and an officer and are preparing to kill them. At the last moment, the hero brings soldiers who save the captives and drive off the hostiles.

The Maiden of the Pie-Faced Indians (Edison, 1911)

A savage tribe captures the hero and tortures him before he is rescued. An *MPW* reviewer, pointing out that the hero walks away with the tree to which he is tied, notes that the film "clearly illustrates the absurdities which often creep into the usual Indian story." (18 Apr., 782)

A Prisoner of the Mohicans (Pathé, 1911)

Mohicans capture a white girl who had earlier helped a poor, starving Native American. This man shows his gratitude by rescuing her from the Mohican camp and returning her to her parents. This film juxtaposes the hostility of the savage Mohicans to the gratitude of a noble character, a common technique, and one that makes a neat classifications of the films difficult.

The Totem Mark (Selig, 1911)
A warlike tribe kidnaps a white woman, and a group of women in the tribe, envious of her beauty, denounce her as a witch and set her adrift in the rapids of a river.

Geronimo's Last Raid (American, 1912). John Emerson
The Apaches of Geronimo capture the hero and are about to burn him at the stake when the cavalry comes to the rescue. An *MPW* reviewer notes that the film has "action and lots of it, for those who like clashes between Indians and settlers and who are stirred by dashing attacks of the U. S. Cavalry and cowboys on the redskins." (14 Sept., 1054)

On Fortune's Wheel (Kay Bee, 1913)
In Arizona, a tribe captures a banker who has been cheating them on land deals and takes revenge by tying him to a wagon wheel and burning him.

The Thundering Herd (Selig, 1914)
The tribe of Chief Swift Wing (Wheeler Oakman) captures the hero and his sweetheart, whom the Chief wants for his own. However, a young woman from the tribe named Starlight (Princess Redwing) befriends the captives, rescues them and eventually accompanies them to their home land. A *Variety* critic bemoans the stock, disrespectful treatment of the Native Americans: "the former kings of the plains are also permitted to run into the range of the camera fire occasionally and help lengthen out the feature." (6 Aug., 1915)

Cardigan (American, 1922). John Noble
The Cayuga tribe of Chief Logan (Frank Montgomery) starts a war and captures the hero. A Native American runner arrives at the last moment to save him from being burned at the stake. A *Variety* critic notes that the tribe is "costumed as the old Biograph company presented their Indians." (24 Feb.)

The Pale Face (First National, 1922). Buster Keaton
   In this comedy, a tribe captures the hero and tries to burn him at the stake, but his asbestos clothing saves him. Because he doesn't burn, they think he is a god and adopt him into the tribe as Little Chief Paleface. Later he saves the tribe from being cheated by crooked oilmen.

Winning of the West (Aywon Film Corp., 1922)
   In this film, hostile warriors again contrast to a noble Native American young woman. Cared for by a white woman, the girl shows her gratitude by rescuing the woman's daughter after warriors have kidnapped her. As the hostiles pursue the two girls, the cavalry comes to the rescue.

North of Nevada (Monogram, 1924). Albert Rogell
   The hero brings to justice Joe Deerfoot (George Magrill), an unscrupulous, college-educated Native American who deceives a boy and kidnaps a white woman in order to get his hands on a ranch.

Sioux Blood (MGM, 1929). John Waters
   Two brothers are separated during a Sioux uprising; one is reared by whites and the other is captured by the Sioux. The former becomes a scout who hates Native Americans and the latter, who takes the name Lone Eagle (Robert Fraser), becomes a hostile brave taught to hate whites by a medicine man, Crazy Wolf (Chief Big Tree). Eventually, the brothers meet and Lone Eagle leaves the tribe to join his brother in white society. In the process both learn some tolerance.

Native Americans in the Serials

   Hostile Savages, who attack, kidnap and torture whites are also typical antagonists for the hero in the early serials, though some of these films also have noble characters.

Kit Carson (American Mutoscope and Biograph, 1903)
   The hero fights with hostile warriors and is befriended by

a noble young woman from the tribe. *The Biograph Bulletin* refers to part nine, *In the Indian Camp:* "Squaws and their papooses, young bucks and Indian maidens are seen at their various occupations. Here we have real Indian life." (Niver, 215)

Perils of Pauline (Pathé, 1914). Donald McKenzie
   In this famous early serial, a tribe at first accepts Pauline as a goddess and then rolls a huge boulder down a hill at her to see if she is immortal.

Hands Up (Pathé, 1918). James W. Horne
   Inca warriors capture a white woman and, thinking she is a goddess, are about to offer her as a sacrifice. In true serial fashion, she is rescued at the last moment.

Winners of the West (Universal, 1921). Edward Laemmle
   Hostile warriors challenge the hero in chapters such as "Blazing Arrow."

White Eagle (Pathé, 1922). W.S. Van Dyke, Fred Jackman
   A white woman whom the tribe calls Princess White Eagle is a main character in this serial with chapters such as "The Red Man's Menace" and "The Flaming Arrow."

In the Days of Daniel Boone (Universal, 1923). William Craft
   A warlike tribe threatens the hero in chapters such as "Chief Black Fish Attacks" and "Running the Gauntlet."

The Sante Fe Trail (Arrow, 1923). Ashton Dearholt, Robert Dillon
   Mixed-bloods and a hostile tribe fight with the heroes in chapters such as "The Half Breed's Treachery," "The Red Menace" and "Pueblo of Death."

Leatherstocking (Pathé, 1924). George Seitz
   In this serial based on Cooper's novels, savage tribes threaten the heroes in chapters such as "The Warpath," "Rivenoak's Revenge" and "Mingo Torture."

Way of a Man (Pathé, 1924). George Seitz

In this more sympathetic serial, the hero deals with Native Americans in chapters like "Redskins and White" and "White Medicine."

Fighting With Buffalo Bill (Universal, 1926). Ray Taylor

In this serial based on Cody's *The Great West That Was,* savage warriors threaten the hero in chapters such as "The Red Menace" and "The Blazing Arrow."

Hawk of the Hills (Pathé, 1927). Spencer Bennet

A savage mixed-blood (Frank Lackteen) and a hostile tribe threaten the hero in chapters like "Doomed to Arrows."

The Indians are Coming (Universal, 1930). Henry MacRae

Also based on Cody's *The Great West That Was,* this serial portrays hostile braves menacing the hero in chapters such as "The Red Terror," "Redskins Revenge" and "Frontiers Aflame."

Hostile Mixed-bloods

Another variety of the Savage is the evil mixed-blood, a standard villain in the early Westerns.

From Out of the Big Snows (Vitagaph, 1915)

When Jean La Salle (George Cooper), a mixed-blood, finds out his white lover has rejected him for a doctor, he seeks his revenge by tying the man to a tree so he can be devoured by wolves. A *Variety* reviewer notes the villain is a "half-breed, who with inborn cunning professes friendship for the white man so that he may later dispose of him." (13 Aug.)

The Ghost Wagon (Bison, 1915)

An evil mixed-blood abducts a white girl whose parents have been killed by hostile braves. After the girl is rescued by her lover, the mixed-blood retaliates by inciting a hostile tribe to go on the warpath.

A Fight for Love (Universal, 1919). John Ford
A treacherous mixed-blood (Joseph Harris) kills a Native American in a fight over a woman from his tribe. After the hero is blamed for the crime, he hunts down the mixed-blood and kills him.

The Half Breed (Assoc. First National Pics., 1922). Charles Taylor
Based on the play, *Half Breed: a Tale of Indian Country*, this film tells the story of Delmar Spavinaw (Wheeler Oakman). An educated man, he finds various ways to take his revenge on a judge who evicted his Native American mother from her land and stood in the way of his love for a white woman.

Unseeing Eyes (Goldwyn Cosmopolitan, 1923). E. H. Griffith
Singing Pine (Frances Red Eagle) rescues the heroes and nurses one of them back to health. Then, with the help of Eagle Blanket (Louis Deer), the heroes triumph over the villain and his treacherous mixed-blood companions (Paul Panzer and Dan Red Eagle).

The Pony Express (Paramount, 1925). James Cruze
A mixed-blood, Charlie Bent (Frank Lackteen), leads a band of Sioux on an attack of a town.

Hawk of the Hills (Pathé, 1929). Spencer Bennet
In this film based on the 1927 serial, Hawk (Frank Lackteen) is a mixed-blood leader of a band of renegade whites and Native Americans, one of whom is Chief Long Hand (Chief Yowlachie).

Drunkenness

In addition to the hostility and treachery, the traits of drunkenness and vengeance are also associated with the image of the Savage. For example, in several of the above films "fire water" is part of the motivation for vicious attacks. This pattern of Native American characters made more hostile by alcohol persists throughout the history of the Western. Though they play off the stereotype, several of the following films reveal some sympathy for characters plagued by alcohol.

Curse of the Red Man (Selig, 1911)

A Native American who learns to drink while going to college struggles with alcoholism after he returns to live with his tribe.

Love In a Tepee (Imperial, 1911)

Bad Eye wants his daughter, Hyacinth, to marry a Mexican whom she detests. He is foiled by his drinking when the Mexican thinks that Bad Eye, who is lying under a blanket in a drunken stupor, is the daughter and carries him away. This allows his daughter to go away with the cowboy she really loves.

Last of the Line (Bison, 1914). Jay Hunt

The son of Chief Gray Otter (William Eagleshirt),who returns from college a hopeless alcoholic, joins some renegades who break a peace treaty made by his father. Because of this, Gray Otter is forced to kill his son, though he does it in a way that makes the young man look like a hero.

Wild and Woolly (Artcraft, 1917). John Emerson

In this comedy, the unlikely hero fights hostile drunken warriors. A *Variety* critic comments, "You've got to laugh when the hero rides into the midst of a bunch of drunken Indians, swings the girl on the back of his horse and makes a getaway without being shot." (22 June)

Vengeance

The Justice of the Redskin (Pathé, 1908)

A Native American accused of killing a little girl trails the actual murderer. When he finds the man with the body of the child, he throws him off a cliff.

The Red Man and the Child (Biograph, 1908). D.W. Griffith

In this film, subtitled "The Story of an Indian's Vengeance," outlaws kill an old miner and kidnap his grandchild while their Native American friend (Charles Innslee) is away. When he returns, he rescues the child and avenges the killing of his old friend by killing all the outlaws.

Indian Runner's Romance (Biograph, 1909). D. W. Griffith

A cowboy kidnaps the wife of Blue Cloud (James Kirkwood), a Sioux runner, and tortures her to make her tell the location of a hidden mine. Blue Cloud hunts him down, kills him, and brings his wife home. A *Variety* critic comments on the acting: "'Made-up Indians are usually a travesty, but in this case both in appearance and action the redskin is natural." (28 Sept.)

Ogallah (Powers, 1911)

A Sioux pursues a kidnapper of one of his people and finally takes his vengeance by killing him. An *MPW* reviewer, who has been encoded by the Savage image, notes that the film has "no mawkish sentimentality. . . . It is savage and cruel, as Indians are by nature." (18 April, 782)

The Yaqui (Blue Bird, 1916)

After Tambor (Hobart Bosworth), the chief of the Yaqui, loses his wife and child to Mexican slave dealers, he rallies his tribe to take vengeance on the Mexicans.

Out of the Snows (Selznick, 1920)

In the Canadian Northwest, a Native American woman kills a white man who slanders her. When whites kill her in retaliation, a man from her tribe takes harsh revenge on them.

The Lonely Trail (Primex Pictures, 1922)

A Native American guide, Pierre Benorte (Fred Beauvais), rescues a white woman from the villain. When Pierre realizes that the villain is the one who had seduced and deserted his sister, he takes his revenge.

The Man Who Paid (Producer's Security Corp., 1922). Oscar Apfel

The tribe of Songo (Frank Montgomery) helps an evil trapper kidnap a white woman. However, when they find out he has double-crossed them, they kill him.

The Wild Bull's Lair (Film Booking Offices, 1925). Del Andrews

The tribe of Eagle Eye (Frank Hagney), a well-educated man who resents the loss of tribal lands, trains a wild bull to lead the cattle of whites to their own remaining land. A *Variety* reviewer notes that the film "is inhabited by a tribe of Indians (not the nice wild old Injuns of former days, but a group of college trained redskins who want to reclaim their land from the palefaces). . . ." (26 Aug.)

Open Range (Paramount, 1927). Clifford Smith

Brave Bear (Bernard Siegel), a chief bitter about white encroachment on his lands, seeks revenge by joining the villain in a plot to steal cattle from the ranchers.

IMAGES OF THE NOBLE RED MAN

The vengeance of the Savage is always excessive; in the Noble Red Man this emotion is tempered into a strong sense of justice. Though the line between justice and vengeance is a thin one, the noble characters are always on the side of justice and peace. They also value friendship, loyalty, generosity, gratitude, honor and courage, all of which, of course, are traits that make them appealing to white audiences.

Friendship and Loyalty

Pioneer Days (Edison, 1907)

Hostile warriors kidnap two children from the cabin of a pioneer family. Aided by a friendly woman from the tribe, the father trails the warriors and rescues his children.

A Kentucky Pioneer (Selig, 1910)

Warlike braves kidnap a woman betrothed to a young pioneer, but she escapes with the help of a young woman from their tribe. As the hostiles pursue both women, other settlers come to the rescue. A *Variety* critic notes that the contrasting of a noble character to her savage tribe is "a theme displayed many times before." (8 Oct.)

A Mohawk's Way (Biograph, 1910). D. W. Griffith

Mohawks wronged by a white woman's evil husband are about to kill the woman. At the last moment, a woman from the tribe, whose baby had earlier been saved by the white woman, comes to her rescue. A contemporary film review comments on the noble character in this film: "Here is the noble red man of James Fenimore Cooper . . . the Indian of romance who, as some people claim, never existed, but who is nevertheless the ideal type for story telling." (Friar, 117)

Red Wing's Loyalty (Bison, 1910)

A cavalry lieutenant who helps the maiden, Red Wing, after she had been hurt by an evil mixed-blood, later unknowingly kills her father in a battle. Despite this, she remains loyal and comes to his rescue after her tribe has captured him and is about to burn him at the stake. She brings soldiers who save the man's life and then reward Red Wing for her loyalty to the lieutenant.

The Little Indian Martyr (Selig, 1912)

A rebellious mission tribe tries to make Chiquito, a boy from the tribe who works for a kindly priest, promise to kill the man. However, the boy remains loyal, warns the priest, and then is killed by his own people.

Deerslayer (Vitagraph, 1913)

The noble Chingachgook helps his friend, Natty Bumppo, fight the Hurons. These well known companions also appear in *The Last of the Mohicans* (Thanhouser, 1911), *The Last of the Mohicans* (Associated Producers, 1920), and *Leatherstocking* (Pathé, 1924).

The Friendless Indian (Pathé, 1913)

A man rejected by his own tribe rescues a little white girl, but is then also rejected by the whites. An *MPW* reviewer comments: "Condemned to walk alone, a Red Man saves a life and is given only a nod for thanks—after all, he is a Indian." (12 July, 232)

The Raiders (Selig, 1921)

In the wilderness of the Canadian Northwest, Uncas, a faithful guide, helps the Mounties track down a gang of whiskey smugglers.

The Woman Conquers (Assoc. First National Pics, 1922). Tom Forman

In the Hudson Bay area, Lawatha, a loyal guide, dies while trying to save the white heroine.

Kit Carson (Paramount, 1928). Alfred L. Werker

When Kit Carson rescues Sing-in-the-Clouds (Dorothy Janis), the daughter of a Blackfeet chief, the tribe declares their lasting friendship. Later, when a villain kills the young woman, Carson takes revenge by throwing him off a cliff into the Blackfeet circle of death.

Generosity and Gratitude

The Red Man (World, 1909)

A Native American repays a white man who had helped him earlier by recovering the man's money from a thief. An *MPW* reviewer notes that the film "shows that singular gratitude of the Indian which was often displayed in these days." (26 June, 884)

Red Wing's Gratitude (Vitagraph, 1909)

White settlers save Red Wing (Princess Redwing) from a beating by her own people. Later Red Wing shows her gratitude by helping a white girl captured by her tribe escape. As the two young women flee, the settlers come to their rescue, but Red Wing is wounded and dies in the arms of the white girl's father.

A Broken Doll (Biograph, 1910). D. W. Griffith

In this film, subtitled "A Tragedy of the Indian Reservation," a white man brutally kills a Native American. When his tribe prepares to take revenge, a girl from the tribe who had been given a doll by a white child shows her gratitude by warning the whites, only to be killed in the fighting.

Mesquite's Gratitude (Kalem, 1911)

A cowboy stops other ranch hands from taunting a young Native woman, Mesquite. Later she helps him in a time of need, and he falls in love with her. At the end, he comes to the camp of her tribe and asks her to marry him.

Iola's Promise (Biograph, 1912). D. W. Griffith

Discussed in the introduction (18–19), this film, subtitled "How the Little Indian Maiden Paid Her Debt of Gratitude," tells the story of Iola, whom a prospector helps when she is in trouble. Later she repays his kindness by rescuing his fiancée as her tribe is preparing to burn her at the stake. The white woman escapes but Iola is fatally wounded.

The Sign Invisible (First National, 1918). Edgar Lewis

Lone Deer (Mitchell Lewis), a mixed-blood separated from his beloved Winona, is wounded in a fight to save a white woman and loses his sight. At the end he is reunited with Winona, who is happy to devote the rest of her life to caring for him.

Danger Valley (Independent Film Assoc., 1921)

After a white man saves a Native American's life in a saloon fight, he shows his gratitude by leading the man to a hidden mine.

The Mine within the Iron Door (Principal Pictures, 1924). Sam Wood

The hero rescues Natachee (Robert Frazer), an educated man who had grown to hate whites because of their

prejudice towards him. Natchee repays the man by showing him the location of a gold mine and by killing the villain.

Honor and Courage

Indian Brothers (Biograph, 1911). D. W. Griffith
    In this film, subtitled "The Story of an Indian's Honor," a
renegade brave kills the ailing chief of the tribe. When the
man's brother finds out about the murder, he captures the
man and punishes him.

Heart of an Indian (Bison, 1913). Thomas Ince
    The chief of a tribe (J. B. Sherry) steals a baby from a white
woman to replace the dead child of his daughter. However,
when his daughter sees how much the woman loves her
baby, she gives it back to the mother. Meanwhile, the
whites, not knowing about this honorable and courageous
act, kill many of the tribe in revenge. Iron Eyes Cody notes
that the film showed "some tender exchanges between a
white woman and an Indian maiden on the theme of
motherhood." (Cody, 32)

The Winner (Box Office Attraction G., 1914)
    The hero is blamed for killing a cowboy who had actually
been murdered by a mixed-blood he had cheated and
ridiculed. The mixed-blood shows his honor by sending a
letter admitting his guilt.

Wyoming (MGM, 1928). W. S. Van Dyke
    Chief Big Cloud (Charles Bell), the son of Chief Chapulti
(Goes in the Lodge) and childhood friend of the hero,
breaks a treaty by attacking the hero's wagon train. The
peace-loving old chief kills his own son to uphold the honor
of his tribe and stop the fighting.

Romances between Native American Women and White Men

    Many of these positive traits of the Noble Red Man (and
several of those associated with the Savage) also motivate

the Native American characters in films which involve romances between Native Americans and romances between Native Americans and whites. In the standard pattern for mixed-romance plots, the Native American finally is rejected or dies.

The Kentuckian (Biograph, 1908)

A rich young man goes West and marries a Native American woman. Later, when she realizes her husband is struggling with the question of whether to return to the East with a socially unacceptable spouse, she understands his dilemma and solves his problem by committing suicide.

Pocahontas: A Child of the Forest (Edison, 1908)

Pocahontas saves Captain Smith from Kunder-Wacha, a hostile brave who thinks she belongs to him. Then she persuades her father, Powhatan, to let her marry Captain Smith. A *Variety* critic notes the lack of accuracy: "The Indians in *Pocahontas* look like Chinese ballet girls must appear, if they have ballet girls in China." (3 Oct.)

Pale Face's Wooing (Kalem, 1909)

Little Red Heart loves a cowboy, but her father wants her to marry a man from their tribe whom he has chosen for her. To stop this romance, her father and the man capture the cowboy and are about to kill him. However, she rescues the cowboy, who kills his rival and threatens to kill her father. When Little Red Heart intercedes, he relents. Then her father forgives them and agrees to their marriage. A *Variety* reviewer notes that such "Indian subjects are always interesting. They have the freshness of the wild." (27 Nov.)

Comata, the Sioux (Biograph, 1909). D. W. Griffith

Clear Eyes leaves her tribe to live with a white man and they have a child. After the man abandons her for a white woman, she goes off towards the Black Hills with Comata, who has loved and watched over her from the beginning. However, they come to a sad end on their trip.

The Heart of a Sioux (Lubin, 1910)

A Sioux girl falls in love with her white teacher, and, though her love is unrequited, she saves the man's life twice. A reviewer for *MPW* argues that such movies are showing that the Indians, contrary to the stereotype of them as "stolid, unemotional people," experience strong emotions. He believes that this film will "go far to remove the stigma which this oft-repeated assertion, that Indians lack heart, has placed upon them." (20 Aug, 365)

Pocahontas (Thanhouser, 1910)

Pocahontas saves the life of Captain John Smith and eventually marries John Rolfe, with whom she goes to England. Shortly after her arrival, she dies while dreaming of her native wilderness.

A Romance of the Western Hills (Biograph, 1910). D. W. Griffith

A young Native American woman, adopted by a white family, falls in love with a white man who cruelly rejects her. Later, she falls in love with a man from her tribe. Before returning to their native land, they take revenge on the man who rejected her. *The Biograph Bulletin* describes the film as "a powerful illustration of one of the many indignities the redskins suffered." (Bowser, 185)

Little Dove's Romance (Bison, 1911)

Little Dove falls in love with a white man, but after he explains that he cannot marry her, she agrees to marry the Native American who loves her. An *MPW* critic comments that the film shows "something of Indian manners and customs . . . in a way that shows a sympathetic understanding of the Indian mind." (9 Sept., 692)

The Yaqui Girl (Pathé, 1911). James Young Deer

A young Yaqui woman falls in love with a Mexican singer. When she finds out he is a bandit and has another lover, she bitterly rejects him.

At Old Fort Dearborn (Bison, 1912). Frank Monty

Singing Bird (Mona Darkfeather) loves a soldier who is captured by her tribe. When she tries to rescue him, her own people kill her. An *MPW* reviewer notes that "Little Mona Darkfeather . . . has a role that will prove to be popular—that of friend of the soldiers." (28 Sept., 1267)

The Invaders (Kay-Bee, 1912)

Sky Star (Ann Little), a young woman from the Sioux tribe of Chief Eagleshirt, loves a surveyor who has entered the land of her tribe. At the end, however, she dies in a battle.

The Vanishing Race (American, 1912)

A family, the last members of the "Hoppe" tribe, face extinction because a white man rejects the love of the young daughter. Her brother kills the men, and then the whites kill him and his father, leaving only the mother and disgraced daughter to wander away.

The Squaw Man (Paramount, 1914). Cecil B. DeMille

Based on the play by Edwin Royle, this film deals with an Englishman who marries Nat-U-Rich (Princess Redwing), the daughter of the Ute Chief Tabywana (Joe Singleton). After she rescues her husband twice and has a child with him, she finds out her husband loves a white woman and wants to return to his homeland. At the end, when her husband accidentally shoots her, she tells him that she is happy he will no longer be held back by her, and then she dies.

Neola, the Sioux (Exposition Players Corp. and 101 Ranch, 1915)

A white man who raped Neola (Neola May) is forced to marry her and later abandons her. Red Deer (Pedro Leon) finds her and asks her to join him as a performer in the 101 Ranch Western Show. Later, Red Deer kills Neola's evil husband, and then they pledge their love for each other.

The Sealed Valley (Metro, 1915)

Nahnya Crossfox (Dorothy Donnelly) lives with her

parents in a valley full of gold called Indian's Paradise. Later, Nahnya seals herself in the valley to live the rest of her life alone, after deciding that the white man she loves should be free to live with a white woman.

The Red Woman (World, 1917). E. Mason Hopper
The daughter of a chief, Maria Temosach (Gail Kane), gains high honors in an eastern college but returns to her tribe in New Mexico because she never was accepted by white society. Later she saves the life of a rich white man, falls in love with him and bears him a child. He abandons her for a while, but then returns, marries her and lives with her in the West.

The Woman God Forgot (Paramount, 1917). Cecil B. DeMille
Though the daughter of Montezuma (Raymond Hatton), Tecza (Geraldine Farrar), loves a Spanish soldier, her father insists that she marry his nephew, Guatemoco (T. Kosloff). After her tribe has captured the soldier and is about to kill him, she rescues him by bringing other Spanish soldiers, who spare her but kill all the rest of her people.

The Goddess of Lost Lake (Paralta, 1918)
A Native American legend tells that whoever sacrifices his life for that of a brave killed at the lake long ago will inherit the gold at the bottom of the lake. The father of the mixed-blood heroine fulfills the legend when he allows himself to be killed by Eagle (Frank Lanning), one of the many who have waited at the lake since the original killing. His daughter takes the gold and then marries an Englishman.

The Squaw Man (Paramount, 1918). Cecil B. DeMille
In this second of three versions produced in the Silent period, Naturich (Ann Little), the daughter of Tabywana (Noah Beery), marries an Englishman and dies before he returns to England. A *Variety* critic reveals contemporary stereotypes of Native Americans in his praise for Ann Little's acting, noting "her wonderful characterization of the female redskin with her expressionless features changing little in suffering or joy." She "displays the stealth of the

Indian" and shoots a villain "in a cool and calculating manner, just as an Indian would do it." (8 Nov.)

The Heart of Wetona (Select, 1919). Sidney Franklin
Based on a contemporary play, this film tells the story of Wetona (Norma Talmadge), a Blackfeet educated by the whites, who was seduced by a cowardly white man. Her father, Chief Quannah, gains vengeance by killing the man, and later Wetona marries a good Indian agent.

Behold My Wife (Paramount, 1920). George Melford
Based on the novel, *The Translation of a Savage*, this film tells the story of Lali (Mable Scott), whom an Englishman marries as revenge on his very proper family. He sends her to England to embarrass his family, but she learns their manners and gains their respect and that of her husband, who reunites with her.

Lonely Heart (Affiliated Dist., 1921). John O'Brian
In the setting of the Oklahoma oil fields, Lonely Heart (Kay Laurell), who is betrothed to Peter Blue Fox (Escamilio Fernandez), falls in love with a white man. When Blue Fox is murdered, she is accused, but is then exonerated when another member of her tribe confesses. At the end, she marries the white man.

The Mohican's Daughter (American, 1922). E. V. Taylor
Based on a Jack London story, "The Story of Jees Uck," the film deals with the romantic struggles of Jees Uck (Nancy Deaver), a mixed-blood whom Chatanna (Nick Thompson), the chief of her tribe, wants to marry. Though she loves a white man, she surrenders herself to the evil Chatanna. However, when the white man proves that the chief is guilty of killing Nashinto (Mortimer Snow), she is able to marry him.

The Son of the Wolf (R. C. Pictures, 1922). Norman Dawn
A white man who falls in love with Chook-Ra (Edith Roberts), the daughter of Chief Thling Tinner (Thomas Jefferson), abandons her for a dance-hall girl. When Chook-

Ra's father makes her return to the tribe, the man sees the error of his ways and wins her back by killing her suitor, the Bear (Fred Stanton).

Jamestown (Pathé, 1923)
   The colonists hold Pocahontas (Dolores Cassinelli) hostage to force her father, Powhatan, and his tribe to join them in fighting the Spanish. At the end, the marriage of Pocahontas and John Rolfe brings peace between the tribe and the whites.

The Heritage of the Desert (Paramount, 1924). Irvin Willat
   With the help of a friendly tribe, the hero rescues Mescal (Bebe Daniels), a mixed-blood whom he eventually marries.

The Gold Hunters (Davis Dist., 1925). Paul Hurst
   The hero, who rescues Minnetake (Hedda Nova) from a gang of villains after gold, eventually finds the gold and falls in love with the young woman. Other Native American characters are Mukoki (All Hallett) and Wabigoon (Noble Johnson).

Scarlet and Gold (Davis Dist., 1925). Frank Grandon
   A loyal Mountie marries Haida (Yvonne Pavis) because she is carrying the child of another Mountie. When she discovers that he loves a white woman, she kills herself so he can be free to marry the woman.

Frozen Justice (Fox, 1929). Allan Dawn
   Talu (Lenor Ulris), a mixed-blood Eskimo who leaves her husband, Lanak (Robert Frazer), to go off with a wicked captain of a ship, suffers for her choice and returns to die in her husband's arms.

Romances between Native American Men and White Women

The Call of the Wild (Biograph, 1908). D. W. Griffith
   In this film, subtitled "The Sad Plight of the Civilized Redman," George Redfeather, from the Carlisle Indian School, proposes to a white woman. When she refuses to

marry him, he angrily returns to the land of his tribe. Later, when the woman ends up in his area, he captures her and is about to take revenge when she uses a religious argument to persuade him to have mercy on her.

The Indian Land Grab (Champion, 1910)

A young man sent by his tribe to fight against land grabbing fails to secure the land rights of his tribe because he is tricked by the daughter of a crooked politician. After he returns home and is about to be punished for his failure, the daughter, who has repented and realizes she loves the young man, appears with a document protecting the tribe's land. Then he and the woman are married and live among his people.

Chief White Eagle (Lubin, 1912)

White Eagle, educated in an Eastern school, murders a white woman who cruelly rejected his love. After he goes home to become chief of his tribe, a reluctant white man hunts him down and kills him. At the end both the man and the tribe pray for White Eagle.

Strongheart (Biograph, 1914)

Based on a contemporary play, this film tells the story of Strongheart, who leaves his tribe and goes to college in the East. He becomes a football star and falls in love with a white woman, but gets in trouble when he lies to help a white friend who has cheated. When he finds out that his father has died and his tribe needs him, he respects his duty and sadly leaves his sweetheart behind.

Where the Trail Divides (Lasky, 1914)

How (Robert Edeson) marries a white woman but later lets her go so she can live in comfort in the East with a rich white man. When this man, who turns out to be a criminal, dies, How brings her back to the West and they renew their marriage.

The Captive God (Triangle, 1916). Thomas Ince

The Aztecs of Montezuma capture Chaipa (W. S. Hart), a

Spaniard adopted by peaceful Cliff Dwellers. As he is about to be killed, his lover Lolomi (Enid Markey), the daughter of Montezuma, comes to his rescue. A *Variety* critic notes that the story "is at once thrilling and carries an air of mystic romance that is compelling." (7 July)

Dawn Maker (Triangle, 1916)

Joe Elk (W. S. Hart), a mixed-blood, falls in love with a white woman and struggles over whether to be loyal to his white or his Native American values. When the woman and her lover are captured by Chief Trouble Thunder's tribe, he decides to rescue them. At the end, badly wounded, he accepts the Native American way by doing the dance of The Dawn Maker before he dies.

The Half-Breed (Triangle, 1916). Allan Dawn

Based on a story by Bret Harte, this film tells the story of Lo Dorman, the son of a Native American woman who had been seduced by a white settler. He spends his early life alone in the forest because the whites drive him from the town. Later he is rejected by one white woman and then finds happiness with another.

The Danger Trail (Selig, 1917). Frederick A. Thompson

A mixed-blood, Jean Croisset (W. Lawson Butt), rescues a white woman and falls in love with her, but finally decides to let her return to her white lover.

The Savage (Bluebird, 1917). Rupert Julian

The title character is Julio Sandoval (Monroe Salisbury), a mixed-blood who falls in love with a white woman and captures her. However, he finally decides to bring her home, and further shows his honor by giving up his life while rescuing her lover.

The Red Red Heart (Bluebird, 1918). Wilfred Lucas

Kut-Le (Monroe Salisbury), a young man educated at an Eastern college, falls in love with a white woman. When she rejects him, he kidnaps her and goes to the mountains of the

West. Eventually she returns his love, and they decide to be married.

The Last of His People (Select, 1920). Robert N. Bradbury
Wolf (Mitchell Lewis), who has been raised by a white man, falls in love with the man's daughter and remains in white society.

The Third Woman (Robertson Cole, 1920)
An educated mixed-blood (Carlyle Blackwell), who is struggling to decide whether to help the people of his tribe and marry one of them or return to a white woman he loves, finally chooses to work for his tribe.

Blazing Arrows (Western Pictures, 1922). Henry McCarty
Sky Fire (Lester Cuneo), a student at Columbia, falls in love with a white woman who rejects him because of his race. Later he returns to the West and rescues the same woman from the evil Gray Eagle (Clark Comstock). At the end, he marries her after he finds out that he is really a white man who had been adopted by a Native American.

The Huntress (Assoc. First National Pics. 1923). Tom Forman
A white woman adopted by the tribe of Musq'oois (Snitz Edwards), Beavertail (Lalo Encinas) and Otebaya (Chief Big Tree), finally leaves so she can avoid marrying a man from the tribe and give herself to the white man she loves. A *Variety* reviewer comments: "The story deals with Indians and the old theme of the girl who thought she was a member of the redskins but who found out later that some careless parents had deserted her. And with the discovery that she isn't Indian comes a desire to capture a white husband." (11 Oct.)

Braveheart (Producers Dist. Corp., 1925). Alan Hale
Braveheart (Rod La Rocque), a scholar and All-American football player at an Eastern college, lies to protect a white friend. When he is found out, he has to return in disgrace to his homeland. Later he vindicates himself by winning fishing rights for his tribe. Then, after Ki-Yote (Frank

Hagney) incites his tribe to kidnap a white woman, Braveheart come to her rescue and realizes she is the person he loved in college. However, at the end he decides to marry a woman from his tribe, Sky Arrow (Jean Acker).

The Red Rider (Universal, 1925). Clifford Smith
When White Elk (Jack Hoxie) rejects a woman he is betrothed to because he loves a white woman, Chief Black Panther (Jack Pratt) condemns him to death. However, after White Elk and the white woman escape, he finds out he is really a white man and they get married. Other Native American characters are Natauka (Natalie Warfield), Silver Waters (Marin Sais), Brown Bear (Francis Ford) and the Medicine Man (Frank Lanning).

The Scarlet West (First National, 1925). John Adolfi
Cardelanche (Robert Frazer), an educated man rejected by his tribe, rescues the Cavalry from hostile warriors and becomes an officer. He falls in love with a white woman, but after learning of Custer's death, gives up his commission, returns to his tribe and marries Nestina (Helen Ferguson).

The Vanishing American (Paramount, 1925). George Seitz
Discussed on pps. 20–21, this film tells the story of Nophaie, who falls in love with Marion, the teacher on his reservation. At the end, he dies while trying to stop the fighting between his tribe and the whites. A *Variety* critic's comment on the film reveals a common contemporary stereotype of Native Americans living on reservations: "The story itself calls attention to the vanishing of the real American, the Indian, off the face of the North American continent. Nothing is said about the Indians who are living in Oklahoma at this time and drawing down a weekly royalty of $1,750 and riding around in sedans which they discard immediately after a tire blows, so as to get a new car." (21 Oct.) Two comments by other *Variety* reviewers reflect a similar prejudice: on *Fool's Paradise* (1921), "Oil did it, the same as oil made it possible for the Injun to move a player piano into his tent, while his fat squaw rocked herself in front and when she wanted a smoke, removed her corncob pipe

from a jeweled chatelaine bag." (16 Dec.). On *The Big Show* (1926): An Indian chief sits in a "majestic pose" with "folded arms and impassive face" as he dictates a letter to his daughter which instructs "his bank in Oklahoma to credit him with oil royalties immediately to cover his checks drawn for a new runabout for his daughter." (14 July)

Red Clay (Universal, 1927). Ernest Laemmle
   Though Chief John Nisheto (William Desmond), a scholar and star college football player, saves the life of a white man in wartime, the man objects to a romance between Chief Nisheto and his sister. After Chief Nisheto is fatally shot, the man repents for his prejudiced attitude. A *Variety* critic notes that the film "runs to the realistic, showing the probable results of an attempt by an Indian to mix with a white girl." (20 Apr.)

Romances between Native Americans

Ramona (Biograph, 1910). D. W. Griffith
   In this film, subtitled "A Story of the Whiteman's Injustice to the Indian," Ramona, a mixed-blood, is the target of prejudice because of her marriage to Chief Alessandro. An *MPW* reviewer notes that the film shows "graphically the injustice which preceded the settlement of a considerable proportion of the United States." (4 June, 942)

A True Indian Brave (Bison, 1910)
   When settlers insult a young Native American woman, and the man from her tribe who loves her comes to her defense, the whites try to lynch them. An *MPW* critic comments that the filmmaker gave "a truer picture than he intended. He may have shown why some of the difficulties between whites and Indians began . . . and the conclusions will not be wholly flattering to the white man." (23 Sept., 689)

The Yaqui Cur (Biograph, 1913). D. W. Griffith
   A young man, who learns white customs like smoking cigarettes and reading the Bible, loves a woman from his

Yaqui tribe who will have nothing to do with him. Later, he refuses to fight with his tribe when they attack the whites, but finally gives his life to save the woman he had loved and lost.

Ramona (Clune, 1916). Donald Crisp
   This is the second adaptation of Helen Hunt Jackson's novel about the tragic love of the mixed-blood Ramona (Adda Gleason) and Chief Alessandro (Monroe Salisbury). A *Variety* critic sees the film as "a plea for justice for the red man who has been robbed of his land by the constant encroachment of the American on his vested domain." (7 Apr.)

The Squaw Man's Son (Lasky, 1917). E. J. Le Saint
   An English mixed-blood (Wallace Reid) leaves his wife in England, comes to America to live with his tribe, and falls in love with Wa-Na-Gi (Anita King), a Carlisle graduate who is teaching at the Indian agency. When she finds out her beloved is married, she is about to commit suicide. However, after she learns that his English wife has died, she marries her mixed-blood lover.

The Great Alone (American, 1922). Jaques Jaccard
   Silent Duval (Monroe Salisbury), a mixed-blood football star, leaves Stanford because of prejudice towards him. He returns to the Yukon and, though he rescues a white woman who had helped him in college, finally falls in love with a mixed-blood woman who has loved him for years.

Justice of the Far North (Columbia, 1925). Norman Dawn
   Umluk (Arthur Jasmine), an Eskimo, returns to his igloo to find that the woman he is to marry, Wamba (Marcia Manon), has been enticed away by a white man. Umluk struggles to get her back but ends up marrying Nootka (Laska Winter), her faithful and loving sister.

Red Love (Davis Dist., 1925). Edgar Lewis
   Thundercloud (John Lowell), a Sioux and graduate of Carlisle, goes away with Starlight (Evangeline Russell), the

mixed-blood daughter of the sheriff. His brother, Little Antelope, a tribal policeman, arrests him for kidnapping. However, at the end Thundercloud is exonerated and marries Starlight. Other Native American characters are Two Crows (Frank Montgomery) and Scar Face (Dexter McReynolds).

Ramona (UA, 1928). Edwin Carewe (Chickasaw)

In this third adaptation of the famous novel, Ramona (Dolores Del Rio), a mixed-blood raised by a cruel white man, defies her guardian and marries Chief Allesandro (Warner Baxter). Eventually she loses both her husband and child, and wanders in a state of amnesia until friends finally rescue her.

Redskin (Paramount, 1929). Victor Schertzinger

Wing Foot (Richard Dix), a Navajo educated in the East and an outcast from his tribe, falls in love with a classmate, Corn Blossom (Gladys Belmont), a member of a rival Pueblo tribe. When he returns to his home, he discovers oil in the desert and uses an offer of oil rights to stop a war between the Pueblo tribe and his people. At the end, he and Corn Blossom are married.

Native American Life before Contact with Whites

These films, many of which are love stories, were very popular during the early part of the Silent period. Because the Native American characters, whether heroes or villains, are central characters, their way of life is the focus in a way very different from that of the Westerns. Contemporary film critics were much taken by this type of film and their comments on them reflect the stereotypes of the times.

Hiawatha (Laemmle, 1909)

In this early adaptation of Longfellow's famous poem, Hiawatha, an Ojibway, overcomes many obstacles before he can marry Minnehaha, a member of the hostile Sioux tribe. A *Variety* critic reflects a common stereotype when he notes that "the actors, both men and women, seemingly cannot secure the natural abandon of the Indian." (30 Oct.)

The Mended Lute (Biograph, 1909). D. W. Griffith
Sioux warriors, Little Bear and Standing Rock are vying for the chief's daughter, Rising Moon, and her father gives her to the highest bidder, Standing Rock, the one she doesn't love. After she leaves her new husband for Little Bear, the two are captured and are about to be burned at the stake when Standing Rock, impressed by their love and bravery, sets them free.

Cheyenne Brave (Pathé, 1910)
Warriors from two different tribes fight for the hand of a maiden. Her Cheyenne lover wins and takes her to the land of his people. An *MPW* reviewer calls the film "one of most, if not the most, remarkable Indian pictures ever produced. . . . All the actors taking part in this picture are real Indians or sufficiently well made up to pass as such." (6 Aug., 299)

The Maid of Niagara (Pathé, 1910)
When his beloved Red Doe is sacrificed to the Spirit of the Falls, Esoomet, a young Iroquois, drowns himself so he can be with her in the afterworld.

Song of the Wildwood Flute (Biograph, 1910). D. W. Griffith
After hearing Gray Cloud (Chief Dark Cloud) play the flute, Dove Eyes (Mary Pickford) decides to marry him rather than another suitor. When Gray Cloud falls into a bear pit, his rival for the affection of Dove Eyes sees how she is suffering and shows his honor by rescuing her beloved. A *Variety* critic notes that the "poor attempt by the principal characters to act as Indians is pitiable." (3 Dec.)

The Squaw's Love (Biograph, 1911). D. W. Griffith
White Eagle (Chief Dark Cloud), betrothed to Silver Fawn, helps his exiled friend, Gray Fox, by bringing into the forest Wild Flower, who is betrothed to Gray Fox. Silver Fawn sees the two of them and thinks her lover has chosen

another woman. After she takes revenge by throwing Wild Flower into the river, Gray Fox rescues her, and, after the mistake is cleared up, all four lovers escape from the hostile tribe that is pursuing them.

Indian Romeo and Juliet (Vitagraph, 1912)

In this adaptation of Shakespeare's famous play, two lovers, one a Huron and the other a Mohican, die because of the hostility between the tribes.

On the Warpath (Bison, 1912)

An old man dreams of ancient battles between fierce Apaches and peace-loving Yumas and of a romance between a man of one tribe and a woman of the other.

A Pueblo Legend (Biograph, 1912). D. W. Griffith

The high priest tells the tribe about a turquoise stone which fell from the heavens, a stone that would bring great happiness and wealth. Then the tribe chooses one of its leaders to go and find the stone. An *MPW* reviewer writes that the film is "a most beautiful portrayal of early Indian symbolism." (14 Feb., 1914)

The Red Man's Honor (Eclipse, 1912). Gaston Roudes

Though really innocent, Red Hawk is accused of killing Seated Bear, his rival for the love of June Dew. The chief of the tribe rules that he must be executed one year later, and Red Hawk shows his honor by returning at the appointed time and dying with his beloved June Dew.

The Tribal Law (Bison, 1912). Otis Turner

A Hopi maiden, Starlight, and an Apache, Jose Seville, marry despite a Hopi law against such a match. Starlight's jilted lover, Gray Wolf, tries to have them killed, but a Hopi man whom Jose had helped earlier rescues them. An *MPW* critic notes that the film is "not of the orthodox sort— burning, raiding, soldiers to the rescue, and all of the regular program. It is a story of Indians as Indians, and in it are shown the habitations, the mode of life, some of the customs." (9 Nov., 536)

Hiawatha (Moore, 1913). F. E. Moore

This adaptation of Longfellow's poem about the adventures of Hiawatha, the Ojibway, and his love for Minnehaha, the Sioux, uses all Native American actors. An *MPW* reviewer comments on the acting and subject matter of the film: "we have had such a surfeit of bloodthirsty Indians, scalping Indians, and burning Indians in the cheap films, that it was like a breath of fresh air to see real human Indians enacting before us an old Indian legend. . . . The Indians of these reels show all that stoic and impressive calm which the white man has never quite been able to understand." (8 Mar., 980)

In the Long Ago (Selig, 1913). Colin Campbell

In an ancient legendary era, by playing a wind pipe made from the thighbone of a great chief, a young man revives his lover, Starlight, who has been under a spell. Then two modern lovers are compared to the legendary ones.

Nanook of the North (Pathé, 1922). Robert Flaherty

This famous film uses an all-native cast to show the struggles of an Eskimo family to survive in the far North.

Kivalina of the Ice Lands (B. R. C. Productions, 1925). Earl Rossman

In this film with an all-Eskimo cast, Aguvaluk, who is told by the witch doctor that he must kill 40 seals and a silver fox before he can marry Kivalina, accomplishes the feats and marries his beloved. A *Variety* critic notes that in this film "all the various activities of the tribe are depicted." (1 July)

The Silent Enemy (Paramount, 1930). H. P. Carver

Discussed in the introduction (21–23), this film tells the story of an Ojibway tribe that struggles to survive in the far North. Bulak becomes chief after the death of Chetoga and though he loves Neewa, the daughter of Chetoga, he cannot marry her until he survives the treachery of Dagwan, who also wants Neewa for his wife. At the end, Bulak saves the tribe and marries Neewa.

Noble Native Americans as Victims

Though numerous films could be categorized under this heading, these are singled out as representative examples of victimization and white prejudice.

Lo, the Poor Indian (Kalem, 1910)
A man who doesn't know or understand the laws of the white man is put in jail for stealing a horse to save the lives of his wife and child. An *MPW* reviewer notes that the film "should arouse a sense of the injustice which has been meted out to unfortunate Indians on the supposed intention of following the white man's ideas of justice." (9 Apr., 553)

The Red Man's Penalty (Bison, 1911)
A mean and crooked Indian agent gives a tribe rotten meat. When the tribe retaliates because of this injustice, the cavalry attacks them and many are killed.

The Indian Servant (Great Northern, 1914)
This comedy makes fun of a Native American whose behavior is inappropriate in white society. Brought home to be a servant by a foreign diplomat, he takes bonnets from the heads of young women in a millinery shop, improperly flirts with them, and then almost wrecks the house of the diplomat when he paints himself and the children and does a war dance with them.

Lone Star (1916). Edward Sloman
On a Nebraskan reservation, a man (William Russell) who gains fame as a surgeon is scorned by his tribe for following white ways and rejected by the whites because he is a Native American.

Captain of Gray Horse Troop (Vitagraph, 1917). William Wobert
Ranchers use their influence in the U.S. Government to steal land from the tribe of Crawling Elk (Otto Lederer). A *Variety* critic comments: "Instead of making all 'Injuns'

merely firewater drinkers, it places them in the attitude of being the abused nation." (18 May)

Drums of the Desert (Paramount, 1927). John Waters
When Chief Brave Bear (Bernard Siegel) and his Navajo tribe try to resist the efforts of oil-hungry villains to force them off their land and desecrate their sacred altars, the cavalry comes to their aid.

* * *

These categories represent some of the perspectives from which one can look at the images of the Savage and Noble Red Man in the Silent period. Obviously, a significant number of films could fit under several categories. This question of categorization will perhaps stimulate the reader to think about other ways of connecting the films. The reader should also note that a connection, or subtext, exists in the opinions of contemporary film reviewers on the portrayal of the Native American characters. Though most of the critics probably knew relatively little about the history and cultures of the Native American tribes (and indeed sometimes reveal very stereotyped views), they evaluate the characters as if they really know Native American peoples. In all likelihood, much of what they knew was drawn from the movies and the print media, especially popular fiction, newspapers and advertising (though this must remain speculation). To the degree that this is true, the early reviewers are good examples of the encoding. Examples of such stereotyping and encoding on the part of the film critics will appear in each of the remaining periods and will at least hint at the evolution of this process.

CHAPTER THREE

THE EARLY SOUND FILMS (1931–1949)

During this period, as the Western grows into a distinct genre, the image of the Noble but doomed Red Man becomes less dominant than that of the Savage. Native American characters more often are hidden enemies in a hostile landscape or savage adversaries of the white hero. Frequently, a fierce and sudden attack on vulnerable whites is their main function in the plot, as happens in John Ford's *Stagecoach* (1939). After Ford builds the threat of an attack by Geronimo and his warriors through most of the film, the attack itself starts with a close shot of an arrow hitting one of the people in the stagecoach. Then the chase begins with the camera following the action at high speed and cross-cutting from close-up reaction shots of those in the stage to low-angle shots of Apaches being shot off their horses and hitting the ground. After the fast-paced editing builds to the point where the people on the stage are about to be killed, the sound of the bugle signals the arrival of the cavalry, and the attack is over as fast as it began. Thus the Apaches in *Stagecoach* have significance only as an absent threat early in the film, and then as a vehicle for cinematic excitement.

In varying degrees, notable historical romances of this period, *The Last of the Mohicans* (1936), *Drums along the Mohawk* (1939), *Northwest Passage* (1940) and *They Died with Their Boots On* (1942), diminish the Native American tribes in a way similar to *Stagecoach*. Though such films are predominant, another representative type is domestic drama such as *Duel in the Sun* (1946). In these films, which expose racial prejudice, individual Native American characters struggle to survive in white society.

The first of the representative historical romances, *The Last of the Mohicans* (1936), differs from Cooper's novel by changing the nature of the companionship between Hawkeye and Chingachgook. At the end of the novel, as Chingachgook is mourning the loss of Uncas, Hawkeye says, "Sagamore, you are not alone" (212). Then Cooper describes their expression of feeling for each other: "Chingachgook grasped the hand that, in the warmth of feeling, the scout had stretched across the warm earth, and in that attitude of friendship these two sturdy and intrepid woodsmen bowed their heads together, while scalding tears fell to their feet, watering the grave of Uncas like drops of falling rain" (212). At the end of the novel, then, Hawkeye and Chingachgook affirm the depth of their friendship as lonely heroes. The film, however, diminishes this relationship so that Hawkeye can become the central hero and fall in love with the heroine. In the Hollywood fashion, the romance of Hawkeye and Cora Monro dominates the plot, and the noble Mohicans become sidekicks.

As friends of the hero, Chingachgook (Robert Barrat) and Uncas (Phillip Reed) are Noble Red Men; however, the film's composition and dialogue reduce their stature, especially in comparison to the novel. The placement of Hawkeye and his two friends in the frame depicts Chingachgook and Uncas as subservient to the hero. In their first appearance, they are walking together behind Hawkeye. This pattern continues in many other shots where the two Mohicans are on either side of the hero, who is slightly more in the foreground. Only at the end of the film, after the death of Uncas and Hawkeye's commitment to his beloved Cora, do Hawkeye and Chingachgook walk together, with the British hero on his horse between them. In addition, Chingachgook's dialogue is typically clipped and gruff. For example, when Uncas offers food to his beloved Alice, his father says, "Mohican chief no wait on squaw." Later, when Hawkeye asks about the condition of the wounded Uncas (who had just been visited by Alice), Chingachgook answers, "Bad, got squaw fever." Chingachgook's son speaks a little more poetically when he refers to his beloved Alice as "the one with the moon in her hair," but generally his dialogue, and that of his father, is less eloquent than that of their counterparts in the novel.

The dialogue of the evil antagonist of Chingachgook and Uncas, Magua (Bruce Cabot), also is reduced to typical Native American movie talk. This savage character, who in the novel incites the hostile Hurons to violence with powerful orations, has lines in the film like "You take em trail, me follow." However, Magua's evil actions, typical of the Savage, speak loudly for him. Driven by vengeance, he captures the daughters of Colonel Monro and demands Alice as his "squaw" because Monro had once ordered him to be whipped, and he convinces the Hurons to attack Monro's British fort, which had already surrendered. Near the end, he also shoots Uncas, whom he has trapped on the edge of a cliff with Alice. After Uncas falls, Magua, seen in a menacing close-up, approaches Alice and she jumps to her death (where her beloved Uncas crawls to her and holds her hand before he dies). Then Magua and Chingachgook have a fierce hand-to-hand battle before the noble Mohican gains his revenge and drowns his evil adversary.

Just as the Savage antagonist is punished at the end, so also is the savage tribe, the Hurons, who resort to ambushes, a savage attack on a surrendered fort, and torture of the hero. These enemies of the Mohicans and allies of the French are portrayed in the classic image of the Savage. Led by the treacherous Magua and sporting the typical "mohawk" hair cuts of villainous characters, they ambush the party of Heywood, Alice and Cora, only to be driven off by the hero and his Mohican companions. When they continue their pursuit of the hero and his party in canoes, Hawkeye leads them away from the others and eludes them by pulling into a backwater while they continue to paddle feverishly down the river, apparently oblivious to the fact that the hero's canoe is no longer in front of them. As is often the case with Savages, they are not only fierce, but also stupid. Later, they attack the British fort, a sequence described by a contemporary film critic: "The massacre of Fort Henry is by far the bloodiest, scalpingest morsel of cinematic imagery ever produced . . ." (NYT, 3 Sept.). This intensely edited sequence begins with a shot of the Hurons breaking down the gate and then cuts from a close-up shot of a brave scalping a colonist, to shots of the Hurons burning the houses, and to Magua shooting Monro and capturing his daughters . The Hurons' final act of violence is their torturing and burning at the stake of the hero, who is rescued at the last moment by a troop of British soldiers and American colonists, who then rout the Hurons decisively.

Such Savages are also the fierce antagonists in another historical romance of this period, *Drums along the Mohawk* (1939). The hero of this film is Gil Martin, a newly married colonist whose attempt to build a successful farm is thwarted by the Savages, who are allies of a wicked royalist. Martin's Native American friend, Blue Back (Chief John Big Tree), is the only Noble Red Man in the film. A convert to the Christian faith, he first appears in the hero's cabin, where he terrifies Gil's new wife. Seen from a low angle, he is a striking presence, wrapped in a long red blanket and holding a flintlock. After the woman recovers, Blue Back returns and gives Gil a stick to discipline his wife. Like Chingachgook, Blue Back is not only a male chauvinist but also a man of few words; when the hero is fussing over his wife as she is about to give birth, he says, "Having babies, that woman's business. She better go far off by herself, leave husband alone." Throughout the film this noble character is often seen in low-angle close-ups, the most notable of which is the final shot which shows him putting on the eye patch of the villain, whom he has caught and killed.

The hostile Savages (Iroquois), on the other hand, are depicted as almost naked, painted warriors (again with "mohawk" haircuts) who burn the crops and cabins of the settlers. In one scene, two drunken savages come into the home of a feisty old woman and are so weakened by drink that they let her browbeat them into carrying her out of the house on her bed before they burn it down. In another scene, a man who has tried to run for help is captured by the tribe and pulled into the view of the fort in a cart filled with straw. As they start the fire, a preacher from the fort shoots the man to stop his agony. While the people in the fort, who call them "greasy devils" and "filthy pagan heathens," prepare for the final attack, the hero outruns three stocky hostiles and brings soldiers, who rescue the people in the fort and quickly drive off the savage but inept warriors.

In another historical drama, also set on the east coast, *Northwest Passage* (1940), virtually all the Native American characters are diminished to the image of the Savage. Based on the Book I of the Kenneth Roberts novel, the film makes heroes out of Major Rogers and his Rangers. Unlike Gil Martin, Rogers has only disdain for Native Americans and even looks down on his devoted but drunken Stockbridge guide, Konkapot. Other Native Americans, like the Mohawks who accompany him on part of his trek are viewed as treacherous "snakes." However, for the Abenaki , allies of the French and the tribe who attacked his people, Rogers has the deepest hatred. He says of them, "Those red hellions hacked and murdered us, burned our homes, stole women, burned babies, scalped stragglers, roasted officers over slow fires." Though he has this reason for his feelings, his hatred really overreaches the motivation. In fact, Rogers is one of the more notable heroes who hate all Native Americans, a type that reappears throughout the history of the Westerns. And his hatred is based on a thorough knowledge of his adversaries: as one of his Rangers says, "The smartest Indian alive can't think like an Indian like Rogers." Implicit in heroes like Rogers is the idea that to know Native Americans is to hate them. In fact, hatred and revenge are the primary motivation for the heroic trek of the Rangers to the land of the Abenaki and their French allies.

When the Rangers get close to the Abenaki town, they hear the tribe celebrating and Rogers, with his characteristic attitude, says, "they're probably all drunk, but we can't count on it." In the early morning, the Rangers attack, and the still dazed Abenaki run in different directions as waves of Rangers shoot and bayonet them. Shots from the perspective of the Rangers show the Abenaki being picked off like targets, hacked with hatchets and bayoneted. The rapid pace of the editing and the variety of close shots give the audience an exciting sense of being part of the killing of the hated tribe. The whole short attack sequence also reduces the fierce Abenaki tribe to cowardly sheep being slaughtered by the superior Rangers. After several high-angle shots of the town burning and the ground strewn with Abenaki bodies, Rogers looks through a pile of moccasins left on the outskirts of the town and says, "Don't any of the redskins have man-sized feet," and then concludes with "there's nothing but roast Indian left in the town." Such vicious comments by the hero about a massacre which the film depicts as a heroic action are typical of the racist tone in *Northwest Passage*.

Though a much less hateful film than *Northwest Passage*, the later historical drama, *They Died with Their Boots On* (1942), diminishes the Native American characters in a somewhat different way, by making them a very insignificant part of the plot. This film follows the career of George Armstrong Custer from his days at West Point through the Civil War to his final battle. The major part of the film, which focuses on his life before he comes to the plains to fight the hostile tribes, portrays him as a jaunty, courageous leader who wins battles during the Civil War with the flair of the all-out cavalry charge. Seen throughout the film in low-angle shots, he grows in heroic stature right up to the final battle. In this process of turning Custer into a mythic hero, the filmmakers, of course, play havoc with history, as a contemporary *Variety* critic noted: "In westerns . . . major errors in history and persons mean little to producers or audiences. The test of a yarn is not its accuracy but its speed and excitement" (1941, 19 Nov.) One of the ways this film distorts history is by making one Sioux warrior, Crazy Horse (Anthony Quinn), the antagonist to Custer. The film disposes of Custer's other fights with hostile tribes in a montage of battle scenes, after noting that the Seventh Cavalry "Cleared the Plains for a Ruthlessly Spreading Civilization That Spelled Doom for the Red Race." After dismissing all that history, the film focuses on Crazy Horse. In the first confrontation between Custer and Crazy Horse, they charge each other on horseback and Custer cuts his rival's lance and reins with his saber, then knocks him off his horse and takes him prisoner. This meeting establishes their rivalry and shows that the best of the Sioux horsemen is no match for Custer in a one-to-one fight.

However, the two men accept each other as great warriors. Later, after Crazy Horse escapes, he will only trust Custer when he is ready to make a treaty. When the treaty is broken by the action of greedy businessmen, Custer shows his respect for the Sioux warrior when he says, "If I were Indian, I would fight with Crazy Horse until my last drop of blood." The director of the film, Raoul Walsh, explained the reason for such a portrayal of Custer and Crazy Horse: "Most westerns had depicted the Indian as a painted, vicious savage. In *They Died . . .* , I tried to show him as an individual who turned violent when his rights as defined by treaty were violated by white men." (*Motion Picture Guide*, Vol. 7, 3355). Though Walsh may have had such a general purpose, his depiction of the Battle of Little Big Horn belittles the adversaries of Custer.

As Custer and his cavalry move toward the battle, the hostiles hide behind rocks, or in trees or the high grass. The camera looks from the perspective of the hostiles in the hills down on Custer and his men in the valley and thus emphasizes their vulnerability. The only close-up view of the Native American characters is in a brief scene from their camp in which each chief identifies his tribe, a scene which emphasizes how greatly they outnumber Custer's men. In the actual Battle of Little Big Horn, the moving camera shows Custer making his characteristic cavalry charge, only to find that he is surrounded by warriors who attack in waves. As Custer and his men make their stand, they kill many of their rivals before they are overwhelmed, and Crazy Horse, the worthy rival, shoots Custer, who is standing above his fallen comrades. The sense of movement and the cross-cutting between Custer and the hostile tribes makes for a quick, exciting climax in which the audience sees Custer as the mythic hero depicted in the many paintings of his last stand.

At the end of the film, Custer comes across as a man who had the courage to sacrifice himself to save the other soldiers in the area and the settlers who, according to Custer, would have been killed by the united hostile plains tribes if he had not engaged them at Little Big Horn. At the very end, Custer's wife, Libby, reads a letter of her husband which will bring to justice the villains who broke the treaty and forced him to fight Crazy Horse. After hearing it, General Sheridan promises that Crazy Horse will get his treaty rights and tells Libby, "Your soldier won his last fight after all." Though the ending has no historical basis, it does nicely complete the glorification of Custer at a time when Americans needed military heroes.

Each of the above films has such a patriotic ending, though only in *They Died with Their Boots On* are the hostile tribes treated with any respect. In *The Last of the Mohicans*, the heroes march off to conquer the French in Canada only after they have defeated the savage Hurons, the allies of the French in the American colonies. At the end of *Drums along the Mohawk*, the colonists cannot defeat the British and become Americans until they have routed the savage Iroquois, who have been incited to violence by the British royalists. And at the end of *Northwest Passage*, Rogers promises his men that the savage allies of the French are nothing compared to the great tribes of the plains that they will meet and conquer on their quest for the Northwest Passage. In each of these three films, the tribes portrayed in the image of the Savage are connected to and manipulated by the royalist or French antagonists of the heroes. As such, they are obstacles to progress that must be eliminated before the British or Americans can achieve their patriotic destinies in North America.

In contrast to these historical films, *Ramona* (1936) and *Duel in the Sun* (1946) focus on the domestic life of Native Americans who are victims of white society and their own natures. In each, the central characters are mixed-blood females who are living with rich families and eventually become involved in tragic love affairs. Though her story is different from that of Ramona because she falls in love with a white man rather than a Native American, Pearl Chavez (Jennifer Jones), the doomed mixed-blood lover in *Duel in the Sun*, is typical of characters in such films which both play on the stereotypes and attempt to expose the prejudice of white society.

A voice-over narrator describes the setting of the beginning and end of the film, Squaw's Head rock, as the place where, according to Comanche legend, Pearl died and then grew into a desert flower. Within this frame, the film tells the story of Pearl Chavez, the daughter of a Native American mother and a Creole father. The primitive and deadly sensuality of Pearl's mother is established early in the film. Wearing a long skirt and beaded headband and standing on a circular bar in the saloon, she does a wild dance which drives the male crowd wild. Seen from a high angle, she shoots a pistol at the height of her dance before she throws herself at her white lover and leaves with him. Shortly thereafter, Pearl's father shoots his wife and her lover, for which he is condemned to be hanged. Pearl's mother is the typical dark, passionate Native American femme fatale, and this heritage is what her daughter must struggle with when she goes to live with the McCanles family on the huge Spanish Bit Ranch. The two McCanles sons, Jesse, an educated, kind man like his genteel Southern mother, and Lewt, a wild, uncontrollable man like his dominating rancher father, represent the forces that will play on Pearl in this setting.

Pearl, whose dark hair is long and curly, dresses like her Native American mother in a long dark skirt and exudes the same "native" sensuality. She responds to the respect and kindness shown to her by Jesse and his mother by promising them to be a "good girl." On the other hand, Lewt sees Pearl as a "bob-tailed little half-breed" he can possess, and his father, the Senator, looks down on her Native American heritage. Commenting on Pearl's outfit, the old man says "Is that what they're wearing this season in wigwams?" And later, referring to her sarcastically as "Pocahontas" or "Minnehaha," he makes Lewt promise not to marry her because he doesn't want the ranch turned "into no Indian reservation." Lewt, who is used to making conquests of women, gives her his Pinto and then on a stormy night comes to her room and embraces her until she gives in and makes love with him. Thus she becomes Lewt's girl and finally has to tell Jesse, who finds Lewt in her room. In a close-up, with tears in her eyes, she says to Jesse, "I couldn't help it. You must think I'm trash like my Ma." Jesse, who like his mother treats Pearl with respect, rejects her at this point and leaves her alone to face her destiny.

Pearl decides, however, to regain respectability by persuading Lewt to marry her. She comes to a dance at the ranch in a white dress and, after Lewt teaches her the ballroom dances, she begs him to marry her but he refuses. After this rejection, she tries for respect (and revenge on Lewt) by agreeing to marry Sam, the foreman of the ranch. Lewt, however, shoots Sam, claiming that he has his "brand" on Pearl. In one last desperate attempt, Pearl hides Lewt from the sheriff, but he refuses to take her with him to Mexico even though she clings to his leg as he leaves. At this low point, Jesse returns and promises to let Pearl live with him and his betrothed so that they can care for and educate her. However, when Lewt hears of this, he comes and shoots Jesse, an act that finally drives Pearl to vengeance.

When Pearl learns that Lewt is at Squaw's Head rock, she puts on a dark blouse, pulls her hair back into a ponytail, takes a rifle and rides her Pinto to carry out her revenge. Her wild look and horse (the Pinto being the "Indian" horse) emphasize her change to the Savage avenger, a role she pursues with an animal-like intensity, shown in a scene where she gets off her horse and lowers herself to the ground to drink with him out of the same water hole. When she finds Lewt, she shoots him twice before he shoots her. After Lewt tells her he loves her, she crawls to him, tells of her love, and they kiss and die. Ultimately, Pearl seems to be doomed just like her mother, and dies a similar violent death with her white lover. Though the film reveals the prejudice that Pearl suffered because of her heritage, it also fosters the stereotype of the mixed-blood femme fatale and reduces her character to a variation of the Noble but doomed Red Man.

IMAGES OF THE SAVAGE

As has been suggested by the representative films, attacks by hostile tribes are common in the plots of Westerns during this period. Again, these attacks provide cinematic excitement and establish the Savage characters as antagonists to the heroes and obstacles to the westward expansion promulgated by the Monroe Doctrine. During this period, however, evil whites often incite the attacks and the hostile warriors are further diminished because they end up fighting and dying for the benefit of the villains.

Attacks on Covered Wagons

Fighting Caravans (Paramount, 1931). Otto Brower and David Burton
Stirred up by the villain, a hostile tribe attacks a wagon train. A *Variety* critic notes that "It's a long wait for the inevitable Indian attack" (1 Apr.). In 1934 Paramount released another version of this film called *Wagon Wheels*.

Rainbow Trail (Fox, 1932). David Howard
The tribe of Lone Eagle (Robert Frazer) and Singing Cloud (Laska Winter) threaten a wagon train. A *Variety* critic comments that this adds "some Indian menace stuff" (2 Feb.).

Wheels of Destiny (Universal, 1934). Alan James
Incited by the villains, the tribe of Scalp-em-Alive (Fred Sale, Jr.) attacks wagon trains.

Ride, Ranger, Ride (Republic, 1936). Joseph Kane
The Comanches of Little Wolf (Chief Thunder Cloud), aided by Tavibo (Monte Blue), a Native American interpreter for the army, attack a wagon train. Texas Ranger Gene Autry and the cavalry come to the rescue.

Arizona (Columbia, 1940). Wesley Ruggles
Incited by the villains, Apaches attack a wagon train, but the cavalry and the hero, who drives a herd of cattle into the charging Indians, save the day.

Kit Carson (UA, 1940). George Seitz
The hero, who leads soldiers and a wagon train to California, fights off an attack by the Shoshone tribe.

Prairie Schooners (Columbia, 1940). Sam Nelson
Wild Bill Hickok, a guide for the wagon train, fights the hostile tribe of Chief Sanche (Jim Thorpe) who are struggling to protect their land. A *Variety* critic comments: "The plot does the redskins dirt; maybe Indians encamped in Colorado at that time were that dumb but it hardly is conceivable. . . . Another quaint twist is the failure of the Indians to come out victorious although outnumbering the white settlers about two to one" (13 Nov.).

The Pioneers (Monogram, 1941). Al Herman
In this film based on the Cooper novel, villains intent on laying claim to a rich valley incite the tribe of War Cloud (Chief Many Treaties) and Lone Deer (Chief Soldani) to attack a wagon train on its way to the valley.

Saddlemates (Republic, 1941). Lester Orleleck
The heroes save a wagon train from an attack by the tribe of Chief Wanechee (Peter Lyon). Other Native American characters are Thunder Bird (Matty Faust), Little Bear (Glenn Strange) and Black Eagle (Iron Eyes Cody).

Lawless Plainsmen (Columbia, 1942). William Berke
The tribe of Tascosa (Stanley Brown) and Ochella (Nick Thompson) attacks a wagon train because one of their people had been killed by the whites. The hero tries to make peace and is captured, but the cavalry comes to the rescue. A *Variety* critic notes that "the story's a standard one of the unscrupulous white man making a deal with the Indians to attack a wagon train" (10 June).

Bad Bascomb (MGM, 1946). Sylvan Simon
Warriors attack a Mormon wagon train, and, in what may be the ultimate put-down of their fighting ability, a girl fends them off with a pea shooter.

Blazing Across the Pecos (Columbia, 1948). Ray Nazarro
The Durango Kid deals with villains running guns to a hostile tribe and later stops their attack on a wagon train.

Apache Chief (Lippert, 1949). Frank MacDonald

Black Wolf (Russell Hayden) leads a band that attacks wagon trains, and Young Eagle (Alan Curtis) leads a band that believes the Apache can live in peace with the whites. At the end, Young Eagle kills Black Wolf in a hand-to-hand fight, establishes peace, and wins the love of the beautiful maiden, Watona (Carol Thurston). Other Native American characters are Big Crow (Trevor Howard), Mohaska (Francis McDonald), Pani (Ted Hecht), Lame Bull (Roy Gordon), Gray Cloud (Billy Wilkerson), Tewa (Rodd Redwing) and White Fawn (Hazel Nilsen).

Attacks on the Cavalry or Soldiers in Forts

Texas Pioneers (Monogram, 1932). Harry Fraser

Using guns sold to them by a villain, a hostile tribe attacks a fort.

Last of the Mohicans (UA, 1936). George Seitz

Discussed in the introduction (65–67), this film chronicles the battles between the English and French during which savage Hurons, incited by the evil Magua, attack the hero and his friends Chingachgook and Uncas and later massacre the inhabitants of Fort William Henry.

The Plainsman (Paramount, 1937). Cecil B. De Mille

Wild Bill Hickok and Buffalo Bill battle the Comanches of Yellow Hand (Paul Harvey) and Painted Horse (Victor Varconi). Though captured and tortured by the Comanche, Hickok finally escapes and rescues the woman he loves. The film also depicts General Custer's fight with the Sioux and Cheyenne at Little Big Horn.

Drums Along the Mohawk (20th Century-Fox, 1939). John Ford

Discussed on pps. 67–69, this film tells the story of the colonists' struggles with the British loyalists and their allies, the savage Iroquois. At the end, the hero brings reinforcements and they stop the vicious Iroquois attack on the fort at German Flats.

Geronimo (Paramount, 1939). Paul Sloane

Geronimo (Chief Thunder Cloud) and his band of hostile Apaches, provided with guns and ammunition by the villain, kill women and children and wipe out almost an entire troop of soldiers before the hero captures him.

Northwest Passage (MGM, 1940). King Vidor

Discussed on pps. 68–69, this film tells the story of Roger's Rangers who make an arduous trek to take revenge on the Abenaki tribe for an earlier attack on the settlers.

Ten Gentlemen from West Point (20th Century-Fox, 1942). Henry Hathaway

Using a strategy they learned at the military academy, new cadets stop a Shawnee uprising led by Tecumseh (Noble Johnson).

They Died with Their Boots On (Warner, 1942). Raoul Walsh

Discussed on pps. 69–71, this film follows the career of George A. Custer from his days at West Point to his last battle at Little Big Horn. In the last part of the film, the Sioux warrior Crazy Horse is Custer's main antagonist.

Deerslayer (Republic, 1943). Lew Landers

In this adaptation of the Cooper novel, the hero, aided by the Delaware tribe, struggles with hostile Hurons who attack a fort and riverboat. A *Variety* reviewer comments on the title character: "Deerslayer is a super-hero who continually eludes the Indians, and, when he's captured, easily escapes in the most convenient spots for script purposes" (10 Nov.).

Buffalo Bill (20th Century-Fox, 1944). William Wellman

In one part of his story, the hero kills his former friend, Yellow Hand (Anthony Quinn), in a hand-to-hand fight, and thus allows the cavalry to come to the rescue in a large battle in which many Cheyenne are killed. Dawn Starlight (Linda Darnell) a Native American school teacher who loves the hero, dies during this battle. Once again the love of a Native American woman for a white man makes it necessary for her to die before the film ends.

Fort Apache (RKO, 1948). John Ford
Angered by a crooked Indian agent, Cochise and his Apaches massacre a troop of cavalry led by an inexperienced and arrogant officer. At the end, Cochise brings the flag of the troop to the hero and then rides away into exile.

Fury at Furnace Creek (20 Century-Fox, 1948). Bruce Humberstone
Spurred on by a villain who wants control of a silver mine, the tribe of Little Dog (Jay Silverheels) attacks a cavalry troop at Fort Furnace Creek.

Massacre River (Monogram, 1949). John Rawlins
A tribe led by Chief Yellowstone (Iron Eyes Cody) fights several battles with soldiers from an army post. When a woman is killed in one of the attacks, Chief Yellowstone promises peace and lets the settlers enter his land.

Attacks on Trains (railroad and telegraph workers) and Stagecoaches

The Telegraph Trail (Vitagraph, 1933). Tenny Wright
Urged on by the villain, a warlike tribe attacks the camp of men working on the transcontinental telegraph line. A *Variety* critic comments: "This outline has been used before: the white man uses his Indian allies to check the march of progress" (4 Apr.).

The Glory Trail (Crescent, 1937). Lynn Shores
Hostile warriors attack railroad workers and soldiers to halt the progress of the rail line.

Prairie Thunder (Warner, 1937). Reeves Eason
Supplied with guns by the villain, a hostile tribe attacks a construction camp and town of railroad and telegraph workers. A *Variety* critic comments that "the plot is reminiscent of past Indian epics and carries stock shots of war dances, etc. from them" (1 Dec.).

Wells Fargo (Paramount, 1937). Frank Lloyd
The hero and his friend, Pawnee (Bernie Siegel) fight a hostile tribe who attacks the Wells Fargo stagecoaches.

Stagecoach (UA, 1939). John Ford
Geronimo (Chief White Horse) and his Apaches attack the stagecoach and are driven off by the cavalry. Discussions of selected techniques from this film are in the first chapter and the introduction to this period.

Susannah of the Mounties (20th Century-Fox, 1939). William Seiter
The Blackfeet tribe of Little Chief (Martin Good Rider), Chief Big Eagle (Maurice Moscovich) and Wolf Pelt raid a railroad construction camp and a post of the Mounties. After they capture the hero, a girl goes to their camp and persuades them to release him and make peace.

Union Pacific (Paramount, 1939). Cecil B. De Mille
Warriors disrupt the building of the railroad by derailing and looting the train.

My Little Chickadee (Universal, 1940). Edward Kline
In this comedy, the heroine skillfully picks off warriors attacking the train she's on, and the hero has an educated Native American friend named Milton who only speaks in grunts.

Western Union (20th Century-Fox, 1941). Fritz Lang
The tribe of Chief Spotted Horse (Chief Big Tree) attacks the builders of the telegraph line after villains supply liquor

to some young braves. However, when the hero shows the power of electricity to the tribe, Spotted Horse lets the line be built.

The Omaha Trail (MGM, 1942). Edward Buzzell
Railroad men struggle with a hostile tribe and a wagon train leader who wants to stop the railway.

Wild Horse Stampede (Monogram, 1943). Alan James
Horse rustlers incite a warlike tribe to attack workers building a railroad through the Southwest.

Canadian Pacific (20th Century-Fox, 1949). Edwin Marin
An evil fur trader incites a tribe to attack the railroad workers.

She Wore a Yellow Ribbon (RKO, 1949). John Ford
The hostile warriors of Red Shirt (Noble Johnson), who belong to the tribe of wise old chief Pony That Walks (Chief Big Tree), attack a stage depot. However, the hero stops an all-out war by attacking the hostiles in their camp.

Attacks on Settlers and Other Representatives of Progress

The Conquering Horde (Paramount, 1931). Edward Sloman
By killing a woman from the tribe of White Cloud (Chief Standing Bear), the villain incites them to attack a group of cattlemen.

Daniel Boone (RKO, 1936). David Howard
Led by a gun-selling villain, a tribe attacks the hero's settlement and is about to break through when rain washes out their tunnels. A *Variety* critic notes that the film uses "a lot of phony histrionics and make-believe hysterical Indian fighting. . . . It's an Indian opera a la mode" (28 Oct.).

The Texas Rangers (Paramount, 1936). King Vidor
Hostile warriors attack a farmhouse and then battle the

hero and his Rangers by throwing large stones from a mountain top.

Hills of Old Wyoming (Paramount, 1937). Nate Watt
When an evil lawman on a reservation, who has mixed-bloods rustle cattle for him, causes trouble between a tribe and the cattlemen, Hopalong Cassidy saves the day.

Overland Express (Columbia, 1938). Drew Eberson
A warlike tribe and stagecoach line owners threaten the founders of the Pony Express. A *Variety* critic comments that "a couple of Injuns on the warpath sequences drag in library clips that don't jive with the groups [of Native Americans] actually in the production" (11 May).

The Texans (Paramount, 1938). James Hogan
Hostile warriors attack cowboys on a cattle drive.

Allegheny Uprising (RKO, 1939). William Seiter
The hero stops the villains from selling liquor and guns to a hostile tribe that threatens the settlers.

Bad Lands (RKO, 1939). Lew Landers
Apaches pick off a posse one-by-one until soldiers save the last survivor.

Northwest Mounted Police (Paramount, 1940). Cecil B. De Mille
Louis Riel, the leader of mixed-bloods called Metis, revolts against the Canadian government and, with his Cree allies, fights the Mounties. A beautiful Metis woman, Louvette Corbeau (Paulette Goddard), entices the Mountie hero to leave his post so the tribes allied with the Metis can attack. Later, the hero redeems himself and makes peace with the wise Cree chief, Big Bear (Walter Hampden).

Pony Post (Universal, 1940). King Vidor
Warlike braves threaten the hero at a Pony Express station.

Young Buffalo Bill (Republic, 1940). Joseph Kane
The hero helps the cavalry stop the tribe of Akuna (Chief Thunder Cloud) as they attack a ranch.

Badlands of Dakota (Universal, 1941). Alfred E. Green
Angered by the gold rush to the Black Hills and the presence of Custer's soldiers, Sioux attack a white village.

Apache Trail (MGM, 1943). Richard Thorpe
Apaches, who have had a sacred pipe stolen from them, attack white settlers. A *Variety* reviewer comments that "the film's major detail, the uprising of the Apaches against the whites, is something that's long since seen its best picture days . . ." (14 Jan.).

Canyon Passage (Universal, 1946). Jacques Tourneur
In Oregon, a hostile tribe attacks settlers and sets fire to their cabins.

My Darling Clementine (20th Century-Fox, 1946). John Ford
At the beginning of the film the drunken Indian Joe (Charles Stevens) terrorizes the citizens of the town until Wyatt Earp stops him.

Along the Oregon Trail (Republic, 1947). R. G. Springsteen
The villains steal rifles to arm hostile warriors for an uprising that will benefit their evil purposes.

Buffalo Bill Rides Again (Screen Guild, 1947). Bernard B. Ray
The hero thwarts the efforts of oil-hungry villains who are inciting the tribe of Chief Brave Eagle (Chief Many Treaties), White Mountain (Charles Stevens) and Young Bird (Shooting Star) to attack the settlers.

Last of the Redmen (Columbia, 1947). George Sherman
Hawkeye and Uncas (Rich Vallin) escort children through the wilderness and are attacked by Magua (Buster Crabbe) and his hostile Huron allies in this film based on Cooper's *Last of the Mohicans*.

The Prairie (Screen Guild, 1948). Frank Wisbar
In this film based on Cooper's novel of the same name, the tribe of the evil Matoreeh (Chief Yowlachie) massacres a pioneer family. Other Native American characters are Eagle Feather (Chief Thunder Cloud) and Running Deer (Jay Silverheels).

Rachel and the Stranger (RKO, 1948). Norman Foster
Hostile braves attack homesteaders in a cabin but are driven off. A *Variety* critic comments: "A socko Indian raid . . . flaming arrows and war whoops pinpoint pioneer danger" (4 Aug.).

Red River (UA, 1948). Howard Hawks
Attacks by Comanches are just one of the obstacles that the hero and his cowboys overcome as they establish the Chisholm Trail. Quo (Chief Yowlachie) is a friendly Native American who accompanies the hero on the cattle drive. A *Variety* critic notes that the film accurately depicts "the marauding Indians that bore down on the pioneers" (14 July).

Gun Runner (Monogram, 1949). Lambert Hillyer
Outlaws smuggle guns to hostile warriors who raid the settlers.

Native Americans in the Serials

In this period , the serials reached the high point of their popularity. Though many of the Native American characters are savage antagonists to the heroes, some of the serials depict Noble Red Men as members of peace-loving tribes and faithful companions of the hero.

Battling with Buffalo Bill (Universal, 1931). Ray Taylor
Based on Cody's *The Great West That Was*, this serial has chapters such as "Captured by Redskins" and "Cheyenne Vengeance." Though the villains have provoked the tribe of Swift Arrow (Jim Thorpe) and Chief Thunderbird (Chief

Thunderbird) to attack by killing one of their women and stealing horses, the hero finally persuades them to make peace.

The Lightning Warrior (Mascot, 1931). Armand Schaefer and Ben Kline
In chapters such as "Drums of Doom" and Flaming Arrows," villains incite the warriors of a tribe to make war, but Rin-Tin-Tin, whom the tribe calls Lightning Warrior, helps to restore the peace.

Heroes of the West (Universal, 1932). Ray Taylor
In chapters like "The Red Peril" and "Captured by Indians," hostile warriors threaten the hero, who is trying to build part of the transcontinental railroad.

Last of the Mohicans (Mascot, 1932). Reeves Eason and Ford Beebe
In twelve chapters such as "Redskin's Honor," "Flaming Arrows" and "The End of the Trail," Hawkeye, Chingach-gook (Hobart Bosworth) and Uncas (Junior Coughlin) battle Magua (Robert Kortman) and the hostile Hurons. This serial is probably the most thorough rendition of Cooper's novel.

Clancy of the Mounted (Universal, 1933). Ray Taylor
In a chapter called "The Breed Strikes," renegade mixed-bloods threaten the hero and his woman.

Fighting with Kit Carson (Mascot, 1933). Armand Schaefer and Colbert Clark
In chapters like "The White Chief" and "Red Phantoms," the hero and his faithful companion, Nakomas (Noah Beery, Jr.), battle hostile tribes.

The Miracle Rider (Mascot, 1935). Armand Schaefer and Reeves Eason
A chapter called "The Vanishing Indian" gives a history of American heroes who have helped tribes whose existence was threatened by villains. Then the hero, an adopted

member of the Ravenhead tribe of Chief Black Wing (Robert Frazer), joins the chief's daughter, Ruth (Jean Gale) and triumphs over the villains who are aided by the hostile Longboat (Robert Kortman). In gratitude the tribe sends the hero and Ruth to be their representatives in Washington.

Rustlers of Red Dog (Universal, 1935). Louis Friedlander
In chapters like "Hostile Indians" and "Flaming Arrow," a tribe attacks a wagon train, stagecoach and fort. The hero saves prisoners taken during the attacks just before they are to be burned at the stake.

Custer's Last Stand (Stage and Screen, 1936). Elmer Clifton
Chapters like "Warpath" and "Red Panthers" lead to Custer's final fight with the Sioux and their allies at the Battle of Little Big Horn.

The Phantom Rider (Universal, 1936). Ray Taylor
In a chapter called "The Indian Raid," hostile warriors attack. Another version of this serial, with a chapter, "The Captive Chief," came out in 1946 (Republic; Spencer Bennet).

The Painted Stallion (Republic, 1937). William Witney and Ray Taylor
After villains incite warriors to attack a wagon train, a white woman, worshiped by the Comanches because of her blonde hair, rides a horse and shoots arrows to warn the whites in a chapter called "The Whispering Arrow."

Wild West Days (Universal, 1937). Ford Beebe and Cliff Smith
In chapters such as "The Redskin's Revenge" and "Rustlers and Redskins," the tribe of Red Hatchet (Chief Thunderbird) threatens the heroes.

Flaming Frontiers (Universal, 1938). Ray Taylor and Alan James
In chapters such as "The Savage Horde" and "Half-

breed's Revenge," hostile braves menace Buffalo Bill and heroine.

The Great Adventures of Wild Bill Hickok (Columbia, 1938). Mack Wright and Sam Nelson
In chapters like "The Apache KIller" and "Savage Vengeance" the tribe of Gray Eagle (Chief Thunder Cloud), Little Elk (Ray Mala) and Snake Eyes (Roscoe Ates) threatens the hero.

The Lone Ranger (Republic, 1938). William Witney and John English
In chapters like "Red Man's Courage," Tonto (Chief Thunder Cloud) makes his first appearance as the faithful companion of the hero.

The Lone Ranger Rides Again (Republic, 1939). William Witney
In this serial, the hero and Tonto (Chief Thunder Cloud) protect a wagon train of settlers.

Adventures of Red Ryder (Republic, 1940). William Witney and John English
In this serial, the hero is aided by his young Indian companion, Little Beaver (Tommy Cook).

Winners of the West (Universal, 1940). Ford Beebe and Ray Taylor
In chapters such as "Trapped by Redskins" and "Sacrificed by Savages," an evil mixed-blood, Snake Eye (Charles Stevens), leads raids on railroad construction camps, telegraph stations, stagecoaches and wagon trains. At the end, Chief War Eagle (Chief Yowlachie) signs a peace treaty.

Perils of the Royal Mounted (Columbia, 1942). James W. Horne
In chapters such as "Burned at the Stake" the tribe of Black Bear (Nick Thompson), an evil medicine man, joins the villain in his plots against the Mounties. Other Native American characters are Flying Cloud (Art Miles) and Little Wolf (Richard Vallin).

Daredevils of the West (Republic, 1943). John English
In a chapter called "Redskin Raiders" a hostile tribe threatens the hero.

Black Arrow (Columbia, 1944). Lew Landers
In chapters such as "An Indian's Revenge" and "Black Arrow Triumphs," Black Arrow (Robert Scott), the son of a Navajo chief, triumphs over the villain, Snake-That-Walks (George Lewis). At the end, Black Arrow finds out that he is really a white man.

The Scarlet Horseman (Universal, 1946). Ray Taylor and Lewis Collins
In chapters like "Comanche Avalanche" and "Staked Plains Massacre," the hero, who takes on the identity of a Comanche legend, the Scarlet Horseman, fights hostile Comanches led by Loma (Victoria Horne), a mixed-blood.

Ghost of Zorro (Republic, 1949). Fred Bannon
The tribe of Yellow Hawk (Alex Montoya) and the villain are the antagonists of the hero.

Vengeance

Though vengeance is often a motive of the Savage characters for their attacks, in some of the following films, the line between this motive and noble striving for justice is sometimes a thin one.

Oklahoma Jim (Monogram, 1931). Harry Fraser
When a young woman who had been seduced by a white man kills herself, the hero and a young man from her tribe (Andy Shuford) stop her people from taking revenge on the whites by bringing the man to justice.

The Thundering Herd (Paramount, 1934). Henry Hathaway
A tribe attacks buffalo hunters who are slaughtering their herds.

Treachery Rides the Range (Warner, 1936). Frank McDonald

After evil buffalo hunters break a treaty, the Cheyenne tribe of Little Big Wolf (Carlyle Moore), Chief Red Smoke (Jim Thorpe), Little Big Fox (Frank Bruno) and Antelope Boy (Dick Botiller) start a war. However, the hero captures the villains and convinces the tribe to make peace.

Tulsa (Eagle Lion, 1949). Stuart Heisler

Redbird (Pedro Armendariz) is the friend of mixed-blood oil wildcatter Cherokee (Susan Hayward). After being treated badly by the villain in court and finding some of his cattle dead, he takes revenge by setting the oil wells on fire.

IMAGES OF THE NOBLE RED MAN

Because of the greater use of Native American characters as antagonists in this period, there are fewer clear-cut examples of generosity, gratitude, honor and courage, though some of the characters in the other categories also have these traits.

Friendship and Loyalty

SOS Iceberg (Vitagraph, 1933). Tony Garnett

Friendly Eskimos use their kayaks to rescue whites marooned on an iceberg.

Annie Oakley (RKO, 1935). George Stevens

The heroine performs in Buffalo Bill's Wild West Show with her friend Sitting Bull (Chief Thunder Cloud) and his Sioux tribe. Sitting Bull shows his friendship by helping her to win the man she loves. His character also adds humor when he has trouble dealing with some of the modern conveniences of civilized life.

Across the Plains (Monogram, 1939). Spencer Bennet

Cherokee (Jack Randall), a white man raised by a friendly tribe, rescues his brother from a gang of villains with the help of the tribe that adopted him.

Frontier Fury (Columbia, 1943). William Berke

When villains capture a good Indian agent and steal supplies, the tribe of Chief Eagle Feather (Billy Wilkerson) and Gray Bear (Stanley Brown) rescues the agent and gets their food back.

Outlaw Trail (Monogram, 1944). Robert Ransey

Thundercloud (Chief Thunder Cloud) becomes one of the three Trail Blazers and shares in their heroic exploits. This character also appears in *Sonora Stagecoach*, another 1944 Trail Blazers film.

Stagecoach to Denver (Republic, 1946). R. G. Springsteen

Red Ryder and his companion, Little Beaver (Bobby Blake), break up a land grab plot.

Oregon Trail Scouts (Republic, 1947). R. G. Springsteen

By kidnapping the grandson of the chief, Little Beaver (Bobby Blake), the villains try to break a treaty Red Ryder made with the tribe. However, the hero rescues the boy and takes him as his companion on his quest to establish law and order in the West. This character, known for his response "You bet-ch-em," also appears in two other 1947 Republic films directed by R.G. Springsteen, *Marshall of Cripple Creek* and *Rustlers of Devil's Canyon*, about which a *Variety* critic comments: "young Bobby Blake as an Indian kid will appeal to the juves" (9 July).

The Dalton Gang (Lippert, 1949). Ford Beebe

The friendly tribe of Chief Irahu helps the hero track the gang of outlaws.

Ma and Pa Kettle (Universal, 1949). Charles Lamont

Crowbar (Chief Yowlachie) and Geoduck (Lester Allen) are the humorous Native American friends of Pa. These characters, portrayed by various actors, appear in most of the Ma and Pa Kettle movies.

Roll, Thunder, Roll (Eagle Lion, 1949). Lewis Collins

Red Ryder and Little Beaver (Don Kay Reynolds) stop a

gang of bandits. A *Variety* critic notes that Little Beaver "is given some sharp lines which will garner laughs, and his role as Red Ryder's junior detective should give juves some vicarious participation in the wild and woolly adventures" (11 May). These characters appear in three other 1949 films, *Cowboy and the Prizefighter, The Fighting Redhead* and *Ride, Ryder, Ride.*

Stallion Canyon (Astor, 1949). Harry Fraser
When his companion, Little Bear (Billy Hammond), is falsely charged with a murder, the hero clears his name. A *Variety* critic comments that the actor "rides well as Little Bear but overdoes the heap-big Injun Talk" (1 June).

Romances between Native American Women and White Men

The Squaw Man (MGM, 1931). Cecil B. De Mille
In yet another version of the well-known play, Naturich (Lupe Velez), daughter of Chief Tabywana (Mitchell Lewis), dies so that her English husband and son can return to England. A *Variety* critic feels that these characters are out of date: "Indians no longer sell cattle; they own oil and many go to college" (22 Sept.).

Behold My Wife (Paramount, 1935). Mitchell Leisen
Based on Sir Gilbert Parker's *Translation of a Savage,* the film tells the story of Tonita Stormcloud (Sylvia Sidney), the daughter of a chief, who saves the life of a white man. When the man marries her to get back at his family, she realizes his motives and tries to avenge herself. Eventually, they are reconciled and live happily together.

Fighting Pioneers (Resolute, 1935). Harry Fraser
After the death of her father, the chief of the tribe, Wa-Na-Na (Ruth Mix) leads her people against the soldiers, but finally falls in love with the hero.

Rose Marie (MGM, 1936). W. S. Van Dyke
Wanda (Joan Taylor), the daughter of Black Eagle (Chief

Yowlachie), falls in love with a Mountie in this musical with lavish numbers like "Totem Tom Tom" and "Indian Love Call."

Wolf Call (Monogram, 1939). George Waggner
In the North to find out about a mine owned by his family, the hero falls in love with the beautiful Towanah (Movita).

Duel in the Sun (Selznick, 1946). King Vidor
Discussed in the introduction (71–73), this film tells the story of Pearl Chavez, a young mixed-blood desired by two brothers, one good and the other bad. A victim of prejudice and her own passionate nature, she dies in the arms of her lover, the bad brother, who refuses to marry her.

Spoilers of the North (Republic, 1947). Richard Sale
The white villain charms a mixed-blood, Laura Reed (Evelyn Ankers) so he can start a fish cannery and recruit members of the local tribe for illegal fishing.

Unconquered (Paramount, 1947). Cecil B. De Mille
The villain marries Hannah (Katherine De Mille), the daughter of the Seneca Chief Guyasuto, who persuades her father to capture the heroine and have her killed. At the last moment, the hero rescues her, and then helps those in the fort fight off a bloody attack by the Senecas, which had been incited by the evil son-in-law of the chief. A contemporary film critic notes that "it is also deplorably evident that *Unconquered*, in this year of grace, is as viciously anti-redskin as *Birth of a Nation* was anti-Negro long years back" (*NYT*, 19 Oct.).

Arctic Manhunt (Universal, 1949). Ewing Scott
An Eskimo woman, Narana (Carol Thurston) loses the white man she loves when he dies in the wilderness.

Colorado Territory (Warner, 1949). Raoul Walsh
Colorado Carson (Virginia Mayo), a mixed-blood lover of the outlaw leader, dies with him at the end.

See also *End of the Trail* (1932), *Northwest Mounted Police* (1940) and *Buffalo Bill* (1944)

Romances between Native American Men and White Women

See *Last of the Mohicans* (1936) in which the romance of Uncas and Alice Monro ends in the death of both characters.

Romances between Native Americans

Call Her Savage (Fox, 1932). John F. Dillon
   After some wild and rebellious behavior, Nasa (Clara Bow), the daughter of a white woman and Moonglow (Gilbert Roland), finds out about her Indian heritage and falls in love with a young mixed-blood man.

Igloo (Universal, 1932). Ewing Scott
   Chee-ak, an Eskimo hunter from another tribe, marries Kyatuk, the daughter of the chief, and leads her starving tribe to the sea during the winter. Despite a revolt along the way, they make it to the sea and find food. Like *The Silent Enemy*, this film has an all-native cast.

Laughing Boy (MGM, 1934). W. S. Van Dyke
   Based on Oliver La Farge's *Laughing Boy*, this film tells the tragic love story of Slim Girl (Lupe Velez) and Laughing Boy (Ramon Novarro), a young Navajo. After the two are married, Slim Girl takes a white lover and plays him against her husband. Finally Laughing Boy finds her in a house near the railroad tracks where she meets her lover, and he kills her with an arrow intended for the man she is with. Other Native American characters are Laughing Boy's father (Chief Thunder Cloud), mother (Catalina Rambala), Wounded Face (Tall Man's Boy), Yellow Singer (F. A. Arments), Squaw's Son (Deer Spring) and Red Man (Pellicana).

Massacre (First National, 1934). Alan Crosland

In this film based on Robert Gessner's novel, Joe Thunder Horse (Richard Barthelmess), a college-educated Sioux, rides in a wild west show and flirts with white women. However, he finds a new sense of responsibility when his father, the chief, calls on him to help his tribe fight villains who are exploiting them on their reservation. Joe Thunderhorse goes to Washington, wins back his tribe's rights and marries an educated Native American woman (Ann Dvorak). A *Variety* critic comments on the presence of the lead white actor: "Worst of all, when surrounded by other big chiefs who are Indians on the up and up, he doesn't look like an Indian any more than Jimmy Durante looks like a Chinaman" (23 Jan.).

Ramona (20th Century-Fox, 1936). Henry King

In this version of Helen H. Jackson's novel, Ramona (Loretta Young) marries Chief Alessandro (Don Ameche) and suffers at the hands of prejudiced whites.

Wagon Tracks West (Republic, 1943). Howard Bretherton

The heroes help Fleetwing (Rick Vallin), a doctor in love with Moonbush (Ann Jeffreys), to handle a corrupt Indian agent and Clawtooth (Tom Tyler), an evil medicine man. A *Variety* critic comments on the character of Moonbush: "The Femme lead could have been handled by a totem pole wired for sound. Ann Jeffreys, as the Indian maid doesn't even get to smile [and] has very few lines . . ." (27 Oct.).

Black Gold (Monogram, 1947). Phil Karlson

Charley Eagle (Anthony Quinn) and his wife, Sarah (Katherine DeMille), become millionaires when oil is discovered on their land. They use their money to adopt a Chinese boy and buy a race horse they name Black Gold. After much trouble with the horse, the boy rides him to a win in a big race for Charley Eagle who is dying. A *Variety* critic notes that the film "is commendable for there is not a single Indian-uttered 'ugh' in the dialogue" (15 Oct.).

Daughter of the West (Film Classics, 1949). Harold Daniels

In this film based on Robert Callahan's novel, an educated Navajo, Navo (Phillip Reed), who is in love with Lolita Moreno (Martha Vickers), a mixed-blood, brings to justice an Indian agent who gives liquor to the tribe so he can steal their mineral rights. Other Native American characters are Okeema (Marion Barry), Wateeka (Luz Alba), Ponca (Tommy Cook) and a Medicine Man (Willow Bird).

See also *The Cowboy and the Indians* (1949)

Native Americans as Victims

In this period, Native American characters often become objects of paternalism and avoid being victims of the villains only because the heroes intervene and rescue them.

End of the Trail (Columbia, 1932). R. Lederman

The hero, the beloved of Luana (Luana Walters), thwarts the gun-running villains and negotiates a treaty with the tribe of Chief Red Cloud (Chief White Eagle). The hero, played by Tim McCoy, an actor very sympathetic to the plight of the western tribes, often talks about the victimization of Native Americans throughout the film.

White Eagle (Columbia, 1932). Lambert Hillyer

White Eagle (Buck Jones), a pony express rider, joins his father, Gray Wolf (Frank Campeau), to bring to justice villains disguised as Native Americans who have caused hostility between their tribe and the whites. At the end, White Eagle finds out that he is really a white man. This film was remade as a serial in 1941 (Columbia; James W. Horne).

Desert Gold (Paramount, 1936). James Hogan

In this film based on Zane Grey's novel, Chief Moya (Buster Crabbe) and his tribe prevail over villains who are after their gold. In the process, Moya also rescues a white woman.

West of Nevada (First Division, 1936). Robert Hill

After villains try to steal gold from the peaceful tribe of Bald Eagle (Dick Botiller), the hero helps the tribe bring them to justice. A *Variety* critic notes that "juvenile audiences will thrill to see that redskins are once again in favor with the Hollywood chiefs" (22 July).

Where the Buffalo Roam (Monogram, 1938). Al Herman

The hero brings to justice villains who have been killing buffalo, contrary to a treaty that allows only the tribe to hunt these animals for food.

Thunder Over the Prairie (Columbia, 1941). Lambert Hillyer

When a Native American medic gets in trouble for revealing that a construction company mistreats its Native American workers, the hero comes to his rescue and proves he has been framed by the villain.

Valley of the Sun (RKO, 1942). George Marshall

Apaches led by Geronimo (Tom Tyler) and Cochise (Antonio Moreno) are driven to war by an evil Indian agent. However, a good agent stops the evil one, and this brings peace between the Apaches and whites.

The Law Rides Again (Monogram, 1943). Alan James

The heroes bring to justice a crooked Indian agent who is starting trouble with the tribe of Eagle Eye (Emmet Lynn) and Barking Fox (Chief Many Treaties) for his own evil purposes.

Romance of the West (PRC, 1946). Robert Emmett

Villains intent on getting land rich with silver try to provoke the tribe of Chief Eagle Feather (Chief Thunder Cloud), but a good Indian agent stops the villains and makes peace.

Under Nevada Skies (Republic, 1946). Frank McDonald

Roy Rogers leads the tribe of Flying Eagle (George L. Lewis) to a victory over the villains.

Dangerous Venture (UA, 1947). George Archainbaud

When villains disguised as Native Americans and a scientist try to exploit the isolated tribe of Talu (Patricia Tate), descendants of the Aztecs, Hopalong Cassidy comes to the rescue.

The Last Round-up (Columbia, 1947). John English

To stop a possible uprising, Gene Autry gets new and fertile lands for a tribe (led by a chief played by Trevor Bardette) whose valuable land and water had been appropriated by the townspeople.

Indian Agent (RKO, 1948). Lesley Selander

When a crooked agent diverts funds for the reservation, the tribe of Red Fox (Noah Beery, Jr.) and Wavoka (Iron Eyes Cody) threatens war. However, the hero foils the villain and keeps the peace.

The Cowboy and the Indians (Columbia, 1949). John English

A crooked Indian agent reduces a tribe to starvation by confiscating their stock and selling their food for his own profit. Gene Autry, aided by a mixed-blood doctor, Nan Palmer (Sheila Ryan), gets food for the tribe and brings the villain to justice. At the end, Nan and young Chief Lakohna (Jay Silverheels) fall in love. Other members of the tribe are Lucky Broken Arm (Claudia Drake), Broken Arm (Charles Stevens), Blue Eagle (Frank Lackteen) and Chief Long Arrow (Chief Yowlachie).

Laramie (Columbia, 1949). Ray Nazarro

The hero saves the day after gun-runners try to start a war with the tribe of Chief Eagle (Shooting Star). Another Native American character is Running Wolf (Jay Silverheels).

Ranger of Cherokee Strip (Republic, 1949). Phillip Ford

The hero comes to the rescue of Joe Bearclaw (Douglas Kennedy), a Cherokee who has been framed by cattlemen intent on pushing the tribe from their territory. Other

Native American characters are Chief Hunter (Monte Blue) and Tokata (Neyle Morrow), a school teacher.

* * *

In the late 1930s and early 1940s, the patriotism of the historical romances resonated with public sentiment before and during World War II. A *Variety* critic alludes to this phenomenon when he describes *They Died with Their Boots On* as a "surefire western, an escape from bombers, tanks and Gestapo . . . American to the last man" (19 Nov., 1941). Characters like General Custer (Errol Flynn) in this film, Gil Martin (Henry Fonda) in *Drums Along the Mohawk* and Major Rogers (Spencer Tracy) in *Northwest Passage* provided Americans with patriotic heroes who fought the Savage tribes, just as the allies were fighting the savage Germans and Japanese.

After the end of the World War II, the image of the Savage begins to yield to that of the noble, peace-loving chief. For example, in *Apache Chief* (1949), Young Eagle, a peaceful chief, overcomes the hostile Black Wolf, and establishes peace with the whites. Another example is Chief Yellowstone (Iron Eyes Cody) in *Massacre River* (1949). In this film, Chief Yellowstone wants peace but must first control the hostile young braves of his tribe. After these braves attack some settlers and kill a white woman, Chief Yellowstone expresses his sorrow for her death and not only promises peace, but also gives his land to the settlers. This peace-loving and wise chief character type becomes a dominant one in the films of the '50s.

CHAPTER FOUR

THE FILMS OF THE 1950S

In this decade, not only do Westerns reach the height of their popularity, they also show more sensitivity towards the history and social problems of their Native American characters. In 1950, *Broken Arrow* starts this trend with its characterization of the Apache chief, Cochise, as a peace-loving friend to a white man. Since the Apache were usually portrayed as the most hostile of the Savage tribes, this film marks a significant change in Hollywood's depiction of Native Americans, one that continues in *Battle at Apache Pass* (1951), *Conquest of Cochise* (1953), and *Taza, Son of Cochise* (1954). This new version of the Noble Red Man, a historical chief as a central positive character, becomes well established in the first half of the 1950s with the above films about Cochise plus *Seminole* (1953), *Sitting Bull* (1954) and *Chief Crazy Horse* (1955). Though notable films of the period such as *The Searchers* (1956) and *Run of the Arrow* (1956) still depict Native American tribes as savage and cruel, Westerns like *Devil's Doorway* (1950) focus on the other side of the issue, the cruelty and prejudice of white society.

Broken Arrow (1950), based on Elliot Arnold's *Blood Brother*, a 1947 historical novel about Tom Jeffords and Cochise, is the first of the major Westerns to portray a historical Native American leader as a heroic central character. Employing a technique common to sympathetic portrayals, the film begins with voice-over by Jeffords in which he acknowledges the Apache language and by implication their culture as he tells the audience, "when the Apaches speak, they will be speaking in our language." Another such voice-over occurs a little later after Jeffords has nursed a wounded Apache boy back to health and, for this good deed, has been spared by Apache warriors, who shortly thereafter kill and torture miners for invading their land. He says, "I learned something that day. Apache women cried over their sons and Apache men and a sense of fair play." Throughout the film, as Jeffords learns more about the Apaches through his friendship with Cochise (Jeff Chandler) and his marriage to Sonseeahray (Deborah Paget), his voice-overs become a commentary aimed at building respect for Apache culture and Cochise.

The friendship of Jeffords and Cochise grows because they are both men of courage, intelligence and honor. When Jeffords first meets Cochise, the camera favors the chief with low-angle and close-up shots which emphasize his authority. As the film continues, such perspectives become a pattern, establishing him as a central character equal to Jeffords. From the beginning, Cochise is imbued with an intelligence that shows through in his dialogue with Jeffords and his interactions with his people. For example, when he tries to persuade the assembled bands of the Apache to accept his peace plan, he uses a pithy analogy: "If a big wind comes, a tree must bend or be lifted out by its roots." He also has a sense of humor, one example of which occurs when he sees Jeffords trying to impress Sonseeahray by what turns out to be a feeble shot of an arrow; he says to her, "Never mind, by the time he's a grown man, he'll know how." In addition to the cleverness of his dialogue, his intelligence comes out in the way he leads his warriors.

A good example of his military shrewdness occurs when a large wagon train, with soldiers hiding in the wagons, enters his land. Seen from a vantage point above the wagons, he directs his carefully planned and orchestrated attack by having lookouts in key locations shoot arrows to signal each group of his braves to attack at the appropriate times. With almost no casualties, his warriors rout the soldiers and take over the wagons and all the supplies in them. In the entire attack sequence, the camera angles show the confusion and vulnerability of the soldiers with high-angle, long-shot perspectives, and the superiority of Cochise and his men with low-angle medium and close-up views. This sequence, which marks a complete reversal in the portrayal and outcome of attacks on U.S. soldiers, is a significant instance of how this film attempts to alter the stereotypes of Native Americans in the Westerns.

However, despite such good intentions on the part of the filmmakers, the characterization of Cochise as the heroic, peace-loving chief ultimately conforms to the Noble Red Man image. Just as Cochise's friend Tom Jeffords is contrasted to the crass townspeople and treacherous ranchers who kill his wife, so Cochise is set off against the savage Apache Geronimo (Jay Silverheels) and the other Apache rebels. Ultimately, Cochise is a heroic character because he learns the way of peace from his white friend and has the wisdom to accept the inevitability of white dominance in the west. Geronimo, on the other hand, is the hostile, rebellious Savage because he refuses to give in to the whites and honor a peace treaty. Near the end of the film, after Cochise stops an attack by Geronimo's warriors, he says, "Let this peace hold. If it is broken, it must not be by Indians, not even bad Indians." As is true of characters drawn to the image of the Noble Red Man, Cochise is so good in all the ways that will make him pleasing to the white audience that he is diminished as a believable fictional character. As a character drawn to the reverse Savage image, the same is true of Geronimo. A contemporary film critic picks up on this excess: "No, we cannot accept this picture as either an exciting or reasonable account of the attitudes and ways of American Indians. They merit justice, but not such patronage" (*NYT*, 24 July).

Another way to appreciate how the film falls back on the image of the Noble Red Man is to compare it to the novel. The film focuses on just a small part of Cochise's biography and never touches on the novel's depiction of Cochise's continuing depression over his brutal killing of a Mexican or his drinking and disillusion in later life, all "negative" but humanizing characteristics. In addition to sanitizing the character of Cochise, the film adds a subplot that doesn't exist in history, the romance between Tom Jeffords and Sonseeahray. On one level, the marriage of the hero and an Apache woman heightens the theme of friendship between whites and Native Americans. However, as with the characterization of Cochise, the film ultimately conforms to a formula, namely the killing off of the Native American woman involved in such a mixed marriage. At the end of the film, after Sonseeahray is shot by evil whites, she becomes not a believable character but only a symbol, a vehicle for concluding the theme of peace. When Tom Jeffords vows revenge for the killing of his wife, Cochise tells him, "You will bear this. Your loss has brought us together." Jeffords accepts the advice of his friend, and, as he rides off alone, says in a voice-over, "The death of Sonseeahray put a seal on the peace. . .I always remembered my wife was with me." Like Nophaie in *The Vanishing American*, the Native American character who loves a white can ultimately only exist in the mind of his beloved, as a memory and as a martyr for the greater peace.

The theme of the peace-loving Noble Red Man continues with the depiction of Cochise in *Battle at Apache Pass* (1951). This film is a sequel to *Broken Arrow* in that the two central characters of Cochise (Jeff Chandler) and Geronimo (Jay Silverheels) are played by the same actors and are again the contrasting friendly Noble Red Man and hostile Savage. However, unlike Tom Jeffords, the white friend of Cochise is a marginal character displaced by a power-hungry government agent who hates Cochise and his band because their attempt to keep the peace prohibits him from taking their land. To force Cochise to make war and thus break the treaty that protects his land, the evil agent aligns himself with Geronimo. The fierceness of Geronimo is established at the beginning of the film when he is seen from a low-angle rallying his rebellious band, and reinforced when he attacks a wagon train. As his men kill and mutilate men, women and children, he grabs a terrified little girl and one of his braves carries off a woman.

While Geronimo is killing the families of the settlers, Cochise is first seen in a warm domestic setting with his beautiful wife, Nona (Susan Cabot), who is expecting a child. Though treated badly by the evil agent, he still insists on peace at a council meeting, during which Geronimo asks the warriors of Cochise to fight with him against the whites.

However, Cochise persuades his people to keep the peace and enhances his status as leader by killing in hand-to-hand combat the hostile brave of Geronimo's band who had captured the woman from the wagon train. In an attempt to restore the peace, he takes the white woman to the fort, where a military doctor shows his gratitude by treating the wound Cochise received in the fight to save her.

This peaceful gesture only heightens the efforts of the villain, who gives guns to Geronimo and incites him to attack a ranch. After this attack, the arrogant young lieutenant who has replaced the friend of Cochise as commander of the fort tries to capture the chief and takes his wife as a hostage. When the lieutenant has some Apache prisoners hanged, Cochise must finally wage war. As he prepares for the battle, he tells his wife he is reluctant to leave her but now must go out and fight because "the soldiers like snakes have turned against the Apache." Cochise shrewdly traps the soldiers in a valley but cannot compete with their fire power. When the soldiers start killing and wounding not only the warriors but also women and children with their cannon fire, Cochise is forced to stop his attack. During this time of truce, the military doctor and the woman rescued by Cochise treat the wounds of his wife, Nona, and his friend takes control of the soldiers after the death of the villains.

Cochise, however, has only a moment of peace before Geronimo, who wants to continue the fighting, challenges him to a hand-to-hand battle. After a violent fight, he subdues Geronimo but refuses to kill him, so "he will live in shame, an outcast." Then he goes to his wife, who, with the help of the white woman, has just given birth to a son. After his friend tells him that the evil agent and Geronimo have been responsible for all the troubles between his tribe and the whites, Cochise says to him, "When the wounds heal, we will again speak of peace." At the end of this film, Cochise is a sadder and more skeptical character than in *Broken Arrow* because he has seen more hostility from the whites and his own people and found that he lives in a world he can no longer control. This ending has a more realistic feeling than that of *Broken Arrow* and may be part of what prompted a contemporary critic to write: "Apache

Pass rates a large 'A' for its handling of Indian character and customs. The redmen emerge as human beings instead of in the characteristic rigging to which they are usually fated" (*Variety*, 2 Apr., 1952).

In *Conquest of Cochise* (1953), Cochise (John Hodiak) again is committed to peace even though he faces hostility from white villains, his own tribe and his former allies, the Comanche. This version of the story, which one contemporary film reviewer sees as a "sympathetic treatment of the problems of Indians" (*Variety*, 26 Aug.), begins with scenes of warriors attacking a Mexican settlement and a voice-over that tells of the earlier alliance of the dreaded Apache and Comanche. Against this historical background emerges Cochise, who has decided to keep the peace with whites because he knows great numbers of them will keep coming to the West. After meeting with the hero, who will become his friend, Cochise promises to advise his Apache warriors to keep the peace with the whites. Seen from a low-angle perspective which reinforces his stature as a hero (a perspective that becomes a pattern), he tells a council of his tribe that he wants peace, but if war becomes necessary the tribe should fight the Comanche rather than the Americans. One of his rebellious warriors, Tukiwah (Steven Ritch), opposes him and warns of the danger of fighting the Comanche. The contrast between a peace-loving character and a Savage one occurs again when Cochise meets with the Comanche at their camp. The hostile chief of the Comanche, Running Cougar (Joseph Waring), is for war with the Mexicans, and Red Knife (Rodd Redwing), is for peace.

When Chief Running Cougar and his hostile braves decide to attack the Mexicans, Cochise and his loyal warriors intervene and not only rescue the Mexicans but also kill some of the Comanche. This turns Red Knife and Tukiwah against Cochise and both the Comanche and hostile Apaches threaten war against the whites. Cochise, however, still holds out for peace, even after the henchman of the villain kills his beloved Terua (Carol Thurston) with a shot meant for him. After this, his white friend tries to find the killer of Terua and thwart the efforts of the villain who, like the one in *Battle at Apache Pass*, foments war to get land from the Apaches. In the meantime, Cochise attacks the Mexicans and takes one of their women as a hostage.

Though Cochise does this to bring the hero to his camp, the beautiful female allows the filmmakers to expand his character to a romantic lead and spokesman for his culture. Even though the woman interrupts Cochise during the ceremonial funeral of Terua, he seems happy to teach her about Apache culture. He tells her that because "survival is our religion," the boys and girls are taught in the same way and one of their early lessons is to run four miles holding water in their mouths. As he goes on to describe their cosmology and then to courting and marriage customs, the woman is clearly falling for him. When she finally kisses him, he allows that "it is a superior custom." The noble Cochise has won the heart of the woman to whom his white friend is also attracted. At this point, however, a potential war with the Americans, not love, is his main concern. He must once again deal with hostile warriors in his tribe and with the warlike Comanche. After the hero brings the man who killed Terua, Cochise is able to stop the war dance of his warriors.

When Cochise goes to the Comanche camp to ask for peace, the hostile warriors take control and torture him with boiling water, knife cuts from warriors on horses, and burning at the stake. Just as he is about to be killed, his friend and the soldiers come to the rescue. Then, just as the Comanches are about to overwhelm the outnumbered soldiers, Tukiwah and the Apache warriors arrive and drive off the hostiles. Finally, Cochise has not only gained the support of his former rival, Tukiwah, but also has achieved a lasting peace. At the end, the peace-loving chief makes one last noble gesture: he gives up, for complicated reasons, the beautiful Mexican woman, who sadly rides off with the hero.

Such peace-loving Cochise characters, who contrast with hostile warriors in and outside their tribe, also appear in *Fort Apache* (1948), *I Killed Geronimo* (1950), *Indian Uprising* (1952) and *Taza, Son of Cochise* (1954). In this latter film, the story of Cochise (Jeff Chandler) comes to a close when, after his death, Taza (Rock Hudson), his noble son, wins the peace by fighting his hostile brother, Naiche (Bart Roberts), and the warriors of Geronimo (Ian MacDonald) who have been supplied with guns by the villain. The image of the noble, peace-loving historical chief, again contrasted with hostile warriors, continues with the depiction of Tecumseh in *Brave Warrior* (1952) and the title character in *Chief Crazy Horse* (1955) (for further discussion, see Biskind, 230–45). Two other representative examples of this character type are Chief Osceola in *Seminole* (1953) and the title character in *Sitting Bull* (1954).

Described in the beginning as "Taken from the pages of History," *Seminole* (1953) tells the story of Osceola (Anthony Quinn), the peaceful mixed-blood chief, the white woman he loves and his friend, a young officer who has known him from childhood. In contrast to these characters are an ambitious, hateful military leader who thinks the Seminoles stand in the way of progress and a hostile Seminole warrior, Kayjeck (Hugh O' Brian). In a flashback which comprises much of the film, the hero, who had been sent to the fort as junior officer, tells of the events leading to the death of his friend. The sad story begins when the evil commander sends him to the camp of Osceola to persuade his friend to come to the fort for a peace parley. During their meeting, Osceola, seen in low-angle and close-up shots that emphasize his authority, is portrayed as an educated man who acknowledges that his tribe cannot prevail over the ever-growing number of whites. He is a man torn between his responsibilities to his tribe, his appreciation of white culture, derived from his education at white schools, and his love for a white woman. With the help of his wise old friend, Kulak (Ralph Moody), he finally convinces Kayjeck and his warriors that they should not attack the soldiers, until he goes to the fort to negotiate a peace treaty. However, unknown to the hero, the commander's offer of a peace talk is only a trick. When Osceola and his friend return to the fort, the commander has him seized and imprisoned in an underground cage. Though the white woman who loves him tries to bring help, Osceola finally dies in the cage, a victim of treachery and his own divided loyalties. As the story continues, however, his death will ultimately be an occasion for a peaceful resolution of the hostilities between his tribe and the whites.

Meanwhile, the evil commander, who desperately wants to make a name for himself, forces the hero and his troops to make a deadly trek through the swamps to attack the stronghold of the Seminoles. Many of the soldiers die, either from the rigors of the march or during the attacks by the Seminole warriors. When the hero finally rebels against his leader, he is framed and sentenced to death by a firing squad. At the last moment, the white woman rescues him by bringing Kayjeck and the Seminole warriors, who surround the fort and stop the execution. Kayjeck exonerates the hero and reveals the treachery of the evil commander, who will be punished by a general who had come to the fort. As the Seminoles, whom Kayjeck describes as "a proud people," leave the fort in a procession carrying the body of Osceola, the general says, "Perhaps we see the beginning of a new way of life," and the hero replies, "I know these people well and really believe that they would like to live with us in peace."

This ending, with its optimistic promise of a new era of peace between the Native Americans and whites, is typical of the peace-loving chief films. Like Sonseeahray in *Broken Arrow*, Osceola becomes a martyr who helps to establish new opportunities for peace. Such films, which countered the negative stereotypes, appealed to some contemporary film critics. One notes: "Applause for Howard Cristie, the producer of an unpretentious but new type of Indian picture, for he has broken away from a worn-out pattern. For the last 20 years 'savages' have whooped, danced, and chased their enemies while the noble chief looked on as stoic as a cigar-store Indian" (*Natural History*, Apr., 190). Though this film leans towards the other extreme of the Noble Red Man, it does continue a positive new direction. However, the upbeat ending of the film also blatantly distorts history to provide the kind of orderly closure standard in 1950s Westerns.

A final representative film, *Sitting Bull* (1954), follows the same patterns of characters and plot as in the other examples: the hostile adversary in the tribe (Crazy Horse), the military hero sympathetic to the tribe who gets into trouble for his attitudes, the ambitious, disobedient military leader, General Custer, a villainous Indian Agent, and the authority figure, President Grant, who promises peace at the end . The film begins (and ends) with a chorus singing a rather jaunty hymn, "Great Spirit," and then the voice-over of Sitting Bull (J. Carrol Naish) telling of the hostility of the seven warrior tribes because the whites have come in great numbers to the sacred Black Hills . Sitting Bull immediately shows his desire for peace after hostile warriors from his tribe, led by Crazy Horse (Iron Eyes Cody), attack a wagon train. Seen in a close-up, Sitting Bull stops the attack and has his men take only the supplies of miners who are illegally in the land of his tribe. Unlike Crazy Horse and the chiefs of the other hostile tribes, Sitting Bull has the wisdom typical in such peace-loving characters. He understands that, because of the vast number of whites, the only way his people will survive is to make peace with them. However, like the Cochise characters, he will be pushed to the extreme to keep the peace.

Sitting Bull's first test comes when the evil agent at Red Rock kills his son, Young Buffalo (Felix Gonzalez), after the young man helped captured members of his tribe escape from the horrible stockade at the agency. Even after this terrible provocation, Sitting Bull prays to the Great Spirit and decides to make one last attempt for peace by negotiating with President Grant. However, he is tested again when Custer and his soldiers come to the Black Hills during the gold rush and kill some Sioux warriors. After gathering all the tribes, Sitting Bull again argues for peace and gets his way after his white friend not only defeats the warlike Crazy Horse in a traditional hand-to-hand fight, but also promises to bring President Grant to the West for peace talks with the tribe. Finally, however, when Custer disobeys orders and decides to attack the united tribes, Sitting Bull and the other chiefs must declare war and meet Custer in the battle of Little Big Horn.

After the battle and the victory which Sitting Bull never wanted, the hero helps the chief and his tribe escape and then is sentenced to death for his actions. In a scene like the one at the end of *Seminole*, the hero is about to be executed when his woman brings Sitting Bull to the rescue. The chief speaks to President Grant: "For many years I have tried to keep the peace. This man understood and risked his life for peace. For all time the Indians will respect this man. The Great White Chief will let this man live and the Indians and whites can again sit in peace council." The President agrees and the film ends with a low-angle close-up of Sitting Bull and the hymn "Great Spirit" playing in the background. Such an optimistic ending, like that of *Broken Arrow* and the other films with peace-loving chiefs, is, of course, far removed from the brutal history of the Plains Indian wars.

Though the portrayal of historical chiefs as Noble Red Men reflects a growing sympathy for Native American characters, the opposing image of the Savage still appears in some of the best Westerns of this period. The saddest example, which will be treated briefly here, is John Ford's *The Searchers* (1956), possibly the best Western of any period. The hero, Ethan Edwards, knows the culture and language of the Comanche well, and hates the tribe so intensely that he shoots the eyes out of a dead brave to condemn him to a life of wandering in the spirit world, and later keeps firing at a herd of buffalo just so the tribe will have less to eat in the winter. Though he has some reason for his feelings, his hatred overreaches the motivation, much like that of Major Rogers in *Northwest Passage*. Also like Rogers he is clearly the hero, who is literally looked up to in low-angle shots throughout the film, and his attitude is that to know the Comanches is to hate them. Another film of this kind, though not as overtly racist as *The Searchers*, is *Run of the Arrow* (1956), which portrays the Sioux tribe in the image of the Savage.

Though *Run of the Arrow* (1956) also takes a harsh view of white culture after the Civil War, it focuses on the savagery of the Sioux warriors. The hero, who hates the Yankees, escapes from the south to the far west and meets a drunken old Sioux scout, Walking Coyote (J. C. Flippen), who tells him that the word *Sioux* means "fierce enemy." Though the hero responds, "I'd like to be one, I'm a cutthroat too," he eventually finds out that even he cannot live the code of the warrior. Shortly thereafter, the two men come upon Sioux warriors of Blue Buffalo (Charles Bronson) who have attacked and burned a wagon and are drinking whiskey they found on one of the wagons. While they watch, Crazy Wolf (H. M. Wynant), the most hostile of the warriors, captures them and they agree to the run of the arrow, a ritual in which a barefoot captive starts at the distance of an arrow shot from the bow of the pursuer and then tries to out run him. Crazy Wolf easily kills Walking Coyote and then is closing in on the hero when a woman from the tribe, Yellow Moccasin (Sarita Montiel), rescues him. After she nurses him back to health they fall in love, and he decides to join the tribe and live with her.

Soon his adopted tribe comes in contact with the cavalry, led by a cocky young officer who looks down on the Sioux. Despite an attempt at a peace talk, hostility breaks out when Crazy Wolf kills a soldier. After several skirmishes, the Sioux finally attack and burn the camp of the soldiers, a scene which ends in a high-angle shot that emphasizes the devastation. This fierce attack and the torturing of the evil soldier by skinning him alive are too much for the hero, who puts the man, his mortal enemy during the Civil War, out of his misery by shooting him. Yellow Moccasin comments on his reaction, "You could not watch the man be skinned. You are an American (not a Sioux)." Convinced that he can't live by the code of the Sioux warrior, he leaves with Yellow Moccasin and a mute boy for an uncertain future. Though the film offers a cynical view of both white and Native American behavior, it clearly suggests that the uniqueness or "otherness" of Sioux culture is defined by its harshness and cruelty. *Run of the Arrow*, then, despite its complex and grim view of life on the plains after the Civil War, certainly plays upon the racist image of the Savage in its depiction of the Sioux.

On the other hand, the last of the representative films, *Devil's Doorway* (1950), takes a dark look at a white society defined by its greed, cruelty and prejudice. Portraying the Shoshone tribe as noble victims, this film tells the sad story of (Broken) Lance Poole (Robert Taylor), a Shoshone who fought with the whites in the Civil War and won the

Congressional Medal of Honor. However, when he returns to his ranch in Wyoming, he soon finds out from his friend, Red Rock (James Mitchell), and his father that he will not be treated as a hero at home. His father, referring to the whites who have taken much of the Shoshone land and are now after their ranch, tells him, "Our people are doomed. An Indian without land loses his heart and soul with it." Soon Lance finds out that the local whites and sheepherders new to the area, many of them spurred on by a hateful old lawyer, are deeply prejudiced towards him and want his land. He also finds a female lawyer sympathetic to his plight who not only works to secure his rights, but also falls in love with him. However, after he loses an appeal to homestead his land because, ironically, he is not considered an American citizen according to Wyoming law, he decides to fight for his land.

Joined by a starving band of Shoshone led by the old Chief Thundercloud (Chief John Big Tree), Lance makes his last stand on his land, which is known as Sweet Meadows. When the lawyer he loves asks him to make concessions to those who are coming, he tells her, "Its hard to understand how an Indian feels about the land. I know I belong. If we lose it now we might as well be dead." After a big fight with the townspeople and sheepherders, the U.S. Cavalry arrives for the final confrontation. Again his beloved lawyer begs him to surrender, but he refuses, telling her not to cry because "a hundred years from now it might have worked." After putting on his Civil War uniform, he walks out of his house and is shot as he offers to give up if the Shoshone women and children are allowed to go to the reservation. As he is about to die, he tells a boy from the tribe that he is the "man" who will take them back to the reservation. Then, seen in a low-angle shot, he salutes and falls to the ground, a noble character who would have been a hero in a world not filled with greed and prejudice.

Like *Broken Arrow* and the other films with peace-loving chiefs, *Devil's Doorway* attempts to tell the story of the westward expansion from a perspective sympathetic to the tribes involved. One contemporary critic writes, "Perhaps it is too late now to change the course of fiction which has established the American Indian as a ruthless savage, but our movie makers appear to be endeavoring to right some of the wrongs they themselves have done the red man over the years" (*NYT*, 10 Nov.). Though films like *The Searchers* and *Run of the Arrow* keep the racism of the Savage image alive, a significant number of the filmmakers do attempt to "right the wrongs" of this image. In spite of their good intentions, however, their films usually move to the opposite extreme of the Noble Red Men. Though such characters appeal to the sense of law and order in this period, they are finally too good to be believed and too divorced from history to be taken seriously.

IMAGES OF THE SAVAGE

During this period, the attack by hostile warriors is still a staple of the Westerns. However, often these characters are not the stock Savages because their hostility is frequently well motivated by the actions of evil whites.

Attacks on Covered Wagons

Cherokee Uprising (Monogram, 1950). Lewis Collins
An evil Indian agent uses whiskey to incite the tribe of Long Knife (Iron Eyes Cody) and Gray Eagle (Chief Yowlachie) to attack wagon trains. The hero stops the attacks by exposing the evil designs of the agent.

I Killed Geronimo (Eagle Lion, 1950). John Hoffman
The hero stops the smuggling of guns to the Apache and kills Geronimo (Chief Thunder Cloud) while his warriors are attacking a wagon train. A critic from *National Parent Teacher*, commenting on the portrayal of the Apaches as Savages, writes, "Today's social conscience is made uncomfortable when the theme of a supposedly historic picture seems to reinstate the old notion that the only good Indian is a dead one" (Nov., 36).

Bend in the River (Universal, 1952). Anthony Mann
   A small band of hostile Shoshone who attack a wagon train on its way to Oregon are killed by the hero in some rather feeble individual fights.

Wagons West (Monogram, 1952). Ford Beebe
   Cheyenne warriors of chief Black Kettle (John Parrish) and Kaw Chief (Charles Stevens), who are armed with rifles supplied by the villains, attack a wagon train heading for California.

Westward the Women (MGM, 1952). William Wellman
   The hero and a wagon train of women show their grit by surviving attacks by hostile warriors.

The Command (Warner, 1953). David Butler
   A warlike tribe stages a fierce attack on a circled wagon train.

Arrow in the Dust (Allied Artists, 1954). Lesley Selander
   The hero stops deadly attacks by the Pawnee when he destroys their guns and ammunition. A *NYT* critic notes that the film dramatizes "the threat of murderous red savages intent on wiping out settlers and troopers" (1 May).

Massacre Canyon (Columbia, 1954). Fred Sears
   Led by Black Eagle (Steve Ritch) and Running Horse (Chris Alciade), Apache warriors attack a wagon train carrying rifles.

Daniel Boone, Trailblazer (Republic, 1956). Albert Gannaway and Ishmael Roderiguez
   Incited by villains, Shawnee warriors attack a wagon train led by the hero. Eventually, he convinces Chief Black-fish (Lon Chaney, Jr.) to make peace.

The Last Wagon (20th Century-Fox, 1956). Delmer Daves
   Apaches attack a wagon train and kill everyone except the hero and some young people. Finally, the hero, who had lived with the Comanche, kills a number of Apache warri-

ors in hand-to-hand combat and leads the survivors to safety.

Dragoon Wells Massacre (Allied Artists, 1957). Harold Schuster
Apaches, led by a hostile chief (John War Eagle), attack a wagon train passing through their country.

Pawnee (Republic, 1957). George Waggner
Crazy Fox (Charles Horvath), a hostile brave who has taken control of the peace-loving Wise Eagle's (Ralph Moody) tribe, leads an attack on a wagon train. Finally the hero, who grew up with the tribe and is contemplating a return to his adopted people, stops the hostiles by killing Crazy Fox in hand-to-hand combat. At the end he chooses white society and decides to marry a white woman rather than Dancing Fawn (Charlotte Austin), a Pawnee woman who loves him.

Westward Ho, the Wagons (Buena Vista, 1957). William Beaudine
At one point, warlike Pawnee attack a wagon train. Later, the hostile Sioux accept the settlers as friends after a doctor helps Many Stars (Iron Eyes Cody), their medicine man, to save the life of Chief Wolf's Brother's (John War Eagle) son. Thus the savageness of the Pawnee contrasts with friendliness of the Sioux.

Attacks on Cavalry and Soldiers in Forts

Davy Crockett, Indian Scout (UA, 1950). Lew Landers
Aided by his loyal friend, Red Hawk (Phillip Reed), the hero rescues army troops from the hostile tribe of Chief Lone Eagle (Robert Barrat), High Tree (Billy Wilkerson), and Sleeping Fox (Chief Thunder Cloud). Later, the noble Red Hawk falls in love with Frances (Ellen Drew), a mixed-blood who had been a spy for the hostile tribe. A *Variety* critic writes that the film "hews to the formula ingredients of howling Indians, ambushed wagon trains, disloyal mixed-bloods and a slight touch of romance" (11 Jan.).

Rio Grande (Republic, 1950) John Ford

Apaches raid a cavalry outpost, and later the soldiers follow them into Mexico to rescue a group of children from the hostile and drunken warriors. A *NYT* critic notes that "John Ford's continuing war with the Red Man and his romance with the U.S. Cavalry. . .shows a few signs of wear and tear" (20 Nov.).

Winchester 73 (Universal, 1950). Anthony Mann

As the gun passes through various lives, one of the stories is of Young Bull (Rock Hudson), who leads his warriors on a raid of a cavalry encampment. The hero, using his knowledge of the tactics of the warriors who defeated Custer, repulses the attack and kills Young Bull.

The Last Outpost (Paramount, 1951). Lewis R. Foster

When a white man kills an Apache chief, the warriors of Geronimo (John War Eagle) and Grey Cloud (Charles Evans) attack a fort. At the last minute, the hero and his men come to the rescue.

Little Big Horn (Lippert, 1951). Charles Marquis Warren

As a cavalry squad tries to get to Custer to warn him of the impending Sioux ambush, warriors kill all of them before they can complete their mission.

Only the Valiant (Warner, 1951). Gordon Douglas

Apaches led by Tuscos (Michael Ansara) stage a series of attacks on soldiers who are trying to hold a strategic pass. In the final attack only the hero and several others survive.

Slaughter Trail (RKO, 1951). Irving Allen

When a cavalry captain refuses to hand over to Chief Paako (Rick Forman) bandits who have killed several of his Navajo people, the tribe attacks the fort but kills only the bandits.

Warpath (Paramount, 1951). Byron Haskin

A man escapes from the Sioux and warns Custer, who then leads his soldiers against the hostiles. A *Variety* critic notes that this situation has become typical: "Putting the cavalry against the Indians has become a rather common storybook" (6 June).

Bugles in the Afternoon (Warner, 1952). Roy Rowland
The hostile Sioux of Red Owl (John War Eagle) attack Fort Lincoln and later defeat Custer at the Battle of Little Big Horn.

Escape from Fort Bravo (MGM, 1953). John Sturges
Apaches attack a small group of soldiers and a woman who are pinned down in a shallow desert wash. As the warriors shoot barrages of arrows that come ever closer to the group, the cavalry finally comes to the rescue.

Fort Ti (Columbia, 1953). William Castle
In this 3D film, hostile braves attack the fort. The hero, who helps save the fort, chooses a white woman even though Running Otter (Phyllis Fowler) loves him.

Apache (UA, 1954). Robert Aldrich
Based on the Paul Wellman novel of the same name, this film tells the story of Massai (Burt Lancaster), one of Geronimo's (Monte Blue) band, who escapes while being taken to prison and wages a harsh one-man war against the army. When Massai finally stops fighting, the government doesn't punish him because it decides that his resistance was part of a declared war. At the end, he and his beloved Nalinle (Jean Peters) will live together in peace. A *Variety* critic comments on the acting: "Lancaster and Miss Peters play their Indian roles understandingly without usual screen stereotyping. As played, these two top characters are humans, surprisingly loquacious in contrast to the usual clipped redskin portrayals" (30 June).

The Siege at Red River (20th Century-Fox, 1954). Rudolph Mate
The villain sells a Gatling gun to hostile Shawnee led by Chief Yellow Hawk (Rico Alaniz) and helps them attack a Union fort.

The Yellow Tomahawk (UA, 1954). Lesley Selander

The tribe of Tonia (Noah Beery, Jr.), Honey Bear (Rita Moreno) and Fire Knife (Lee Van Cleef) declares war after an evil officer kills some of their women and children and breaks a treaty by preparing to build a fort on their land. After many whites are killed, the hero, a friend of Fire Knife, rescues the survivors, although he has to kill his friend in the process. A *Variety* critic comments: "The story takes the redskins' side to show provocation for their attacks on a cavalry encampment" (19 May).

Fort Yuma (UA, 1955). Lesley Selander

After soldiers kill his father at a peace parley, Mangas (Abel Fernandez) leads his Apache warriors on an attack on the fort in which many of them are killed.

The Gun That Won the West (Columbia, 1955). William Castle

After several attempts at peace with the Sioux of the wise Chief Red Cloud (Robert Bice) and hostile Afraid of his Horses (Michael Morgan), the hero and his soldiers, using the new Springfield rifle, fight the tribe and kill many warriors.

The Last Frontier (*Savage Wilderness*) (Columbia, 1955). Anthony Mann

After being provoked by an excessive officer, the tribes of Red Cloud (Manuel Donde) and Spotted Elk (William Calles) attack the soldiers and drive them back to their fort. With the fire power of cannons and the help of the hero and his friend, Mungo (Pat Hogan), the soldiers survive the attack. A *NYT* critic notes that in the early films the soldiers were noble and the Native Americans were savage until "civilization" reversed the images, and then he remarks that in this film "civilization has got so far that everybody is ornery" (8 Dec.).

Yellowneck (Republic, 1955). R. John Hugh

In the great swamp of Florida, hostile Seminoles attack Confederate deserters called "yellownecks."

Pillars of the Sky (Universal, 1956). George Marshall

The tribe of Chief Kamiakin (Michael Ansara) starts a war because soldiers try to build a road and a fort on land given to the tribe in a treaty.

Quincannon, Frontier Scout (UA, 1956). Lesley Selander

A villain who has smuggled guns to the tribe of Iron Wolf (Ed Hashim) and incited them to attack a fort is brought to justice by the hero.

Seventh Cavalry (Columbia, 1956). Edmund Goulding

The tribe of Yellow Hawk (Pat Hogan) surrounds soldiers who are at the Little Big Horn to bring the bodies of Custer and his men to a proper burial. Through the efforts of the hero and Yellow Hawk the hostile warriors do not attack, and, when Custer's horse appears, they let the soldiers ride away.

Revolt at Fort Laramie (UA, 1957). Lesley Selander

Red Cloud (Eddie Little Sky) and his Sioux warriors demand money before they agree to a treaty. Finally, they attack, but are defeated by Union soldiers aided by Confederates.

Apache Territory (Columbia, 1958). Ray Nazarro

Apaches pin down a group of soldiers and the hero, who has rescued a white woman from them. Finally, they escape in a dust storm.

Fort Bowie (UA, 1958). Howard W. Koch

After soldiers kill a band of Apaches who were trying to surrender, the warriors of Vitorio (Larry Chance) attack and occupy a fort. With help from Chenzana (Jana Davi), a woman from the tribe who loves him, the hero leads the soldiers as they retake the fort. A *Variety* critic comments: "A switch is made from usual films in this category by having the cavalry storm their own fort . . ." (5 Feb.).

Fort Dobbs (Warner, 1958). Gordon Douglas

Using a new repeating rifle, the hero and his men defend

the fort from a series of Comanche attacks. In the process many Comanche warriors die.

Fort Massacre (UA, 1958). Joseph N. Newman
A hateful soldier whose wife and children were killed by the Apache provokes attacks from the Paiute tribe of Moving Cloud (Larry Chance). After numerous attacks in which many of his soldiers are killed, his own men kill the soldier and stop the fighting. The film provokes a snide comment from a *Variety* reviewer about the acting: "Susan Cabot, as an Indian girl is a beaut but no Paiute" (30 Apr.).

Tonka (Buena Vista, 1958). Lewis R. Foster
White Bull (Sal Mineo), the son of Prairie Flower (Joy Page), is a Sioux boy who trains his horse, Tonka, only to have it sold to a cavalry officer. The horse is the only survivor after an arrogant, fanatical Custer leads his soldiers into the Battle of Little Big Horn where they are defeated by the warriors of Sitting Bull (John War Eagle). At the end, White Bull is reunited with Tonka.

The Wonderful Country (UA, 1959). Robert Parrish
When the villain incites the Apache to war so he can get their land for a railroad, the hero rescues a troop attacked by hostile warriors.

Attacks on Trains and Stagecoaches

Rocky Mountain (Warner, 1950). William Keighley
The hero and his men stop an attack on a stagecoach by luring the hostile braves away. Later they are all killed during an attack by a great number of warriors.

Train to Tombstone (Lippert, 1950). William Berke
Hostile warriors stage attacks on trains. A *Variety* critic comments on the lack of reality, noting that the attacks, with the "same Injun repeatedly falling off his pony," are "just plain funny in their ridiculousness" (6 Sept.).

Fort Defiance (UA, 1951). John Rawlins
   A hostile tribe led by Brave Bear (Iron Eyes Cody) attacks a stagecoach.

The Stand at Apache River (Universal, 1953). Lee Sholem
   A band of Apaches led by Cara Blanca (Edgar Barrier) and Dead Horse (Forrest Lewis) attacks some people at a stagecoach station.

Overland Express (UA, 1954). Fred Sears
   The villain gives rifles to the tribe of Chief Dark Thunder (Pat Hogan) and keeps them on the warpath to force railroaders to build on his land.

Around the World in 80 Days (UA, 1956). Michael Anderson
   After the travelers meet a peaceful tribe who smoke the pipe with the engineer and do an orderly circle dance in an idyllic village, they encounter hostile Sioux who attack their train and capture the hero's friend, whom they are about to burn at the stake when the hero and the cavalry come to the rescue. Again, the Savage image plays off that of the Noble Red Man.

Attacks on Settlers and Other Representatives of Progress

Ambush (MGM, 1950). Sam Wood
   The heroes rescue a white woman from the hostile Apaches of Diablito (Charles Stevens) and Tana (Chief Thunder Cloud), both of whom are killed.

The Cariboo Trail (20th Century-Fox, 1950). Edwin Marin
   The warlike tribe of Chief White Buffalo (Fred Libby) attack the hero who is mining gold in their land.

Indian Territory (Columbia, 1950). John English
   Gene Autry brings to justice villains who have been selling guns to the tribe of Soma (Charles Stevens) and leading them on raids against the whites.

The Traveling Saleswoman (Columbia, 1950). Charles F. Riesner
  In this comedy, the heroine gets involved in an uprising led by Chief Running Deer (Chief Thunder Cloud).

Apache Drums (Universal, 1951). Hugo Fregonese
  The Apaches of Chache (Chinto Gusman) attack a town called Spanish Boot.

Cavalry Scout (Monogram, 1951). Lesley Selander
  The hero stops the villains from smuggling guns to hostile Sioux and Cheyenne.

Distant Drums (Warner, 1951). Raoul Walsh
  The hero rescues prisoners of the Seminole by killing their chief, Oscala (Larry Carper), in a hand-to-hand duel under water. Finally, a troop of soldiers rescues the survivors as the hostiles mount their big attack.

Flaming Feather (Paramount, 1951). Ray Enright
  Led by the villain, a warlike tribe attacks the ranch of the hero.

New Mexico (UA, 1951). Irving Reis
  Although the hero tries to stop his friend, Chief Acuma (Ted De Corsia), from fighting the villains after they break a treaty, his tribe, armed with weapons supplied by a crooked politician, finally makes war.

Oh! Susanna (Republic, 1951). Joseph Kane
  In the Black Hills, warlike Sioux attack miners who are breaking a treaty.

The Red Mountain (Paramount, 1951). William Dieterle
  Incited by General Quantrell, Utes attack settlers. A *Variety* reviewer comments on the ending: ". . . an all-out, shoot'em-up, waving flags-charging cavalry, redskins-bite-the-dust finale that uses every cliché in the book" (14 Nov.).

When the Redskins Rode (Columbia, 1951). Lew Landers
   A female French spy incites Chief Prince Hannoc (Jon Hall) and his Delaware to fight against the British by seducing the chief's son.

Apache Country (Columbia, 1952). George Archainbaud
   When villains provide guns and whiskey to the Apache and incite them to attack innocent settlers, Gene Autry comes to the rescue.

Ambush at Tomahawk Gap (Columbia, 1953). Fred Sears
   Apaches attack a group of settlers and try to kill them with flaming arrows.

Arrowhead (Paramount, 1953). Charles Marquis Warren
   Raised by the Apache and loved by Nita (Katy Jurado), the hero becomes a true hater of his adopted tribe. Finally, he defeats the warlike leader, Toriano (Jack Palance), who returns to the Apache and leads them against the whites. He is a notable example in the line of hateful characters who suggest the idea that to know Native Americans is to hate them. A *NYT* critic comments on this attitude in the film: "Whatever feelings of friendship for the American Indian may have been shown in a few open-minded Westerns lately, it is plain that producer Nate Holt is having no truck with any such ideas. To him an Indian is still a treacherous dog" (16 Sept.).

The Charge at Feather River (Warner, 1953). Gordon Douglas
   In this 3D film, the hero rescues two women from the Cheyenne, one of whom is in love with their Chief Thunder Cloud (Fred Carson). His warriors give chase and attack the hero's party at the river.

Pony Express (Paramount, 1953). Jerry Hopper
   After the Sioux have captured Buffalo Bill Cody, he has a hand-to-hand fight with their Chief Yellow Hand (Pat Hogan) and defeats him. Later he comes to the rescue in a climactic battle with the Sioux.

Saginaw Trail (Columbia, 1953). George Archainbaud

A villain disguises himself as a warrior and hires the renegade tribe of Red Bird (John War Eagle), the Huron (Rodd Redwing) and the Fox (Billy Wilkerson) to attack settlers in the Michigan woods.

War Paint (UA, 1953). Lesley Selander

The hero struggles to get a treaty to the tribe of Taslik (Keith Larsen) and Wanima (Joan Taylor) in order to avert a war.

River of No Return (20th Century-Fox, 1954). Otto Preminger

A hostile tribe uses rocks and arrows to attack explorers on a raft.

Southwest Passage (UA, 1954). Ray Nazarro

A tribe that at first thinks camels are a kind of god later attacks the whites traveling on the animals.

Apache Ambush (Columbia, 1955). Fred Sears

Apaches join with Mexican bandits in raids on settlers and have a large battle with a group of post-Civil War soldiers. A *Variety* critic comments: "One thing about this pic; it won't make the distributor very popular in Mexico or with Indians. Both are shown up in the worst possible light" (10 Aug.).

Apache Woman (American, 1955). Roger Corman

The hero finds out that murders thought to be committed by reservation Apaches were actually done by the mixed-blood femme fatale, Anne (Joan Taylor) and her college-educated brother, Armand (Lance Fuller)

Sante Fe Passage (Republic, 1955). William Witney

Chief Satank and his hostile warriors attack a group which includes the hero, his beloved Aurlie (Faith Domergue), a mixed-blood, and her mother, Ptewaquin (Irene Tedrow).

The Tall Men (20th Century-Fox, 1955). Raoul Walsh

The hero saves a woman during an attack by hostile warriors. Later, when the warriors attack men on a cattle drive, the hero starts a stampede to turn them away.

Dakota Incident (Republic, 1956). Lewis K. Foster

Hostile Sioux led by an unnamed chief (Charles Horvath) pin down a group of whites in a gully and eventually kill most of them.

Ghost Town (UA, 1956). Allen Miner

The Cheyenne of Dull Knife (Ed Hashim) attack a small group of whites in a deserted town. The hero and a mixed-blood, Maureen (Serena Sande), survive and fall in love.

Copper Sky (20th Century-Fox, 1957). Charles Marquis Warren

At the beginning of the film, Apaches attack a town and kill all but two of the inhabitants.

Guns of Fort Petticoat (Columbia, 1957). George Marshall

The hero and a group of women work together to fight and defeat Cheyenne warriors led by their chief (Charles Horvath), who is intent on gaining revenge for the Sand Creek massacre.

Ambush at Cimarron Pass (20th Century-Fox, 1958). Jodie Coplean

Apaches attack and harass a small group of whites until the hero rescues the survivors.

Blood Arrow (20th Century-Fox, 1958). Charles Marquis Warren

When hostile Blackfeet led by Little Otter (Richard Gilden) attack a Mormon woman bringing serum to sick families, some whites and Taslatch (Rocky Shahan) come to her rescue.

Escape from Red Rock (20th Century-Fox, 1958). Edward Bernds
The hero and his woman find a baby whose parents had been killed by the Apache, who, in turn, attack them. At the last moment, they are rescued.

The Law and Jake Wade (MGM, 1958). John Sturges
Comanches attack the hero and his people in a ghost town.

Oregon Passage (Allied Artists, 1958). Paul Landres
The Shoshone of Chief Black Eagle (H. M. Wynant), Little Deer (Toni Gerry) and Nato (Paul Fierro) attack and kill some settlers. The hero finally kills Black Eagle in hand-to-hand combat, and thus stops his braves from attacking the fort.

Thunder in the Sun (Paramount, 1959). Russell Rouse
Basques take on a hostile tribe in the mountains and befuddle them with their trilling calls and bounding jumps from rocks. Finally, they and the hero kill many of the hostiles and then move on to their promised land.

Kidnapping

Young Daniel Boone (Monogram, 1950). Reginald LeBorg
The hero rescues two white women kidnapped by the tribe of Little Hawk (William Roy) and Walking Eagle (Nipo Strongheart).

Many Rivers to Cross (MGM, 1955). Roy Rowland
The hero rescues his beloved who has been kidnapped by the tribe of Sandak (Ralph Moody) and Slangoh (Abel Fernandez).

Seminole Uprising (Columbia, 1955). Earl Bellamy
The Seminoles of Black Cat (Steve Ritch) escape from their Florida reservation and go on raids in Texas during which they capture a white woman. The mixed-blood hero

returns the tribe to the reservation and falls in love with the woman.

Shotgun (Allied Artists, 1955). Lesley Selander
The hero rescues a white woman captured by the Apaches of Delgadito (Paul Marion).

The Searchers (Warner, 1956). John Ford
In this film (discussed in various parts of this book), Chief Scar (Henry Brandon) of the Comanche kidnaps two girls and kills their parents in revenge for the killing of his sons. Scar's warriors rape and kill one of them, and he takes the other for his wife. After years of searching, the heroes kill Scar and rescue the young woman.

The Tomahawk Trail (UA, 1957). Lesley Selander
Captured by Apaches and befriended by Tula (Lisa Montell), the daughter of the chief, the heroine is eventually rescued by soldiers.

Trooper Hook (UA, 1957). Charles Marquis Warren
A white woman captured by the Apache chief, Nachez (Rudolfo Acosta), has a son by him. After the hero rescues the woman, her white husband rejects her and the boy. At the end, both Nachez and her husband die, and she and her son leave with the hero.

Native Americans in Serials

Cody of the Pony Express (Columbia, 1950). Spencer Bennet
In chapters such as "The Fatal Arrow" and "Captured by Indians" the hostile tribe of Chief Gray Cloud uses guns supplied by outlaws to threaten the hero.

Roar of the Iron Horse (Columbia, 1950). Spencer Bennet and T. Carr
In chapters such as "Indian Attack," "Captured by Redskins" and "Redskin's Revenge" hostile warriors threaten settlers and railroad builders.

Son of Geronimo (Columbia, 1952). Spencer Bennet
In chapters like "Indian Ambush" and "On the War-path" the Apaches of Geronimo (Chief Yowlachie) and Porico (Rodd Redwing) attack wagon trains and eventually turn against their outlaw allies.

Man with the Steel Whip (Republic, 1954). Franklin Adreon
In chapters like "Redskin Raiders" a villain after a tribe's gold incites them to war.

Blazing the Overland Trial (Columbia, 1956). Spencer Bennet
In a chapter called "Rifles for Redskins," the villain incites a warlike tribe to attack a wagon train.

Perils of the Wilderness (Columbia, 1956). Spencer Bennet
In chapters such as "Menace of the Medicine Man" hostiles threaten the settlers.

Vengeance

Two Flags West (20th Century-Fox, 1950). Robert Wise
After the haughty commander of a fort deliberately kills the son of a Kiowa chief, the tribe attacks and gains vengeance by killing the officer.

Wagonmaster (RKO, 1950). John Ford
The hero makes friends with a band of Navajo and they have a joint celebration. However, when a Mormon molests a woman from the tribe, they threaten war until the hero has the man punished.

Tomahawk (Universal, 1951). George Sherman
After a cruel soldier kills the parents of Movahseetah (Susan Cabot), her Sioux tribe, led by Red Cloud (John War Eagle), attacks the soldiers in fights that became known as the Fetterman and Wagon Box massacres. A *Commonweal* reviewer comments: "This is another in the current cycle of westerns that dares to speak up for the Indians and suggests

that white men haven't always been too honorable in their dealings" (2 Mar., 520).

Apache War Smoke (MGM, 1952). Harold Kress
When the hero refuses to hand over a man who robbed and killed several members of their tribe, Apaches attack a group of whites.

The Battles of Chief Pontiac (Realart, 1952). Felix Kress
When the evil leader of some Hessians tries to wipe out the Ottawa of Chief Pontiac (Lon Chaney) by sending them blankets infested with smallpox, the tribe captures him and gets revenge by wrapping him up in the blankets. At the same time , the hero rescues a white woman who is about to be raped by Hawkbill (Larry Chance).

Fort Osage (Monogram, 1952). Lesley Selander
After villains break a treaty, the Osage tribe attacks a wagon train, but they punish only the villains and let the rest of the people go on their way.

Old Overland Trail (Republic, 1953). William Witney
When a villain sells whiskey and rifles to Apache so they will make war, a good Indian agent stops the hostility. Finally, the tribe gains revenge by killing the villain.

The Tall Texan (Lippert, 1953). Elmo Williams
After whites break a treaty and seek gold on the land of Jaqui (George Steele), his tribe attacks and kills most of them.

Garden of Evil (20th Century-Fox, 1954). Henry Hathaway
Apaches ambush a group of outlaws and many of them are killed.

The Man from Laramie (Columbia, 1955). Anthony Mann
A villain who sells repeating rifles to the Apaches is finally killed by the tribe when a later shipment is destroyed.

Seven Cities of Gold (20th Century-Fox, 1955). Robert Webb
The villain seduces Ula (Rita Moreno), a woman from the tribe of chief Matuwir (Jeffrey Hunter), and the tribe threatens war until the man gives himself up for punishment.

Smoke Signal (Universal, 1955). Jerry Hopper
In the Grand Canyon, the hero escapes from hostile warriors led by Delche (Pat Hogan), who have been mistreated by the military.

Massacre (20th Century Fox, 1956). Louis King
Supplied with guns by treacherous smugglers, Yaqui warriors attack and kill a group of Mexicans. Finally they also kill the smugglers.

Quantez (Universal, 1957). Harry Keller
Apaches led by Delgadito (Michael Ansara) attack a gang of outlaws.

Gunmen from Laredo (Columbia, 1959). Wallace MacDonald
The Apaches of Coloradas (Charles Horvath) and Delgados (X Brands) pursue the hero and a young Mexican woman who was captured and raised by them across the desert. At the end, the hero kills Coloradas in hand-to-hand combat.

IMAGES OF THE NOBLE RED MAN

Friendship and Loyalty

Annie Get Your Gun (MGM, 1950). George Sidney
In this musical, Sitting Bull (J. Carrol Naish) is the friend of the heroine and helps her win the man she loves. He and Little Horse (Chief Yowlachie) adopt her into their Sioux tribe, which also acts during the attacks staged in Buffalo Bill's Wild West Show.

Colt 45 (Warner, 1950). Edwin Marin
The hero and the friendly tribe of Walking Bear (Chief Thunder Cloud) bring a bank robber to justice.

The Iroquois Trail (UA, 1950). Phil Karlson
Based on characters from Cooper's novels, this film follows the exploits of Hawkeye and Sagamore (Monte Blue), his faithful companion, as they fight hostile warriors.

Ticket to Tomahawk (20th Century-Fox, 1950). Richard Sale
Pawnee (Chief Yowlachie), the taciturn friend of the heroine, helps her to overcome villains who are competing with her for a train-line contract. Crooked Knife (Chief Thunder Cloud) and his Arapahoe warriors also help the heroine when her beloved, who was a friend of Crooked Knife in a wild west show, uses fireworks to win over the tribe. Other Native American characters are Trancos (Charles Stevens), Lone Eagle (John War Eagle) and Crazy Dog (Shooting Star).

Snake River Desperadoes (Columbia, 1951). Fred Sears
The Durango Kid, with the help of his young companion, Little Hawk (Don Reynolds), fights villains who disguise themselves as Native Americans to incite a war.

Desert Pursuit (Monogram, 1952). George Blair
The Mission tribe, who at first think Arabs riding camels and pursuing a white couple are holy men, finally see the truth and rescue the couple.

The Half Breed (RKO, 1952). Stuart Gilmore
Charlie Wolf (Jack Buetel), an Apache mixed-blood, joins the hero in bringing to justice villains who are trying to start a war so they can get at gold on the reservation. A *NYT* reviewer notes that the film "does profess concern for Indians of 1867, which is commendable but hardly timely. Perhaps it will give somebody an idea for a motion picture about the plight of the contemporary Indian, the Navajos of the Southwest, for instance" (5 July).

Navajo (Lippert, 1952). Norman Foster

Little Son of the Hunter (Francis Kee Teller), a Navajo boy forced to go to a white school, escapes to a canyon, tricks his pursuers and then rescues them. A critic from *Parent and Teacher* comments: "Serious and moving, this drama points to a new kind of Indian story vastly removed from the commonplace melodrama of pioneer warfare" (Jan., 37).

Pony Soldier (20th Century-Fox, 1952). Joseph Newman

A Mountie and his mixed-blood companion, Natayo (Thomas Gomez), make friends with the Northern Cree of Chief Standing Bear (Stuart Randall), young Comes Running (Anthony Numkena), Konah (Cameron Mitchell), White Moon (Adeline De Walt Reynolds), Roks-Ki (Muriel Landers), Shemawgun (Grady Galloway) and a Medicine Man (Nipo T. Strongheart). Aided by the friendly Chief Standing Bear and Comes Running, who kills the hostile sub-chief Konah, the heroes stop a war and lead the tribe back to Canada. A *NYT* critic comments: "Anything but the old-time movie redskins, full of festering resentments and booze, these are fine and upstanding representatives of a racial minority" (20 Dec.).

Last of the Comanches (Columbia, 1953). Andre De Toth

When the Comanches of Black Cloud (John War Eagle) attack a group of whites trapped in an abandoned mission, Little Knife (Johnny Stewart), who had earlier been helped by whites, shows his gratitude and friendship by helping to rescue them.

The Nebraskan (Columbia, 1953). Fred Sears

Wing Foot (Maurice Jara), the friend of the hero, is unjustly accused of killing a friendly chief. Chief Spotted Bear (Jay Silverheels), the real murderer who wants to kill Wing Foot, starts a war because the hero will not hand over his friend. At the end, Yellow Knife, the son of Spotted Bear, who has been rescued by the hero, rescues him from burning at the stake, kills Spotted Bear and promises that he and Wing Foot will make peace.

The Pathfinder (Columbia, 1953). Sidney Salkow

In this film based on Cooper's novel, the hero and his friends, Chingachgook (Jay Silverheels) and Uncas (Ed. Koch, Jr.), spy for the British on the French and hostile Mingoes of Chief Arrowhead (Rodd Redwing). Other Native American characters are Lokawa (Elena Verdugo), the wife of a British soldier, and Eagle Feather (Chief Yowlachie), Togamak (Ross Conklin) and Ka-letan (Vi Ingram).

Peter Pan (RKO, 1953). Hamilton Luske, Clyde Geronimi and Wilfred Jackson

In this Disney animated film, the Indian Chief (Voice of Candy Candido) protects Peter Pan and the children.

Tumbleweed (Universal, 1953). Nathan Juran

The Yaqui tribe of Aguila (Ralph Moody) and Tigre (Eugene Iglesias) attacks the hero, but one of the warriors, whom he had helped earlier, comes to his rescue.

Drum Beat (Warner, 1954). Delmer Daves

As the hero tries to establish a treaty with the Modoc tribe of the rebellious Captain Jack (Charles Bronson), two friendly members of the tribe, Manok (Anthony Caruso) and Toby (Marisa Pavan) help him. After Toby, who loves the hero, gives her life to save him, he finally kills Captain Jack in hand-to-hand combat.

Four Guns to the Border (Universal, 1954). Richard Karlson

Yaqui (Jay Silverheels), one of the central characters, rescues a woman from the Apaches before he is killed.

Saskatchewan (Universal, 1954). Raoul Walsh

The hero, who was raised by the Cree and is blood brother of Cajou (Jay Silverheels), tries to stop the hostile Sioux of Sitting Bull from inciting the Cree to war. Just as he and his men are about to be overrun by the Sioux, Cajou and his warriors come to the rescue. Other Native American characters are Chief Dark Cloud (Anthony Moreno) and Spotted Eagle (Anthony Caruso).

They Rode West (Columbia, 1954). Phil Karlson
The Kiowa of Santanta (Stuart Randall) join the hostile Comanches of Chief Quannah Parker (John War Eagle) and threaten war. However, the hero keeps the peace by saving the life of Santanta's son. Other Native American characters are Red Wolf (Eugene Iglesias), Asatai (Frank De Kova) and Spotted Wolf (Maurice Jara)

War Arrow (Universal, 1954). George Sherman
The hero, with the help of friendly Seminoles led by Magro (Henry Brandon), puts down a Kiowa uprising incited by the villain and led by Santanta (Jay Silverheels).

Davy Crockett—King of the Wild Frontier (Buena Vista, 1955). Norman Foster
In the first part of this film, the hero wins the respect of the tribe of Chief Red Stick (Pat Hogan) and Charles Two Shirts (Jeff Thompson).

Strange Lady in Town (Warner, 1955). Mervyn LeRoy
A doctor from Boston treats Apaches and Mexicans in Sante Fe. When the white establishment gives her trouble, her patients show their loyalty and friendship by standing up for her.

The Lone Ranger (Warner, 1956). Stuart Heisler
The hero and his companion, Tonto (Jay Silverheels), bring to justice an evil rancher who is fomenting trouble between the whites and Native Americans so that he can take silver from the tribe's land. Warriors kidnap the villain's daughter but finally show their honor by returning her to her mother.

Reprisal (Columbia, 1956). George Sherman
Two people from the tribe of Katola (Phillip Breedlove) and Kelene (Victor Zamudio) are unjustly hanged because of the villains. At the urging of Taini (Kathryn Grant) and a sympathetic white woman, the hero, Frank Madden (Guy Madison), a mixed-blood, takes on the villains and brings

them to justice. At the end he falls in love with the white woman. A *Newsweek* critic notes: "The Indians, in line with current Hollywood practice, look pretty good. In fact, if this new morality continues, moviegoers may never see a bad Indian again" (19 Nov., 135–6).

Walk the Proud Land (Universal, 1956). Jesse Hibbs
Also titled *Apache Agent*, this film tells the story of John Clum, an agent at the San Carlos Reservation who takes care of the Apache of Geronimo (Jay Silverheels), Talito (Tommy Ball), Eskiminiyin (Robert Warwick), Tono (Eugene Mazzola), Alchise (Maurice Jara) and Pica (Marty Carrizosa). Though loved by Tainey (Anne Bancroft), he remains faithful to his wife. Finally he brings peace to the reservation when he convinces Geronimo to surrender and live a life of law and order. A *Time* critic notes that the film is "a western with a difference: the Indians, or most of them, are the good guys" (24 Sept., 92).

Apache Warrior (20th Century-Fox, 1957). Elmo Williams
The Apache Kid (Keith Larsen), a scout who helps the hero hunt down hostile Apaches, goes to jail after he revenges his brother's murder by killing Chato (George Keymas). With the help of the rebel Apache, Marteen (Rudolfo Acosta), he escapes and marries Liwana (Eugenia Paul). Eventually, the hero becomes his friend again and forgives his crime because he realizes the Kid was practicing Apache justice.

Deerslayer (20th Century-Fox, 1957). Kurt Neumann
In this film based on the Cooper novel, the hero who is raised by Mohicans joins his blood brother, Chingachgook (Carlos Rivas), to save a hateful white man and his daughters from hostile Hurons who are intent on getting back the scalps of their warriors.

Flaming Frontier (20th Century Fox, 1958). Sam Newfield
Captain Jim Hewson (Bruce Bennett), a mixed-blood, keeps the peace between his cavalry and a wronged tribe.

The Light in the Forest (Buena Vista, 1958). Herschel Daugherty
   The Delaware of Cuyloga (Joseph Calleia) capture a white boy whom they adopt and name Young True Son (Douglas MacArthur). He lives happily with the tribe until a treaty forces them to return him to his natural parents. Unhappy with white society at first, he finally learns that there are good and bad people in both cultures.

The Lone Ranger and the Lost City of Gold (UA, 1958). Lesley Selander
   When villains try to gain control of a tribal mine, the Lost City of Gold, the hero and his faithful companion, Tonto (Jay Silverheels), thwart the plot and return the mine to the tribe of Chief Tomache (John Miljan), Redbird (Maurice Jara) and Canlama (Belle Mitchell).

The Sheriff of Fractured Jaw (20th Century-Fox, 1959). Raoul Walsh
   In this spoof of Westerns, the English sheriff becomes the blood brother of Running Deer (Jonathan Applegarth) and Red Wolf (Joe Buffalo), who help him to protect the town.

The Peace-loving Chief

These noble characters often contrast with hostile leaders from their tribe. They also often have the other typical traits of gratitude, honor and courage.

Broken Arrow (20th Century-Fox, 1950) Delmer Daves
   Discussed in the introduction (98–101), this film tells the story of Cochise, the friend of the hero who chooses the way of peace for his tribe. In this landmark film many of the minor Apache characters are played by Native American actors: Gokia-Geronimo (Jay Silverheels), Juan (Billy Wilkerson), Nochale (Chris Yellow Bird), Pionsenay (J.W. Cody), Nahilazy (John War Eagle), Skinyea (Charles Soldani) and Teese (Iron Eyes Cody).

Comanche Territory (Universal, 1950). George Sherman
  Chief Quisima (Pedro de Corba) of the Comanche controls his hostile warriors and makes friends with the hero, Jim Bowie, who saves the tribe by finding a treaty stolen by villains and by bringing them guns so they can defend themselves. A *Variety* critic notes: "This is one of the few recent screen vehicles in which the Indians are never cast as villains" (5 Apr.).

The Battle at Apache Pass (Universal, 1951). George Sherman
  Discussed on pps. 101–3, this film tells the story of peace-loving Cochise who prevails over the hostile Geronimo and finally makes a treaty with the government.

Brave Warrior (Columbia, 1952). Spencer G. Bennet
  Aided by Tecumseh (Jay Silverheels), chief of the Shawnee, the hero deals with British villains who are inciting hostile members of the tribe, led by the Prophet (Michael Ansara) and Chief Little Cloud (Billy Wilkerson) to make war against the settlers.

Conquest of Cochise (Columbia, 1953). William Castle
  Discussed on pps. 103–4, this film tells the story of how Cochise keeps the peace despite the efforts of hostile warriors from his tribe and from his former allies, the Comanches.

Fort Vengeance (Allied Artists, 1953). Lesley Selander
  Despite the efforts of Sitting Bull (Michael Granger) and his hostile Sioux, the peace-loving chief of the Canadian Blackfeet, Crowfoot (Morris Ankrum), and the hero avert a war. The hero exonerates son of Crowfoot, Eagle Heart (Paul Marion), from the charge of murder by finding the real murderer, and the tribe agrees to peace.

Hondo (Warner, 1953). John Farrow
  The hero, who grew up with the Apache and respects the honorable Chief Vitorio (Michael Pate), fights against the hostile warriors of Silva (Rodolfo Acosta). A *Variety* critic comments that "Vitorio. . .is shown as a just leader con-

cerned about the problems of his people and bewildered by the white man's violation of treaties" (25 Nov.).

Seminole (Universal, 1953). Budd Boetticher
Discussed on pps. 105–6, this film tells the story of Chief Osceola who dies after being captured by an evil military leader. However, at the end, his tribe, led by the once hostile Kayjeck, makes peace.

Battle of Rogue River (Columbia, 1954). William Castle
The tribe of Chief Mike (Michael Granger), a leader who wants peace, is finally incited to war by a villain. At the end, the hero exposes the villain and makes peace with Chief Mike.

Black Dakotas (Columbia, 1954). Ray Nazarro
War Cloud (John War Eagle), the chief of the Sioux who wants peace, and the hostile, ambitious Black Buffalo (Jay Silverheels) come in contact with a villain who uses a fake treaty that promises gold to the tribe. At the end, the hero overcomes the villain, and the tribe agrees to peace when they get a real treaty and the gold.

Cattle Queen of Montana (RKO, 1954). Allan Dwan
Coloradas (Lance Fuller), a college-educated chief of the Blackfeet, helps a female rancher fight the villain and hostile, whiskey-drinking warriors from his tribe led by Natchakoa (Anthony Caruso). Other Native American characters are Starfire (Yvette Dugay) and Powhani (Rodd Redwing). A *Variety* reviewer writes: "In the picture's favor (but this seems to be a trend lately in Indian territory stories) is an attempt to depict the problems of the Redmen in fighting the encroachment of their land by white settlers. The Indians are not all evil, scalp-hunting devils" (17 Nov.).

Drums Across the River (Universal, 1954). Nathan Juran
To get at their gold, the villain starts trouble with the Ute tribe of Taos (Jay Silverheels), Red Knife (Ken Terrell) and Chief Owray (Morris Ankrum). The hero, whose mother

had been killed by hostile warriors, finally decides to help Chief Owray keep the peace.

Sitting Bull (UA, 1954). Sidney Salkow

Discussed on pps. 106–8, this film tells the story of Sitting Bull, who is driven to war by Custer, but finally makes peace with the whites.

Taza, Son of Cochise (Universal, 1954). Douglas Sirk

Taza tries to keep the peace, but his rebellious brother, Naiche (Bart Roberts), convinces the tribe to join with the hostile Geronimo (Ian MacDonald) and Grey Eagle (Morris Ankrum). When the hostile warriors attack the cavalry, Taza helps the soldiers defeat them so that peace can be reestablished. Other Apache characters are Oona (Barbara Rush), the daughter of Grey Eagle and beloved of Taza, Chato (Eugene Iglesias), Skinja (James Van Horn) and Kocha (Charles Horvath). A *Newsweek* critic notes that the film "is another chapter in Hollywood's long and truculent argument with the American Indian. This one, like many others, pays a kind of lip service to the idea that the Indians may be men of merit, but as usual they take a numerical licking" (1 Mar., 80).

Chief Crazy Horse (Universal, 1955). George Sherman

Crazy Horse is the prophesied leader of the Sioux of Flying Hawk (Keith Larsen), Worm (Paul Guilfoyle), Spotted Tail (Robert Warwick), Red Cloud (Morris Ankrum), Old Man Afraid (Stuart Randall) and He Dog (Henry Wills). Influenced by a white friend and his wife, Black Shawl (Susan Ball), he finally makes peace with the whites, only to be killed by Little Big Man (Ray Danton). A *Time* critic notes that the film "pays a Technicolor installment on Hollywood's debt to the American Indian: after years of getting clobbered, the redskins this time win three battles in a row over the U.S. Cavalry" (10 May 86).

The Indian Fighter (UA, 1955). Andre De Toth

When the hero falls in love with Onahti (Elsa Martinelli), the daughter of Chief Red Cloud (Eduard Franz), and neglects his duties as a wagonmaster, a villain who is after gold incites Grey Wolf (Harry Sanders) and other hostile braves to war. At the end, Grey Wolf is killed, and the hero turns over the villain to Red Cloud, who agrees to peace and allows him to marry Onahti. A *Newsweek* critic notes that Hollywood's "tribesmen have, of late, been getting nobler and nobler, and occasionally they even come out all right, always with the understanding white man passing the peace pipe" (9 Jan., 1956, 71)

White Feather (20th Century-Fox, 1955). Robert Webb
    The hero, who is in charge of moving the Cheyenne of the peace-loving Chief Broken Hand (Eduard Franz) to a new reservation, causes trouble when he falls in love with Appearing Day (Debra Paget), who is betrothed to the son of the chief, Little Dog (Jeffrey Hunter). After the death of Little Dog and his hostile friend, American Horse (Hugh O'Brian), Chief Broken Hand makes peace and the tribe moves off to the reservation. A *NYT* critic comments that "the Red Man. . .is a truly brave warrior but somehow a sad figure, resigned, at last, to the truth that the White Man is strong enough to oust him from his hunting grounds and that he must move to new lands" (17 Feb.).

Comanche (UA, 1956). George Sherman
    Despite the opposition of Black Cloud (Henry Brandon) and his hostile warriors, Flat Mouth (Mike Mazurki) and Little Snake (Tony Carbajal), Chief Quannah Parker of the Comanche (Kent Smith) agrees to peace. Because of the efforts of his white friend, who kills Black Cloud in hand-to-hand combat, Quannah Parker accepts a treaty.

War Drums (UA, 1957). Reginald Le Borg
    Villains push the peace-loving Mangas Coloradas (Lex Barker) and his wife, Riva (Joan Taylor) into breaking a treaty. However, the hero helps them escape an unjust punishment and join other members of their Apache tribe in the mountains, Chino (John Calicos), Nona (Jil Jarmyn), Yellow Moon (Jeanne Carmen) and Delgadito (Ward Ellis).

Yellowstone Kelly (Warner, 1959). Gordon Douglas
The hero, a friend of Gall (John Russell), the just and honorable chief of the Sioux, rescues Wahleeah (Andra Martin), a captive Arapahoe woman who falls in love with him. After the hero kills the hostile Sagapi (Ray Danton), Gall makes peace and, even though he loves her, lets Wahleeah go away with his friend.

Romances between Native American Women and White Men

The female characters in these films have many of the typical traits of the Noble Red Man.

Across the Wide Missouri (MGM, 1951). William Wellman
The hero marries a Blackfeet, Kamiah (Maria Marques), and tries to live on land controlled by the hostile young Ironshirt (Ricardo Montalban). When the chief of the tribe, Looking Glass (J. Carrol Naish), is killed, the hostiles attack and Ironshirt and Kamiah die during the fighting. After the death of his wife, the hero takes their son to the mountains and lives with friends from the tribe.

The Big Sky (RKO, 1952). Howard Hawks
On a river journey, the hero falls in love with Teal Eye (Elizabeth Threatt), a Blackfeet whom the leader has taken along so he will be able to trade with her people. Along with Poordevil (Hank Worden), the group fights hostile Crow and French traders. At the end, the hero and Teal Eyes decide to live with her tribe.

The Wild North (MGM, 1952). Andrew Morton
A woman (Cyd Charisse) from a tribe whose chief is played by John War Eagle falls in love with the hero.

Captain John Smith and Pocahontas (UA, 1953). Lew Landers
Pocahontas (Jody Lawrence) saves the life of John Smith and marries him to keep the peace with the settlers. Her father, the wise old Chief Powhatan (Douglas Dumbrille),

reluctantly approves of the match but the hostile Ope-
chanco (Stuart Randall) rebels and joins the villains. At the
end, John Smith sails for England, and Pocahontas stays
behind to keep the peace. Other Native American characters are Nantaques (Shepard Menken), Mawhis (Franchesca
di Scaffa) and Lacuma (Joan Dixon).

The Savage (Paramount, 1953). George Marshall
    Warbonnet (Charlton Heston), a white man raised by the
Sioux, falls in love with Luta (Joan Taylor). After she dies in
an attack by hostile Crow and Warbonnet refuses to lead
warriors against soldiers, he leaves the tribe and returns to
a white woman who loves him. At the end, he almost
sacrifices his life to convince his tribe not to attack the fort.
Other Native American characters are Running Dog
(Donald Porter), Iron Breast (Ted De Corsia), Yellow Eagle
(Ian MacDonald), Pehingi (Angela Clarke) and Long Mine
(Larry Tolan).

Broken Lance (20th Century-Fox, 1954). Edward Dmytryk
    A white man married to a Native American, Senora De-
vereaux (Katy Jurado), and his family struggle against white
society's contempt and prejudice. After the husband dies,
Senora Devereaux and her mixed-blood son, Joe (Robert
Wagner), keep the peace. At the end, Joe breaks the lance of
war and departs with the white woman he loves. Like
Flaming Star (1960), the film is a strong indictment of racism.

Rose Marie (MGM, 1954). Mervyn LeRoy
    Wanda (Joan Taylor), the daughter of Chief Black Eagle
(Chief Yowlachie), falls in love with a Mountie who eventually jilts her.

The Far Horizons (Paramount, 1955). Rudolph Mate
    This film about the Lewis and Clark expedition focuses
on the romance between Clark and Sacajawea (Donna Reed)
of the Shoshone. After helping the expedition reach its goal,
despite attacks by hostile tribes, Sacajawea decides to leave
Clark and return to her people, even though she still loves
him.

The Last Hunt (MGM, 1956). Richard Brooks
A hateful buffalo hunter vies with his companion for the affections of a young Native American woman (Debra Paget). After beating a mixed-blood (Russ Tamblyn) and killing young Spotted Hand (Ed Lovehill), the evil hunter finally freezes to death.

Mohawk (20th Century-Fox, 1956). Kurt Neumann
Joined by a villain, Pokhawah (Neville Brand) and his hostile Mohawk warriors start a war by killing the son of the wise, peace-loving Chief Kowanen (Ted de Corsia) and his wife, Minikah (Mae Clarke). The hero stops the hostility by killing Pokhawah, and the beautiful Onida (Rita Gam) falls in love with him. At the end, he chooses a white woman.

Ride Out for Revenge (UA, 1957). Bernard Girard
Having rejected his society, the hero lives with Pretty Willow (Joanne Gilbert) and her Cheyenne tribe led by Yellow Wolf (Frank de Kova) and Little Wolf (Vince Edwards). At the end, they are displaced because prospectors discover gold on their reservation.

Run of the Arrow (Universal, 1957). Samuel Fuller
Discussed in the introduction (108–9), this film has a subplot in which the hero marries Yellow Moccasin (Sarita Montiel) after she helps him survive the "run of the arrow" ordeal. At the end, she and the hero leave her Sioux people.

Bullwhip (Allied Artists, 1958). Harmon Jones
The hero tames his strong-willed mixed-blood wife, Cheyenne (Rhonda Fleming).

The Last Train from Gun Hill (Paramount, 1959). John Sturges
The hero hunts down two men who raped and killed his Native American wife.

The Oregon Trail (20th Century-Fox, 1959). Gene Fowler
During an attack on a wagon train, hostile warriors capture the hero, who is then rescued by a Native American woman, Shona Hastings (Gloria Talbot). After helping the

soldiers control the hostiles, he decides to live with his beloved Shona.

See also *Broken Arrow* (1950), *Arrowhead* (1953), *Drum Beat* (1954), *The Indian Fighter* (1955), *Seminole Uprising* (1955), *Seven Cities of Gold* (1955), *White Feather* (1955), *Ghost Town* (1956), *Walk the Proud Land* (1956), *Pawnee* (1957) *Trooper Hook* (1957), *Fort Bowie* (1958), and *Yellowstone Kelly* (1959).

Romances between Native American Men and White Women

Devil's Doorway (MGM, 1950). Anthony Mann
   Discussed on pps. 109–11, this film tells the story of Broken Lance Poole, a military hero who returns to his ranch and must fight to save it. At the end, a female lawyer fails to help him, and he dies defending his land.

Foxfire (Universal, 1955). Joseph Pevney
   Jonathan Dartland (Jeff Chandler), a mixed-blood Apache mining engineer, has trouble living with his white wife. However, his wise old mother, Saba (Celia Lovesky), helps the couple to appreciate each other.

The Vanishing American (Republic, 1955). Joseph Kane
   Blandy (Scott Brady) is a Navajo who loves a white woman living on the reservation. After overcoming a crooked trader, an evil Indian agent and hostile Apaches, he settles down with his beloved white woman. Other Native American characters are Yachi (Gloria Castillo), a young woman threatened by the villain, Etenia (Julian Rivero), Coshonta (George Keymas), Quah-tain (Charles Stevens) and Beeteia (Jay Silverheels).

See also *Jim Thorpe, All American* (1951), *Seminole* (1953), *Broken Lance* (1954) and *Reprisal* (1956).

Romances between Native Americans

Hiawatha (Monogram, 1952). Kurt Neumann
   Based on Longfellow's poem, this film tells the story of

the love between the Ojibway man, Hiawatha (Vince Edwards), and the Sioux woman, Minnehaha (Yvette Dugay). When the hostile Pau Puk Keewis tries to start trouble with the Sioux, Hiawatha stops him and finally gets permission from his tribe to marry Minnehaha.

See also *Davy Crockett, Indian Scout* (1950), *Apache* (1954), *Taza, Son of Cochise* (1954), *Apache Warrior* (1957) and *Yellowstone Kelly* (1959).

Native Americans as Victims

In these films, basically noble characters suffer because of prejudice or the machinations of villains. The hero is often a paternalistic savior of individuals and tribes.

North of the Great Divide (Republic, 1950). William Witney
Roy Rogers, an Indian agent and blood brother of the Oseka tribe of Canada, helps his friends by exposing villains who are tampering with the tribe's salmon fishing rights and causing starvation in the reservation.

Raiders of Tomahawk Creek (Columbia, 1950). Fred Sears
The Durango Kid deals with an evil Indian agent who is exploiting the tribe of chief Flying Arrow (Paul Marion).

Buffalo Bill in Tomahawk Territory (UA, 1952). Bernard B. Ray
Villains who are after gold try to turn the soldiers against the Sioux led by Chief White Cloud (Rodd Redwing) by disguising themselves as warriors and attacking wagon trains. The hero discovers the plot and keeps the peace by offering the tribe a herd of cattle as payment from the government.

Indian Uprising (Columbia, 1952). Ray Nazarro
Villains incite the Apache tribe to war to get at gold on their land. At the end the hero saves the day by tricking Geronimo into surrendering. A *Variety* critic notes: "This basic good vs evil motivation has been done before. As

usual the hero is the peace keeper, the villains are the exploiters and the Indians are the losers" (26 Dec., 1951).

Laramie Mountains (Columbia, 1952). Ray Nazarro
    When villains after gold try to start a war with the tribe of Swift Eagle (Jock Mahoney) and Chief Lone Tree (John War Eagle), the Durango Kid comes to the rescue.

Column South (Universal, 1953). Frederick de Kova
    When the villain incites Navajo led by Menquito (Dennis Weaver) to make war so he can cover up his defection from the Confederacy, the hero foils his plans.

The Great Sioux Uprising (Universal, 1953). Lloyd Bacon
    When villains steal horses from the Sioux of Red Cloud (John War Eagle), the hero averts a war by working out a plan for the tribe to sell horses to ranchers. A reviewer from *Natural History* comments: "These are Hollywood Indians and are always seen dressed in their best, but at least they are represented as humans with normal reactions" (June, 286).

Jack McCall, Desperado (Columbia, 1953). Sidney Salkow
    Villains after gold kill warriors from the Sioux tribe of Red Cloud (Jay Silverheels) and Grey Eagle (Eugene Iglesias).

Masterson of Kansas (Columbia, 1955). William Castle
    A villain tries to stop the tribe of Yellow Hand (Jay Silverheels) from getting rich grasslands by framing his white friend.

Massacre at Sand Creek (Columbia, 1956).
    This TV movie tells the story of Colonel Chivington's attack on unsuspecting Cheyenne women, children and elderly in which many were brutally murdered.

Secret of Treasure Mountain (Columbia, 1956). Seymour Friedman
    Villains after gold threaten the Apache tribe of Vahoe (Pat

Hogan) and Tawana (Susan Cummings). However, the curse that protects the tribe finally stops the villains.

White Squaw (Columbia, 1956). Ray Nazarro
   The villain tries to drive from their reservation the Sioux tribe who have adopted Ectay-O Wahnee (May Wynn), a mixed-blood. The hero comes to the rescue, and finally the villain dies in a burning tepee.

Wild Dakotas (Assoc. Releasing, 1956). Sam Newfield
   When a villain tries to cheat Arapahoes out of their land, the hero exposes his evil scheme and prevents a war.

Yaqui Drums (Allied Artists, 1956). Jean Yarbrough
   A villain trying to steal land from the Yaqui incites the tribe to war.

Naked in the Sun (Allied Artists, 1957). R. John Hugh
   Based on Frank Slaughter's *The Warrior,* this film deals with the struggles between Seminoles led by Osceola and slave traders during the colonial period.

The Oklahoman (Allied Artists, 1957). Francis D. Lyon
   Greedy ranchers after his land try to frame Charlie Smith (Michael Pate), a Native American rancher. The hero, whom Maria Smith (Gloria Talbott) loves, comes to the rescue. A *NYT* critic praises the film for portraying "A hero who is man enough to make a skin-conscious community ashamed of itself" (15 May).

Gunman's Walk (Columbia, 1958). Phil Karlson
   Clee Chonard (Kathryn Grant), a mixed-blood, and Black Horse (Chief Blue Eagle) are victimized by white society. A *Variety* reviewer notes that the film has "contemporary pertinency with the outspoken discussion of racial elements, in this case involving Indians" (18 June).

Contemporary Native Americans

Though a few of the films in the early periods deal with Native American characters in somewhat contemporary settings, this type of film becomes more prominent in this and the following decades.

Jim Thorpe, All American (Warner, 1951). Michael Curtiz
   This film tells the story of Jim Thorpe (Burt Lancaster), the Sauk and Fox athlete from Oklahoma who became a star in baseball, football and Olympic field and track. After the loss of his 1912 Olympic medals, the decline of his professional football career, the death of his son, and divorce from his white wife, he is reduced to driving a dump truck. However, encouraged by his favorite coach, he finally comes back to a productive life by teaching young athletes. Other Native American characters are his friends, Little Boy (Jack Big Head) and Ed Guyac (Dick Wesson), his father, Hiram (Nestor Paiva), Wally Denny (Suni Warcloud) and Louis Tewanema (Al Mejia).

Red Snow (Columbia, 1952). Boris Petroff, Harry Franklin and Ewing Scott
   An Eskimo soldier, Sgt. Koovuk (Ray Mala), finds that the Russians are developing a new weapon in his area. Other Eskimo characters are his wife, Alak (Gloria Sanders), Chief Nanu (Robert Bice) and Tuglu (Phillip Ahn).

The Story of Will Rogers (Warner, 1952). Michael Curtiz
   This film is a sympathetic biography of the famous mixed-blood humorist.

Battle Cry (Warner, 1955). Raoul Walsh
   Crazy Horse (Felix Noriego), a Native American soldier, is a minor character in this World War II film.

The FBI Story (Warner, 1959). Mervyn LeRoy
   In one segment, the agents pursue villains who are after oil and who killed members of the Oklahoma Osage tribe.

Never So Few (MGM, 1959). John Sturges
   In this World War II film, Sgt. John Danforth (Charles Bronson) is a Native American soldier bitter about the way he has been treated by white society.

* * *

Though the above non-Western films mark the beginning of a new vehicle for portraying Native American characters, the Westerns of this decade remain the primary texts. In the tradition of the classic Hollywood cinema, the Western plots of this decade regularly place rebellious and peace-loving characters in opposition. And the resolutions always reward those motivated by peace and punish those motivated by rebellious forces of disorder. As would be expected in the Eisenhower years (1953–61) when devotion to law, order and peace was at a high point, the plots of the Westerns, with some notable exceptions, establish a view of the West as a place where Native Americans and whites can live in peace and work together. This view continues in the early films of the 1960s.

CHAPTER FIVE

FILMS OF THE 1960S

The sympathetic portrayal of Native American characters continues in this decade during which the popularity of the Western begins to decline. The degree to which the positive images of the 1950s had become ingrained is echoed in an early 1960s review of *Geronimo* (1962). The critic begins with an exclamation: "They sure don't make Injun pictures the way they used to." Then, bemoaning the loss of the "uninhibited action ingredients that characterized the early indifferent-to-racial-stereotypes westerns," he concludes: "In some ways the modern Indian picture may be better, but something haunting and stirring has been lost in the metamorphosis" (*Variety*, 25 Apr.). Though "the uninhibited action" of attacks by hostile tribes still occurs in the Westerns of this period, some notable films, like their predecessors in the 1950s, depict Native Americans as positive, heroic central characters who must struggle with life on reservations.

In *Geronimo* (1962), the perennial, rebellious, hostile leader becomes an honorable, peace-loving chief who wins new rights for his people. *Cheyenne Autumn* (1964) depicts Dull Knife and Little Wolf as heroes who lead their people from a bleak Oklahoma reservation on an epic journey back to their homeland. In *Hombre* (1967) and *Tell 'em Willie Boy Is Here* (1969) the heroes fight for their identity and survival in a West where their tribes suffer the indignities of reservation life. Even *The Stalking Moon* (1968), in which the central Apache character is a Savage avenger, expresses hostility in the context of a defeated and driven tribe. Finally, in *Flaming Star* (1960), a heroic mixed-blood and his noble

Kiowa mother suffer the prejudice of both white and Native American society. Though the characters of these films are still drawn to the extremes of the Noble Red Man and Savage images, they do reveal a continuing change of attitude in the Western.

The early positive attitude reveals itself in the plot of *Geronimo* (1962), in which this fierce, proud warrior, driven to rebellion by a crooked Indian agent, finally becomes a family man who is willing to make peace with friendly, honest whites. Like the Cochise character of *Broken Arrow* (1950), Geronimo (Chuck Connors) is clever and persistent in his resistance to evil whites. His adversaries are the Bible-spouting Indian agent who sees Apaches as "children of the devil" and the captain who feels Geronimo's band is "nothing but a pack of dirty wild animals." On the other hand, two good whites, a lieutenant who respects the rights of the tribe and an honorable senator, eventually enable Geronimo to choose a peaceful resolution. The other character who helps Geronimo evolve into a peace-loving chief is Teela (Kamala Devi), the educated woman from his tribe who bears his son and thus gives him a reason for making peace.

Seen in a pattern of close-ups and low-angle shots from the beginning, Geronimo is established as a powerful central character in contrast to the other Apaches. His friend Mangas (Ross Martin) has capitulated and is trying to grow crops in the barren land to support his wife and baby son. And Teela teaches the Apache children to read white man's books. When Geronimo shoots an arrow into her book to show his disdain, she tells him he should learn to read and he responds, "I want them to respect me for what I am, not what they want me to be." However, when the Indian agent sells Apache land to a cattleman, even Mangas joins his friend in declaring war against the evil whites. Though Teela still resists the decision to start a war, she clearly loves Geronimo.

After Geronimo and his warriors steal horses and escape from the reservation, he tells them the strategy behind his declaration of war, "We can win because we don't have a chance. We will fight long enough so Americans will wonder why such a people must fight and will make a treaty that will recognize the honor and dignity of the Apaches." As he and his warriors continue their war, Geronimo shows his skill by silently overcoming a patrol of soldiers and, later, by an efficient attack on a wagon train in which his warriors take over the food wagons with tactics as clever as those of Cochise in *Broken Arrow*. Even during this attack, Geronimo thinks of Teela and takes a book (ironically *The US Army Regulations*) for her. After overcoming her resistance and taking her from the reservation, Geronimo starts to change when they declare their love and Teela tells him she is pregnant. Geronimo responds, "He will be a fine warrior, but maybe he should read." Despite this domestic interlude and signs that his strategy is affecting public opinion, however, hunger and a growing number of soldiers drive Geronimo's band to the point where surrender seems their only answer, especially as the evil captain sets up cannons which can hit their location. Even when his warrior, Natchez (Armando Silvestre), calls for surrender, Geronimo holds out and fights back by shooting a flaming arrow to blow up the soldiers' powder. However, when Teela has their son, he finally changes his mind.

As Geronimo approaches the baby, Teela begs him to surrender so his son will not be killed, and he replies, "I wondered if I am right [to surrender]; when I look at you and the child I stop wondering." And on cue, the honorable senator and good lieutenant walk up the hill and offer Geronimo a fair treaty. Smiling at Teela, Geronimo accepts and he and his people walk down the hill to join the whites in a life of peace. Hence the great hostile warrior of the 1950 films also becomes a peaceful-loving chief. From *Broken Arrow* to this film, such orderly, happy endings are typical of the plots which depict historical chiefs as central heroic characters. Making a statement that could apply to any of these films, a *Variety* critic comments on the ending of *Geronimo*: "The picture has an uplift ending that may fool youngsters into concluding that the Indians ultimately got a decent shake—a false note of resolution contradicted to this day" (25 Apr.). Such fantasy resolutions, however, become more rare later in the period, though the next film, *Cheyenne Autumn* (1964), follows a similar pattern.

Based on the historical novel of the same name by Mari Sandoz, *Cheyenne Autumn* portrays historical chiefs, Dull Knife (Gilbert Roland) and Little Wolf (Ricardo Montalban), as heroic central characters who survive against great odds until they, as was the case in *Geronimo*, are offered a treaty by a good government official. John Ford saw this epic story of the Cheyenne as his chance to make amends for the way he and other directors of Westerns had depicted Native American characters: "There are two sides to every story, but I wanted to show their [Native Americans] point of view for a change. Let's face it, we've treated them very badly—it's a blot on our shield; we've cheated and robbed, killed, murdered, massacred and everything else, but they kill one white man and, God, out come the troops" (Bogdanovich, 104). To accomplish his purpose, Ford not only uses honorable chiefs as central characters, but also establishes a hero, Tom Archer, who respects the Cheyenne and is a sympathetic voice-over narrator, much like Tom Jeffords in *Broken Arrow*.

John Ford also acknowledges the Cheyenne language by using it for the dialogue between members of the tribe. He further builds respect for the uniqueness of the tribe through the attitudes of Tom Archer and his friend, the Polish sergeant. Archer shows his appreciation when he says to the Quaker woman. "All you've seen are reservation Indians. The Cheyenne are the greatest fighters in the world, fierce, smart and meaner than sin." The Polish sergeant shows empathy for the Cheyenne by pointing out the parallel between the Cossacks' attempt to exterminate his people and the U. S. Army's attempt to kill off the Cheyenne. Throughout the film, Tom Archer's voice-overs emphasize the suffering and heroism of the Cheyenne as they escape from the Oklahoma reservation and make the dangerous trek to their homeland in the north.

In addition to using this technique, Ford and the screen-writer also imbue the characters of Dull Knife and Little Wolf with the intelligence to speak with simple eloquence and fight with shrewd tactics. For example, Little Wolf responds to an officer, "We are asked to remember much; the white man remembers nothing." And later he says, "Even a dog can go where he likes, but not a Cheyenne." The cleverness of the Cheyenne leaders, however, goes beyond their words. When superior numbers of the cavalry draw close, Little Wolf and Dull Knife direct their warriors to start grass fires which not only put the cavalry into disarray but also give the warriors a cover from which to shoot. The shrewdness and tenacity of these chiefs, who are emphasized as heroes by patterns of close low-angle shots, enable their people to hold out until Tom Archer and the good Secretary of the Interior can come to their rescue.

As in *Geronimo*, just as the Cheyenne are trapped by the cavalry and have artillery trained on them, the hero and honorable government official praise the heroism of the tribe and offer them a treaty. The official tells them that "you have made one of the most heroic marches in history." Then, when Dull Knife asks him who will tell about Fort Robinson, the place where many of his people were killed, he promises to inform those in government. After the two chiefs accept the treaty, Little Wolf kills the rebellious young son of Dull Knife and Spanish Woman (Dolores Del Rio), Red Shirt (Sal Mineo), because the young warrior had stolen one of his wives. Then Little Wolf gives Dull Knife the medicine bundle which had earlier been given to him by the old Chief Tall Tree (Victor Jory) and, seen from a low angle, he rides off into the horizon. As is typical in the peace-loving chief films, the rebellious warrior must be punished while the noble characters who accept peaceful coexistence with the whites are rewarded with new land and opportunities.

To tell the Cheyenne's side of the story, Ford relies on the image of the Noble Red Man. For example, he depicts Little Wolf as a noble character to the end, even though he kills the son of Dull Knife. On the other hand, in Mari Sandoz's historical novel a drunken Little Wolf kills, for no immediate good reason, a member of his tribe who had earlier flirted with his wives. For this shameful act, he spends the rest of his life in exile. In a much more obvious way than in the novel, Ford contrasts his noble chiefs to cruel, unfeeling whites like the cowboy who kills a starving Cheyenne for his scalp or the fanatical German commander of Fort Robinson. Such a depiction of the two chiefs as Noble Red Men does build the kind of sympathy for the Cheyenne seen by a *NYT* critic who notes that the film "is a stark and eye-opening symbolization of a shameful tendency that has prevailed in our national life—the tendency to be unjust and heartless to weaker people who get in the way of manifest destiny" (24 Dec.). Ford's *Cheyenne Autumn* does tell an important side of American history, but the noble Native American characters are more symbols of white exploitation than believable characters in themselves, as in the novel of Mari Sandoz.

Later in the decade, *Hombre* (1967) also treats the theme of Native Americans reduced to living on reservations and exploited by greedy whites, though with a much less positive ending than *Cheyenne Autumn.* The hero, John Russell, is a white man raised by the Apache who rejects the greed and prejudice of white society and chooses the harsh, but honorably self-contained, life of the Apache. First seen dressed as an Apache with his two friends from the tribe, Russell finds out he has inherited a boarding house from the man who gave him his white name. His Mexican friend encourages him to take the inheritance with a statement that turns out to be sadly ironic: "It pays to be a white man now. Put yourself on the winning side for once." After selling the house, Russell joins a group of people on a stagecoach and encounters the kind of prejudice he knows well as an adopted Apache. One young wife says that she knows what Apaches do to white women, and the other woman, the wife of the crooked Indian agent from the San Carlos Reservation, says she can't imagine eating a dog like the Apache. Russell asks her if she has ever been hungry and then tells her that, as an Apache, he has eaten dog and "lived like one." After hearing this, the wife insists Russell not ride in the stage.

When villains hold up the stage, take the agent's wife hostage and later pin down the rest of the group at an abandoned mine, Russell is the only one who can save them. Accepting this role with quiet resignation, he decides to call the bluff of the villains only after he finds out that the agent has stolen a large amount of money from the Apache at San Carlos. As the wife of the agent, whom the robbers have staked out in the sun, begs for help, Russell at first shows his anger towards the woman's prejudice and refuses to help her. When the one woman in the party who admires him asks why, he responds, "Up there in the mountains, there's a whole people who have lost everything. They don't have a place to spread their blessings. They've been insulted, diseased, made drunk and foolish. I know the men who did this as white men and I don't respect them." Finally, Russell decides to go down and take on the villains because he knows he's the only one who can ensure that the money stolen from his people at San Carlos by the Indian agent will be returned to them.

In the ensuing shootout, Russell is fatally wounded, but he dies knowing that he has paid his debt to his adopted tribe. The last shot of this man who dies for his people is a high-angle close-up of his face followed by a cut to a grainy picture of him as a boy with the Apache. Commenting on this last scene, a *NYT* critic notes that his death is "mindful of the selfless sacrifices made by the Indian hero of *Broken Arrow*" (22 Mar., 41). Though Cochise doesn't lose his life at the end of that film, the comparison is apt because John Russell's devotion to his adopted tribe does transform him into a version of the Noble, but doomed, Red Man.

Another later film that deals with Apaches after they have been conquered and put on reservations is *The Stalking Moon* (1968). In this film, however, the Apache character, Savaje (Nathaniel Narcisco), is a renegade bent on vengeance and a notable example of the Savage image in this period. The beginning of the film emphasizes the sad state of the Apache as the hero and some soldiers round up a small starving band which includes a white woman and her mixed-blood son (Noland Clay). The soldiers reveal their attitude towards the Apache when they look at the woman, and one says, "I wonder what she went through all those years?" Another comments, "God only knows what's going on in that woman's head." Because she knows her Apache husband, Savaje, is close behind, she asks the hero to take her and the boy with him. Finally he agrees and they head towards his ranch in New Mexico, though that place will offer no escape from the fierce Savaje.

As Savaje searches for his son he leaves a bloody trail of destruction, killing three men in a wagon, all the men and women (and even the hero's horse) at two stage stations and a group of Mexicans. When the hero realizes Savaje has arrived at his ranch and the woman, whom he now loves, offers to leave, he says, "Dead people all the way across Arizona. If I can, I have to stop it." Thus starts his deadly confrontation with Savaje, during which the savage warrior beats up the white woman, kills the hero's Mexican farm hand and his dog, and murders his mixed-blood friend, Nick Tana (Robert Forster). Through all this Savaje remains a hidden enemy who is always there but is seen only in flashes until the final fight, during which he charges and jumps on the hero even after being shot several times. The portrayal of this savage character prompts a *Variety* critic, who apparently had read the Theodore Olsen novel of the same name, to comment: "Savaje never is developed so as to project the terror force he is supposed to be. Instead he is little more than a savage Indian" (18 Dec.). Indeed, this character, though he has reasons for his vengeance, over-reaches so violently in his revenge that he becomes the typical Savage.

In another representative film from the more pessimistic last part of this era, *Tell 'em Willie Boy Is Here* (1969), the hero, Willie (Robert Blake), is a renegade like Savaje, but also a sympathetic character victimized by prejudice. The first high-angle shots of Willie as he leaves a freight train and runs through the rocky desert terrain establish him as a pursued man, an image that persists until his death near the end. When Willie arrives in the town near the reservation he immediately encounters the old prejudice: as he buys a yellow scarf for his girl friend, Lola (Katharine Ross), the store keeper says (in a statement that turns out to be ironic), "You're going to make some squaw happy tonight." And when he tries to get in a game at the pool hall, a man tells him, "Why don't you get back to the reservation where you belong?" Willie's real trouble, however, starts when he kills Lola's father. As they start their escape, Willie says to Lola, "One way or the other you die at the end. Nobody gives a damn what Indians do, nobody!" Though on one level what he says is true, his words are also ironic because the murder draws in not only the local sheriff and the female Indian agent who feels she owns Lola and her tribe, but also the press, who make a big story out of the fugitives' attempt to escape the sheriff and his posse.

When Willie eludes the posse by shooting their horses, Lola says to him, "You can't beat them." And he replies, "Maybe, but they'll know I was here." He also dismisses the possibility of surrendering and going back to prison: "Indians don't last in prison. They weren't born for it like whites." Finally, they arrive at the old village and Willie puts on the ghost dance shirt of his father (such shirts were originally believed to stop the bullets of the soldiers). The scene ends with Lola vowing to never leave him. Shortly thereafter, the sheriff finds Lola lying on her back, wearing the white dress she originally wore to please the female Indian agent, with the yellow scarf Willie gave her covering the gunshot wound from which she died. Two members of Lola's tribe who are with the sheriff have different opinions about the mystery of her death; one feels that Willie followed the warrior tradition of killing one's wife to save her from the enemy, and the other thinks she killed herself so she wouldn't hold him back.

Whatever the truth of her death, Willie continues to run, as the camera cuts between tracking shots of him moving through the rough terrain with his rifle on his shoulder and low-angle shots of the sheriff pursuing on his horse. As he promised he would, he finally catches up with Willie, who is sitting on a high rock. Clearly Willie has let him come close, and, when Willie stands up and turns, he shoots him, only to find out that Willie's rifle is empty. Thus the inexorable pursuit by the sheriff, who is the son of an Indian fighter, ends with the death of a Native American who never really had a chance. A *Variety* critic comments on this ending: "(in a sense, repeating the whole white-Indian history in America) is what the film is about" (22 Oct.). This film from the end of the decade reflects the kind of heavy and ironic social criticism typical of the Viet Nam era.

The last representative film (from the beginning of this period), *Flaming Star* (1960) is a less political but even more overt and heavy-handed critique of racial prejudice than *Tell 'em Willie Boy Is Here*. Like *Broken Lance* (1954), this film deals with prejudice towards a Native American wife of a white man, Neddy Burton (Dolores Del Rio), and her mixed-blood son, Pacer (Elvis Presley). These two characters, who are often seen together, first appear at a large dinner at the Burton ranch. As they sit together at the table, the conversation of their friends reveals the first hints of prejudice towards them, a prejudice that grows deadly after warriors from Neddy's Kiowa tribe attack and kill their neighbors. When the other ranchers come to the Burton ranch and question their loyalty because "a Kiowa squaw" lives with them, the deadly battle between their white friends and the Burtons begins with the killing of the Burtons' cattle. Another striking example of prejudice occurs while Neddy and Pacer are alone at the ranch. Two men ride up and ask for food, and Neddy, with her characteristic warmth and hospitality, starts to prepare a meal. However, after they make a comment about "Injuns living in a house like this" and one of them tries to kiss Neddy, she deftly defends herself and kicks them out of the house. Then Pacer takes over and avenges this affront to his mother by severely beating the two men. Pacer and his mother hug at the end of the scene, but this will be their only triumph over the forces of prejudice.

In addition to the prejudice of the whites, Pacer and Neddy must deal with the anger of the Kiowa led by Buffalo Horn (Rudolfo Acosta), who tries to persuade Pacer to fight with him against the whites. Referring to the ranchers' unending encroachment on their traditional lands, he tells Pacer, "We have no place to go. We have to fight or die. This is the great fight of our dreams. If I have a one-half white leave his father's people and fight for his mother's people, I will have great medicine." Pacer resists turning against his father and brother, who truly love him and his mother, but he reluctantly agrees to accompany Neddy to the Kiowa camp and then says, "They ain't my people. To tell you the truth, I don't know who's my people. Maybe I ain't got any." At the camp, Pacer sits in the circle of warriors, exchanges jokes with them and smokes the pipe, while his mother sits with her family. Though this scene establishes the Kiowa as honorable people who have been pushed into fighting the whites, it also shows that Neddy and Pacer no longer fit into the ways of the tribe.

On their way back to the ranch, one of their former friends who had been wounded by the Kiowa shoots Neddy and Two Moons (Perry Lopez), an event that finally forces Pacer to choose sides in the fighting. After a cowardly doctor resists helping Neddy and she dies, Pacer's pent-up feelings about the prejudice come out: "All Ma and me ever got was dirty looks." Now he will go to war against the whites, though he tells Buffalo Horn he will never fight his father and brother. During the fighting, however, his white brother is wounded by the Kiowa, and Pacer goes against the tribe by rescuing him. At this point, Pacer takes off his shirt and uses his brother's blood as war paint and kills some of the warriors in hand-to-hand combat. When his brother tells him that he is hopelessly outnumbered, Pacer responds, "If it's going to be like this for the rest of my life, to hell with it." Pacer's situation is indeed hopeless, and the next day, when he returns (with his shirt on) to the town where his brother was taken, he is fatally wounded. As he rides away into the horizon to face his flaming star of death, he says, "Maybe some day, somewhere, people will understand people like us."

A contemporary *NYT* critic believes that this unhappy ending "seems to underline the sadness of the period when the Indian began to vanish" (17 Dec.). Pacer's final cry for understanding and the reviewer's interpretation of the ending offer an appropriate perspective for a conclusion. During this period, overt sympathy for Native American characters becomes more the rule than the exception. However, the motivation of the sympathy is often a sentimental attitude like that of the above reviewer, one that sees the characters as Noble but doomed Red Men, victims of the inevitable march of white civilization. Though such an attitude is well intentioned, it falls short of any real empathy for the Native American characters.

IMAGES OF THE SAVAGE

As was true in the '50s Westerns, attacks by hostile warriors are often motivated by evil whites.

Attacks On Covered Wagons

Frontier Uprising (Zenith, 1961). Edward L. Cahn
When the Modoc tribe of Chief Taztay (Herman Rudin) attacks a wagon train and traps a troop of soldiers in a canyon, the hero comes to the rescue.

Taggart (Universal, 1964). R. G. Springsteen
Hostile Apaches attack a wagon train and fort. A *Variety* critic notes that "the script is traditional in the attitude towards Indians: the only good ones are dead ones" (9 Dec.).

The Hallelujah Trail (UA, 1965). John Sturges
In this spoof of Westerns, the whiskey-loving Sioux warriors of Chief Walks Stooped Over (Martin Landau), Elks Runner (Jim Burk) and Chief Five Barrels (Robert Wilke) attack a circled wagon train and later circle the wagons themselves as the cavalry attacks them.

The Tall Women (Allied Artists, 1966). Sidney Pink
Apache warriors led by Pope (Luis Prendes) attack a wagon train and kill all but seven women and the hero. Finally, Chief White Cloud (Fernando Hilbeck) acknowledges the courage of the survivors and orders Pope not to attack them again.

Attacks on the Cavalry and Soldiers in Forts

Sergeant Rutledge (Warner, 1960). John Ford
In a series of flashbacks during the trial of a black

cavalryman, the black hero is seen protecting a white woman from hostile Apaches and stopping the cavalry from riding into an Apache ambush.

Thunder of Drums (MGM, 1961). Joseph M. Newman
Hostile Apaches attack soldiers who eventually trick them and kill many of the warriors. A *Variety* critic notes that the "Apaches [are] of the old screen school of all-bad Injuns" (30 Aug.).

Sergeants 3 (UA, 1962). John Sturges
In this comedy, the hostile tribe of Mountain Hawk (Henry Silva), Watanka (Michael Pate), White Eagle (Richard Hale) and Ghost Dancer (Eddie Little Sky) capture the heroes, who later manage to save the cavalry from an ambush.

Fort Courageous (20th Century-Fox, 1965). Lesley Selander
Hostile warriors finally let a small group of soldiers who have fought off many attacks leave the fort as a show of respect for their courage.

The Glory Guys (UA, 1965). Arnold Laven
Soldiers fight warlike Sioux in large, spectacular battles.

The Great Sioux Massacre (Columbia, 1965). Sidney Salkow
Custer, who initially is a friend to the Plains tribes and an enemy of crooked politicians and greedy Indian agents, finally agrees to mistreat the tribes because of his own political ambitions. Sitting Bull (Michael Pate) and Crazy Horse (Iron Eyes Cody) lead the Sioux against Custer in the Battle of Little Big Horn.

Major Dundee (Columbia, 1965). Sam Peckinpah
The hero and his soldiers pursue into Mexico the Apache band of Sierra Charriba (Michael Pate), who have kidnapped children and massacred settlers. A *NYT* critic comments: "This particular West is an ugly place and the director's camera searches intractably for the grimmest aspects" (8 Apr., 45).

War Party (20th Century-Fox, 1965). Lesley Selander
Comanches attack a patrol sent out to bring help for troops pinned down by other members of the tribe. Though most of the men in the patrol die, the hero, with the help of Nicoma (Laurie Mock), manages to blow up the tribe's ammunition, kill the chief and rescue the troop. Nicoma dies in the process of assisting the hero.

Chuka (Paramount, 1967). Gordon Douglas
Although the hero aids Hanu (Marco Antonio), Chief of the Arapahoe, later the starving tribe, helped by a female member from within, kills everyone in the fort.

Custer of the West (Cinerama, 1967). Robert Siodmak
Influenced by politicians, Custer and his soldiers massacre a band of the Cheyenne. Afterwards, he searches his soul and fights for the rights of Native Americans until his last fight with the Sioux and Cheyenne of Dull Knife (Kieron Moore) at the Battle of Little Big Horn.

Fort Utah (Paramount, 1967). Lesley Selander
After a villain kills women and children from their tribe, warriors attack a fort and stagecoach. When the body of the villain is handed over to them, they stop the attacks.

40 Guns to Apache Pass (Columbia, 1967). William Witney
After hostile Apaches led by Cochise (Michael Keep) attack his soldiers and settlers, the hero struggles to stop an evil soldier from selling repeating rifles to the Apaches.

The Legend of Custer (Fox, 1967). Norman Foster
This TV movie chronicles Custer's battles with the Plains tribes.

Attacks on Trains and Stagecoaches

Stagecoach (20th Century-Fox, 1966). Gordon Douglas
In this remake of the John Ford classic, Sioux warriors attack the passengers and are routed by the cavalry.

How the West Was Won (MGM, 1963). John Ford, George Marshall, Henry Hathaway
In one part of this epic western, hostile warriors stampede a herd of buffalo to cover their attack on railroad builders.

White Comanche (Spanish, 1967). Gilbert Kay
Twin sons of a Comanche mother (both played by William Shatner) grow up as Johnny Moon, a peace-loving man, and Notah, a fierce, peyote-crazed warrior. After Notah and his warriors attack a stagecoach and beat up a white woman, Johnny fights him in a one-on-one battle and kills him.

Attacks on Settlers and Other Representatives of Progress

Geronimo's Revenge (Buena Vista, 1960). James Neilson
This Disney movie deals with the conflicts between Texas John Slaughter and the Apaches of Geronimo.

The Comancheros (20th Century-Fox, 1961). Michael Curtiz
The heroes fight the evil Comancheros and the hostile Comanches led by Iron Shirt (George Lewis). A *New Yorker* critic notes that in "Hollywood the only good Comanches are dead Comanches" and then observes: "have you ever noticed in Westerns that the white men can be shot and wounded not once but many times, while Indians who get shot almost always die instantly?" (9 Dec., 235).

The Wild Westerners (Columbia, 1962). Oscar Rudolph
The Sioux warriors of Yellow Moon (Ilse Burkert) and Wasna (Hans Wedemeyer) attack lawmen transporting gold to Union troops.

Blood on the Arrow (Allied Artists, 1964). Sidney Salkow
The Apache tribe of Kai La (Robert Carricart) attack a trading post, kill everyone except the hero, and kidnap a boy. Eventually the hero leads the warriors into a trap and rescues the child.

He Rides Tall (Universal, 1964). R. G. Springsteen
A warlike tribe attacks settlers and kills a white woman.

Young Guns of Texas (20th Century-Fox, 1964). Maury Dexter
Raised by the Comanche, the hero fights hostile Apaches.

Kid Rodelo (Paramount, 1966). Richard Carlson
Cavalry Hat (Jose Villa Sante), a Yaqui chief, pursues the hero who finally kills him.

Red Tomahawk (Paramount, 1967). R. G. Springsteen
After the Battle of Little Big Horn, the hero saves a town from a Sioux attack.

Arizona Bushwackers (Paramount, 1968). Lesley Selander
Supplied with rifles by the villain, Apaches attack a town.

Day of the Evil Gun (MGM, 1968). Jerry Thorpe
In this reworking of Ford's *The Searchers,* Apaches kidnap the hero's family and then attack a town.

Shalako (Cinerama, 1968). Edward Dmytryk
In this film based on a Louis L'Amour novel, the Apaches of Chato (Woody Strode) attack Europeans who are hunting on their land and brutally kill a white woman. At the end, the hero rescues a white woman and beats Chato in a hand-to-hand fight.

Kidnapping

Comanche Station (Columbia, 1960). Budd Boetticher
After the Comanche capture a white woman, the hero trades with them to secure her release. When Comanche warriors later attack the station, they are driven off.

Two Rode Together (Columbia, 1961). John Ford
The cynical heroes bring back to white society a mixed-blood young man, Running Wolf (David Kent), and a

Mexican woman who for years have been the captives of Comanches led by Quannah Parker (Henry Brandon). The whites, however, lynch Running Wolf and reject the Mexican woman, who had been the wife of Stone Calf (Woody Strode), a black man and rival of Quannah Parker in the Comanche tribe.

Savage Sam (Buena Vista, 1963). Norman Tokar

The faithful dog, Savage Sam, leads the heroes to the hostile Apaches of Broken Nose (Pat Hogan) and Bandy Legs (Rudolfo Acosta), who have captured two children. Since this is a Disney film, the harshness of the tribe is rather surprising.

Rio Conchos (20th Century-Fox, 1964). Gordon Douglas

The Apaches of Bloodshirt (Rudolfo Acosta) capture the heroes who are trying to stop villains running guns to the tribe. When the Apaches torture them, a Native American woman, Sally (Wende Wagner), takes pity and helps them escape.

Vengeance

The Canadians (20th Century-Fox, 1961). Burt Kennedy

After villains kill part of a Sioux war party, the survivors, two of whom are the White Squaw (Teresa Stratas) and Chief Four Horns (Michael Pate), take their revenge by driving them off a cliff.

The Purple Hills (Assoc. Producers, 1961). Maury Dexter

Apaches led by Chito (Danny Zapien) attack and kill the villain.

Navajo Run (American, 1964). Johnny Seven

A villain tricks Matthew Whitehawk (Johnny Seven) to get him into the woods so he can hunt him down as he has done before with other Navajos. Matthew, however, survives and takes his revenge by killing the villain with a rattlesnake.

Apache Uprising (Paramount, 1966). R. G. Springsteen
Apaches release white captives in exchange for their Chief Antone (Abel Fernandez) and then take revenge on the villain for his double-dealing.

The Devil's Mistress (Holiday, 1966). Orville Wanzer
Liah (Joan Stapleton), a mixed-blood, uses her magical powers to take revenge on white men who rape her and kill her husband.

Duel at Diablo (UA, 1966). Ralph Nelson
Apaches led by Chata (John Hoyt) and Alchise (Eddie Little Sky) attack and punish the evil husband of a white woman who has rejected her because she had a baby with a member of their tribe. A *Time* critic comments: "If anything, *Diablo* proves that it can be extremely difficult to promote racial harmony while playing cowboys and Indians" (1 July, 78).

Johnny Reno (Paramount, 1966). R. G. Springsteen
When Chief Little Bear (Paul Daniel) finds out that his son has been killed for loving a white woman, his warriors attack the town and take revenge on the killer.

Nevada Smith (Paramount, 1966). Henry Hathaway
The mixed-blood hero (Steve McQueen) avenges the killing of his white father and Native American mother. During his quest, Neesa (Janet Margolin), a Kiowa prostitute, brings him to the camp of her people to recover. Though they fall in love, he leaves her to pursue his revenge.

The Talisman (Gillman, 1966). John Carr
A Cheyenne warrior (Ned Romero) cares for and falls in love with a white woman who is the only survivor from a wagon train attacked by his tribe. After three white men rape her, the warrior gains revenge by burying one in sand where ants will eat his head, tearing another apart with two bent trees, and killing the third with a rattlesnake.

Death Curse of Tartu (Thunderbird, 1967). William Grefe
Tartu (Doug Hobart), a Seminole witch doctor who has been dead for 400 years, takes revenge on students who tamper with his grave.

Navajo Joe (UA, 1967). Sergio Corbucci
Navajo Joe (Burt Reynolds) takes harsh revenge on villains who kill his wife and everyone else in his village. As he kills them one by one, he rescues Estella (Nicolletta Machiavelli), a Native American, and saves the entire town even though the people are prejudiced against him.

The Way West (UA, 1967). Andrew V. McLaglen
After the son of the Sioux chief is accidentally killed, the hero has to hang a man to stop the tribe from taking revenge.

The Scalphunters (UA, 1968). Sydney Pollack
The clever Kiowa Chief Two Crows (Armando Silvestre) takes the furs of the hero and leaves him a slave that his tribe had captured. Then the scalphunters attack the warriors of Two Crows and kill everyone but the chief. At the end, the Kiowa of Two Crows get their revenge on the villains and spare only the hero, his black friend and a white woman of dubious virtue who offers herself to the chief.

The Stalking Moon (National, 1968). Robert Mulligan
Discussed in the introduction (154–55), this film deals with the vengeance of Savaje, an Apache renegade who is trying to get back his son.

Once Upon a Time in the West (Paramount, 1969). Sergio Leone
Cheyenne (Jason Robards), a mixed-blood wrongly accused of a crime, takes his revenge.

The Ramrodder (Entertainment Ventures, 1969). Van Guyloler
A white man rapes a Native American woman and her tribe retaliates by raping a white woman. The hero averts a

war by handing over the man to the tribe, which punishes him with castration. Finally, the hero marries Princess Tuwana (Kathy Williams).

IMAGES OF THE NOBLE RED MAN

Friendship and Loyalty

For the Love of Mike (20th Century-Fox, 1960). George Sherman

Mike (Danny Bravo), Native American teenager, wins a horse race and gives the money to the Catholic church. Other Native American characters are Tony Eagle (Armando Silvestre) and Mrs. Eagle (Elsa Cardenas).

Oklahoma Territory (UA, 1960). Edward L. Cahn

The villain commits a murder and then blames it on Buffalo Horn (Ted de Corsia) to start a war so he can get the tribe's land for a railroad. The hero, who is a friend of Buffalo Horn and his son, Running Cloud (X Brands), and daughter, Ruth Red Hawk (Gloria Talbott), is forced to prosecute but finally wins the acquittal of Buffalo Horn. A *Variety* critic, commenting on the white actors, notes that "Gloria Talbott looks about as much like an Injun as Ted de Corsia, who doesn't" (10 Feb.).

Walk Tall (20th Century-Fox, 1960). Maury Dexter

With the help of Shoshone warriors Chief Black Feather (Felix Locher) and Buffalo Horn (Dave De Paul), the hero stops a villain whose attacks on the tribe could start a war.

Along the Mohawk Trail, The Red Man and the Renegades, The Long Rifle and the Tomahawk and *The Pathfinder* (ITC, 1962). Sam Newfield and Sidney Salkow

Drawn from a TV series based on Cooper's *The Last of the Mohicans*, these TV movies deal with the adventures of Hawkeye and his friend, Chingachgook (Tom Chaney).

Indian Paint (Eagle American, 1963). Norman Foster

Nishko (Johnny Crawford), son of Hevatanu (Jay Silver-heels), the chief of the Arikara, rescues his white stallion from the Comanche. After many adventures, he allows his horse to go free, but the horse follows him when he returns to his people. Other Native American characters are Suta-makis (Pat Hogan), Wacopi (Johnny Crawford, Jr.), Nopa-wallo (George Lewis), Amatula (Joan Hallmark), Sutako (Bill Blackwell), Lataso (Al Doney) and Petala (Cinda Siler).

A Distant Trumpet (Warner, 1964). Raoul Walsh

After the Apache tribe of Chief War Eagle has been driven into Mexico, the hero, whose life War Eagle saves, persuades the government to give the tribe a reservation in Arizona. A *Variety* critic comments on the depiction of the battles: "Hardly a white man bites the dust, yet the Redmen consistently get picked off like ducks at a shooting gallery. How one-sided can you get?" (27 May).

Arizona Raiders (Columbia, 1965). William Witney

The hero rescues Martina (Gloria Talbott), the daughter of the Yaqui chief, and the tribe helps him bring a gang of outlaws to justice.

Cat Ballou (Columbia, 1965). Elliot Silverstein

In this comic Western, Jackson Two Bears (Tom Nardini) is the best-educated member of the gang.

Treasure of Silver Lake (Columbia, 1965). Harold Reinl

Old Shatterhand and his friend, Winnetou (Pierre Brice), pacify a party of hostile warriors and join them to bring a gang of outlaws to justice.

Winnetou I or *Apache Gold* (Columbia, 1965). Harold Reinl and Stipe Delic

This film and various sequels are based on novels about the adventures of a mythical Apache chief by Karl May, a German writer very popular in Europe but little known in the U.S. Old Shatterhand and Winnetou (Pierre Brice), the Apache chief, become friends and thwart the efforts of the villain who is after gold on the tribe's land.

Frontier Hellcat (Columbia, 1966). Alfred Vohrer and Stipe Delic
   Old Surehand and his blood brother, Winnetou (Pierre Brice), join Shoshone warriors to rescue a wagon train from villains disguised as Native Americans.

Rampage at Apache Wells (Columbia, 1966). Harold Philipps
   Shatterhand and Winnetou (Pierre Brice) bring to justice oil swindlers who incite Navajo warriors to attack a wagon train by killing the chief's son.

Winnetou II or *Last of the Renegades* (Columbia, 1966). Harold Reinl
   Old Shatterhand and Winnetou (Pierre Brice), the Apache chief, deal with villains who are trying to incite the tribe to war so they can build a railroad on their land.

Africa Texas Style (Paramount, 1967). Andrew Marton
   John Henry (Tom Nardini) is the Navajo companion of the hero who helps him round up wild animals in an African reserve.

Shatterhand (Goldstone, 1967). Hugo Fregonese
   When villains and renegade Comanches after Apache land make trouble for Winnetou (Pierre Brice), his friend, Shatterhand, helps the Apache chief fight them in a battle in which his son, Tujunga (Alain Tissier), is killed.

The War Wagon (Universal, 1967). Burt Kennedy
   Levi Walking Bear (Howard Keel), a cynical renegade who has learned from the whites how to grab all he can, is the friend of the hero. Starving Kiowa led by Wild Horse (Marco Antonio) also help the hero stop the war wagon, but later attack to get the gold on the wagon.

Welcome to Hard Times (MGM, 1967). Burt Kennedy
John Bear (Royal Dano) helps to rebuild a town after it is terrorized by the villain.

Winnetou III or *The Desperado Trail* (Columbia, 1967). Harold Reinl
After a villain frames Winnetou (Pierre Brice), the Apache chief and his friend, Old Shatterhand, fight a battle with the villain and his renegade warriors. Stepping in front of Old Shatterhand to take a bullet meant for him, Winnetou dies valiantly.

Flaming Frontier (Warner, 1968). Alfred Vohrer
Surehand and his blood brother, Winnetou (Pierre Brice), fight with Comanches who are angered by the murder of their chief's son.

Three Guns for Texas (Universal, 1968). David Lowell Rich, Paul Stanley and Earl Bellamy
Texas Rangers join the tribe of Running Antelope (Cliff Osmond) and Linda Little Trees (Shelley Morrison), who falls in love with one of them, to fight a gang of outlaws.

Hang Your Hat on the Wind (Buena Vista, 1969). Larry Landsburgh
In this Disney film, a Navajo boy named Goyo (Ric Natoli) finds a valuable escaped racehorse and adopts him. Later, however, when he gives the horse back to the owner and then rescues it from bandits, he gets his own pony as a reward.

100 Rifles (20th Century-Fox, 1969). Tom Gries
Yaqui Joe (Burt Reynolds) is a mixed-blood Yaqui who gets rifles for his tribe and decides to live with them. He loves Sarita (Raquel Welch), a leader of rebel warriors.

Smith! (Buena Vista, 1969). Michael O'Herlihy
In this Disney film, the hero tries to hide and help Gabriel Jimmyboy (Frank Ramirez), a Nez Perce who is wrongly accused of murder. When the young man goes to trial, Ol Antoine (Chief Dan George) replaces as interpreter the evil

Walter Charlie (Warren Oates) and helps Jimmyboy prove his innocence. A *Variety* critic notes that the Native American actors from "Hollywood's Indian Actors Workshop of Jay Silverheels (who has a small but winning role in the courtroom) supplements the regional feeling of the film" (26 Mar.).

Undefeated (20th Century-Fox, 1969). Andrew McLaglen
Cheyenne warriors help the hero, whose adopted son, Blue Boy (Roman Gabriel), is from their tribe.

Peace-loving Chief

Geronimo (UA, 1962). Arnold Laven
Discussed in the introduction (149–51), this film deals with the evolution of Geronimo into a family man willing to make a peace treaty.

Cheyenne Autumn (Warner, 1964). John Ford
Discussed in the introduction (151–53), this film deals with the trek of Dull Knife and Little Wolf and their bands of Cheyenne to their homeland, and their acceptance of a treaty.

The Plainsman (Universal, 1966). David Lowell Rich
Supplied with rifles by the villain, Cheyenne warriors led by the hostile Crazy Knife (Henry Silva) capture Wild Bill Hickok and Buffalo Bill, but the noble, peace-loving Black Kettle (Simon Oakland) rescues them.

Hondo and the Apaches (MGM, 1967). Lee H. Katzin
The noble Vittorio (Michael Pate) rescues his friend, Hondo, from hostile Apache warriors led by Silva (Victor Lundin). At the end, Vittorio kills Silva and promises to make peace.

Romances Between Native American Women and White Men

Apache Rifles (20th Century-Fox, 1964). William Witney
When villains after gold incite the Apaches of Red Hawk (Michael Dante) to war, the hero, who changes his hateful

ways after falling in love with a mixed-blood, Dawn Gillis (Linda Lawson), comes to the rescue.

Deadwood '76 (Fairway, 1965). James Landis
   The tribe of Spotted Snake (Gordon Schwenk) captures the hero, who falls in love with Little Bird (LaDonna Cottier). Later, when two cowboys rape her, the hero kills them, only to be lynched by a mob.

The Desert Raven (Allied Artists, 1965). Alan S. Lee
   Though watched over closely by her mother, Rena (Bea Silvern), Raven (Rachel Romen) falls in love with a white man whom she promises to marry when he gets out of prison.

Texas Across the River (Universal, 1966). Michael Gordon
   In this spoof of Westerns, the hero rescues, and eventually falls in love with, Lonetta (Tina Marquand) from the Comanche of the Medicine Man (Richard Farnsworth), Chief Iron Jacket (Michael Ansara) and his bumbling son, Yellow Knife (Linden Chiles). The hero's wisecracking Native American friend is Kronk (Joey Bishop).

MacKenna's Gold (Columbia, 1969). J. Lee Thompson and Tom Shaw
   As the hero searches for gold in a valley sacred to the Apache, a woman from the tribe, Hesh Ke (Julie Newmar), falls in love with him and competes with a white woman for his affection. When Apache warriors attack, Hesh Ke, her companion, Hachita (Ted Cassidy), and everyone but the hero and his woman die in the valley.

See also *The Unforgiven* (1960), *War Party* (1965) and *Three Guns for Texas* (1968).

Romances Between Native American Men and White Women

Johnny Tiger (Universal, 1966). Paul Wendkos
   Johnny Tiger (Chad Everett), a mixed-blood Seminole and grandson of Chief Sam Tiger (Ford Rainey), is caught between a white teacher who wants him to educate himself

so he can teach his people new ways and his grandfather who wants him to be a traditional Seminole. Johnny chooses education, marries the teacher's daughter and promises to use his knowledge to help his people as their new chief.

Stay Away Joe (MGM, 1968). Peter Tewksbury

In this comedy based on the novel by Dan Cushman, the son of Charlie Lightcloud (Burgess Meredith), Joe Lightcloud (Elvis Presley), a mixed-blood Navajo rodeo champion, tries to help his tribe by selling a prize stud bull for a barbecue. His sister, Annie (Katy Jurado), contributes to the mix-up by selling her father's cattle. Both Joe and Annie are in love with whites. A *Variety* critic comments: "The basic story—contemporary American Indians who are portrayed as laughable incompetents—is out of touch with latter day appreciation of some basic dignity in all human beings" (13 Mar.).

See also *The Talisman* (1966).

Romances Between Native Americans

Kings of the Sun (UA, 1963). J. Lee Thompson

After the evil Hunac Ceel (Leo Gordon) attacks the Mayans led by Balam (George Chakiris), they flee to the north where they are confronted by the tribe of Black Eagle (Yul Brynner). However, when Balam saves the life of Black Eagle, even though he has fallen in love with Balam's woman, Ixchel (Shirley A. Field), the tribes unite and defeat the warriors of Hunac Ceel. During that battle, Black Eagle dies while saving the life of Balam, who is then reunited with Ixchel.

Tell 'em Willie Boy Is Here (Universal, 1969). Abraham Polonsky

Discussed in the introduction (155–57), this film, based on *Willy Boy, A Desert Manhunt* by Harry Lawton, tells the story of the tragic love between Willie and Lola.

See also *Geronimo* (1962) and *100 Rifles* (1969)

Native Americans as Victims

Flaming Star (20th Century-Fox, 1960). Don Siegel
   Discussed in the introduction (157–59), this film tells the story of the prejudice toward mixed-blood Pacer Burton and his Kiowa mother, Neddy.

Savage Innocents (Paramount, 1960). Nicholas Ray
   Inuk (Anthony Quinn), good natured Eskimo, marries Asiak (Yoko Tani) and provides for his wife's family. Their happiness is shattered, however, when a missionary who is ignorant of the custom, refuses Inuk's offer of his wife for the night, and Inuk kills him. Two Mounties hunt Inuk down, but one of them, who accepts the differences of Eskimo culture, finally lets Inuk return to his people.

The Unforgiven (UA, 1960). John Houston
   Based on the novel of the same name by Alan LeMay, this film tells the story of Rachel Zachary (Audrey Hepburn), a Kiowa raised by a white family. When her racial identity is revealed, the white man she is to marry rejects her and she suffers prejudice from the whites and the anger of her tribe, one of whom is Lost Bird (Carlos Rivas), who wants her as a wife. When the Kiowa warriors attack her white family, she kills her brother.

McLintock! (UA, 1963). Andrew V. McLaglen
   The hero takes up the cause of Davey Elk (Perry Lopez), Puma (Michael Pate) and Running Buffalo (John Stanley), Comanches just released from prison.

Island of the Blue Dolphins (Universal, 1964). James B. Clark
   A Chumash girl, Karana (Celia Kaye), is abandoned for almost 20 years on an Aleutian island after villains kill her father, Chowig (Carlos Romero). She survives numerous hardships, including the loss of her brother, Ramo (Larry Domasin), before missionaries rescue her.

Hombre (20th Century-Fox, 1967). Martin Ritt
   Discussed in the introduction (153–54), this film tells the

story of a white man who embraces the Apache way of life and sacrifices himself for his adopted people.

Heaven with a Gun (MGM, 1969). Lee H. Katzin
The hero protects a young Native American, Leloopa (Barbara Hershey) and punishes the man who assaulted her.

Contemporary Native Americans

All the Young Men (Columbia, 1960). Hall Bartlett
In this film about the Korean war, a Native American soldier, Hunter (Mario Alcalde), sides with the black hero because he also has experienced prejudice.

All Hands on Deck (20th Century-Fox, 1961). Norman Taurog
In this comedy, Shrieking Eagle (Buddy Hackett) is a Chickasaw who wears a feather in his sailor hat. After seeing a cowboy and Indian movie, he tears apart the theatre and threatens to scalp the admirals.

The Outsider (Universal, 1961). Delbert Mann
This film tells the sad story of Ira Hayes, one of the soldiers who raised the American flag on Iwo Jima, from the time he leaves his Pima reservation to become a soldier to his death from alcoholism ten years later. His inability to handle his fame, the death of his white friend and his tribe's rejection of him lead him to a life of isolation and alcoholism. Though befriended by Jay Morago (Edmund Hashim), the chief of the Pima, and helped by his mother , Nancy Hayes (Vivian Nathan), he dies a broken man.

Requiem for a Heavyweight (Columbia, 1962). Ralph Nelson
Mountain Rivera (Anthony Quinn), an over-the-hill mixed-blood boxer, finally has to dress like a Plains Indian to get a job as a wrestler. At the end, while the crowd laughs at his outfit, he humiliates himself by doing a war dance.

Pajama Party (American, 1964). Don Weis
Chief Rotten Eagle (Buster Keaton) helps some con men crash the party.

Born Losers (American, 1966). T. C. Frank (Tom Laughlin)
Billy Jack (Tom Laughlin), a mixed-blood, rescues a woman from a motorcycle gang and dies at the end. However, the character is resurrected in the *Billy Jack* films.

The Exiles (Pathé, 1966). Kent MacKenzie
Three young Native Americans, Yvonne (Yvonne Williams), Homer (Homer Nish) and Tommy (Tommy Reynolds), leave their reservation and go to Los Angeles. After realizing they don't fit in the city, they go to a hilltop near the freeways and, in a futile gesture, try to sing and dance in the traditional ways.

Run, Appaloosa, Run (Buena Vista, 1966). Larry Landsburgh
In this Disney film, Mary Blackfeather (Adele Palacios), the finest rider of her Nez Perce tribe, wins a big race on her horse, Holy Smoke.

The Hooked Generation (Allied Artists, 1968). William Grefe
Drug dealers hide out in a Seminole village and rape a young woman from the tribe.

The Savage Seven (American Intern., 1968). Richard Rush
Businessmen and a motorcycle gang victimize a group of Native Americans living in a shanty town. Johnny Littlehawk (Robert Walker, Jr.), Grey Wolf (Max Julien) and Running Buck (John Cardos) fight back and try to protect the females in their group. However, when the bikers rape one of their women, the killing starts.

Castle Keep (Columbia, 1969). Sydney Pollack
In this World War II film, Henry Three Ears of an Elk (James Patterson) is one of the soldiers guarding the castle.

Satan's Sadists (Independent, 1969). Al Adamson
Firewater (John Cardos), the Native American friend of

the sadistic leader of a motorcycle gang, finally rebels against him.

* * *

In the numerous films of this period depicting the plight of the Noble Red Man, guilt often mixes with sympathy. A *Newsweek* reviewer snidely catches this feeling in a comment on a film from the beginning of the next decade, *Journey Through Rosebud* (1972): "Recent literature and films have discovered the Indians' humanity" and are "trying to make amends," but in the process "white guilt . . . pours forth enough tears to wash away the wigwam" (24 Apr., 89). Later in this period of the '60s, when the Viet Nam war becomes a painful experience for everyone, political and moral indignation mixes with guilt and produces anti-Westerns such as *Tell 'em Willie Boy Is Here* (1969), which also dominate the first part of the '70s.

CHAPTER SIX

FILMS OF THE 1970S

This decade of the anti-Western with its dark, cynical views of American values, occasioned in part by the Vietnam war, is exemplified in *Little Big Man* (1970). In the words of its director, Arthur Penn, this film "challenges the notion that the heroes of America are the ones you read about in history books. It challenges the glorification of the gunfighter and the simple proposition that the cavalry was the good guys and the Indians the bad guys." (Calder, 213). Such a purpose leads Penn to make the Cheyenne the "good guys," and a similar revisionist purpose informs the portrayal of Native American characters in other anti-Westerns of this era. In *A Man Called Horse* (1970), a film that claims to be an authentic depiction of tribal spirituality and rituals, the culture of the Sioux band which captures the hero ultimately changes him into a warrior. *Ulzana's Raid* (1972) gives a harsh view of Apache warriors whose guerrilla culture cannot survive in a changing West. And in *The Outlaw Josey Wales* (1976), a film that plays against many of the Western formulas, three Native American characters are the only equals to the hero in a grim post-Civil War western landscape. While such revisionist Westerns are playing against the background of Vietnam, two other representative films, *I Heard the Owl Call My Name* (1973) and *When the Legends Die* (1972) mark the beginning of a new trend, the portrayal of contemporary Native American characters who find new identities in the traditional ways of their tribes.

Little Big Man (1970) depicts the Cheyenne and their chief, Old Lodge Skins (Chief Dan George), as the moral center against which the corrupt values of the major white characters can be measured. In Old Lodge Skin's world view everything is alive and connected. When Little Big Man (Dustin Hoffman) asks him why the soldiers killed women and children, he replies, "Because they are strange; they don't know where the center is." Later, after another massacre by the soldiers, Old Lodge Skins elaborates on the difference between the Cheyenne and whites, "The Human Beings believe that everything is alive . . . the white man believes everything is dead. If the Human Beings try to keep living, the white man will rub them out. That is the difference." And indeed each of the main white characters has no respect for human dignity or life. The hypocritical Pendrakes care only for their own sensual desires; the deeply cynical Merriwether rejects any moral order and lives only to exploit others; the paranoid Wild Bill Hickok kills with complete detachment; and the megalomaniac General Custer exterminates women and children at Washita. Each of these characters represents part of the mentality that Penn connects to the victimization of the Vietnam war.

The character of Old Lodge Skins, however, is not just a contrast for emphasis of this political theme; it is also a vehicle for the first Native American to play a major role in a big budget Western. Chief Dan George brings to his part a film presence and sense of humor that make Old Lodge Skins one of the most human and memorable Native Americans in the Westerns. Often seen in warmly lit low-angle close-ups that emphasize his dignity, he delivers his lines with droll understatement and a unique twinkle in his eye. For example, when he is talking to Little Big Man, he asks him about his white wife: "Does she show a pleasant enthusiasm when you mount her? I've never noticed it in a white woman." At the end of the film, he again shows his humor after he lies down to die and then blinks when rain drops hit his face. He asks Little Big Man, "Am I still in this world?" Then, after a groan of recognition, he says, "I was afraid of that—sometimes the magic works; sometimes it doesn't." Such lines, and the fact that he represents the privileged morality of the film, make him a charming and significant character. Unfortunately, however, the director ultimately reduces his characterization to the Noble Red Man image.

Because Penn is so committed to making Old Lodge Skins and his Cheyenne the good guys, he takes away what made them more believable and rounded characters in the Thomas Berger novel on which the film is based. For example, in the novel, the tribe of Old Lodge Skins kills Jack Crabb's family after they make the mistake of giving the warriors whiskey rather than coffee. In the film, the Cheyenne are kept pure by having the Pawnee massacre the family. And, in the novel, during the battle at Washita, Cheyenne braves kill a unit of soldiers, Little Big Man's wife escapes, and Old Lodge Skins leaves the camp with a show of bravery and strength. Whereas, in the film, the soldiers not only kill everyone, including Little Big Man's wife, Sunshine (Amy Eccles), and her baby, but Old Lodge Skins, who thinks he's invisible, must be helped out of camp by Little Big Man. This diminishing of his character continues at the end of the film when Old Lodge Skins fails to die, as he had wanted. At the end of the novel, however, in a crass world where he no longer fits, his death is appropriate and honorable. These changes allow Penn to make his political point about Vietnam and maintain the quirkiness of Old Lodge Skin's character to the end, but they also transform the Cheyenne and their leader into the noble, but doomed Red Men image.

Similar intentions also turn the Sioux tribe in *A Man Called Horse* into Noble but doomed Red Men. Although the filmmakers note at the beginning that the film uses new research on the Sun Dance and depicts authentic Lakota rituals, they ultimately fall back on a pattern noted by a critic in *Film Quarterly:* "Stripped of its pretensions, *Horse* parades the standard myth that the white man can do everything better than the Indian. Give him a little time and he will marry the best looking girl (a princess of course) and will end up the chief of the tribe" (Spring 1972, 28). The Sioux, led by Yellow Hand (Manu Tupou), capture the hero, John Morgan, an Englishman on a hunting trip, and treat him cruelly from the beginning, making him get on his hands and knees and wear a horse blanket and then dragging him behind a horse. The harshness of the Sioux way of life is also exemplified in a mother who cuts off a finger to grieve the death of her son and then gives away all his possessions as other women from the tribe tear apart her teepee and drive her from the camp. After more insults, torture and a failed escape, the hero finally cries out in a sort of Shakespearean anguish, "I am not an animal; I am a man." This impresses some of the women and marks the beginning of the hero's evolution into a Sioux Warrior called Horse.

After Morgan lives through a winter with the tribe and learns the Lakota language, he falls in love with Running Deer (Corinna Tsopei), a beautiful young woman who has rejected an offer of marriage from Black Eagle (Eddie Little Sky). She is quick to recognize Morgan's superiority and reciprocate his love. However, before they can marry, Morgan must have gifts for her family and must prove himself as a warrior. An attack by the Shoshone, during which he kills several warriors and reluctantly scalps one of them, allows him to become a warrior and capture horses that can be given to the parents. However, he still must be initiated into the tribe by participating in the Sun Dance ritual. After doing a sweat ceremony, he goes to the lodge to make his Sun Vow, during which bones are inserted in his chest by a medicine man (Iron Eyes Cody) and he is suspended in the air by ropes attached to the bones. In his agony, he has a vision of sacred animals as he takes on the Lakota identity. After this test, he not only changes from an Englishman to a super leader in the tribe, but also finally gains the right to make love with Running Deer.

His bliss, however, is short-lived because the Shoshone soon make a revenge attack on the tribe, during which Running Deer, Yellow Hand, and Horse's friend, Batise, are mortally wounded. Just when defeat seems inevitable, Horse rallies his tribe by killing in hand-to-hand combat Striking Bear (Terry Leonard), the chief of the Shoshone. Then he has his warriors use long bows (in the medieval English tradition) to drive off the remaining Shoshone. After this battle and the funeral of his wife and Yellow

Hand, he becomes the chief, but he soon leaves the tribe to return to England when his adopted mother, Buffalo Cow Head (Judith Anderson), dies. This ending depicts the tribe as Noble, but doomed, Red Men left without a leader.

In a sequel, *The Return of a Man Called Horse* (1976) the hero returns to the West to again rescue the tribe. Despite what might be good intentions, that film, like the original, clearly diminishes the Native American characters, as a *New Yorker* critic notes: "The attitude of the film towards Indians is patronizing in the extreme. It feeds the notions about the Western white male as omniscient savior which are already too current" (16 Aug., 87).

A Man Called Horse attempts to portray the Sioux as a distinctive culture with its own unique rituals but ultimately fails because it lets the hero preempt the culture. *Ulzana's Raid* (1972), on the other hand, succeeds in portraying the Apache warriors of Ulzana (Joaquin Martinez) as members of a unique culture, though it defines their "otherness" in terms of their fierce (and again doomed) way of life as guerrilla warriors. In this anti-Western, the West is a gritty and grim place in which both the hero and Ulzana die at the end. After Ulzana and his men escape from the San Carlos reservation, the cynical old scout tells a young Christian soldier that "their probable intention is to rape, pillage and maim." As guerrilla fighters in a hopeless cause, Ulzana's warriors do terrorize soldiers and settlers in ways reminiscent of Savaje in *The Stalking Moon*. With harsh efficiency, the Apache attack a woman and her son, and the soldier protecting them shoots the woman and himself. Though the Apache shoot the horses and cut the heart out of the soldier, they do not harm the boy because of their tribal respect for young males. Then, using binoculars taken from the soldiers, they stalk the father of this family, who has stayed behind to guard the farm. After shooting his dog and burning his out-buildings, they trick him out of his hiding place by playing a bugle taken from the soldiers, and then torture him to death. Later they attack a homestead, torture a family and rape the mother.

The Christian soldier, stunned by these acts of violence, asks his Apache scout, Ke-Ni-Kay (Jorge Luke), why his

Apache people are so cruel. Ke-Ni-Kay, explaining that in his culture the killer takes the power of his victims, says, "Here in this land a man must have power. Ulzana will want to kill many." Then the soldier asks the old scout if he hates the Apache, and he replies that hating the Apache would be "like hating the desert because it has no water." Later, after the soldier sees another soldier brutally stabbing the body of an Apache warrior, the old scout comments on his angry reaction, "I see you don't like seeing white men acting like Indians—kind of confuses the issue." As the conflict between the soldiers and the warriors of Ulzana moves towards its grim ending, the line between them does blur, especially when the soldiers use the woman raped by the Apache as bait to lure them into a fight.

In the final fight, the hero is fatally wounded after he kills several of the remaining warriors, and Ke-Ni-Kay kills Ulzana after he has acknowledged his defeat with a death song. At the end, the disillusioned Christian soldier and Ke-Ni-Kay, the Apache who has decided to survive by working for the whites, are the only witnesses in the conclusion to the bitter war with Ulzana. This ending is a sharp contrast to the upbeat conclusion of *Apache* (1954), also directed by Robert Aldrich and starring Burt Lancaster as the Apache warrior. In that film, the soldiers hunt down the hostile warrior but finally allow him to live the rest of his life in peace; in the harsh West of *Ulzana's Raid* no such happy ending is possible for the aging scout (Burt Lancaster) or for Ulzana.

The last of the representative anti-Westerns, *The Outlaw Josey Wales* (1976), also depicts the post-Civil War West as a harsh place, corrupted by politicians, evil soldiers, bounty hunters and vicious Comancheros. In this world, Wales, whose wife and son were killed by soldiers, is one of few truly moral characters, though ironically he is known as an outlaw. His only equals, in the sense of their being outsiders and good warriors, are three Native American characters, Lone Watie (Chief Dan George), Little Moonlight (Gerald-ine Keams) and Ten Bears (Will Sampson). Just as Clint Eastwood plays against the formula of the lonely hero, so also do these characters (all played by Native American actors) play against the images of the Savage and Noble Red Man.

After Wales has escaped to the Indian Nation, he sneaks up on Lone Watie, the old Cherokee who becomes his friend, and tells him that he thought this wasn't supposed "to happen with Indians." Lone Watie replies, "I'm an Indian all right, but here in the nation they call us a civilized tribe because we're so easy to sneak up on. The white man have been sneaking up on us for years." He then tells how he lost his wife and children on the Trail of Tears and how the government gave him medals for being so civilized and dressed him like Abraham Lincoln. In fact, he talks so long that Wales falls asleep. Like Wales, Lone Watie lost his family but never gave up the fight, and this establishes a bond between them. While Wales goes to find a horse for his new friend, he comes upon Little Moonlight, who is being mistreated by a trader and two vile buffalo hunters. After rescuing her and taking the horses of the recently deceased hunters, the lonely hero now has two companions and a dog.

Little Moonlight, a Navajo who had been captured by Cheyenne and raped by the Arapahoe, is just as talkative as Lone Watie, though she speaks in her native tongue. Thus both the characters play against the image of taciturn Native American. Little Moonlight is also a skilled warrior. When she and Wales return, Lone Watie sneaks up on Wales, only to have Little Moonlight sneak up on him. Later, when Wales and Lone Watie have a shootout with soldiers in a town, she stops the pursuers just long enough so that the two can escape. When she catches up with them and Lone Watie, thinking she is one of the posse, jumps from a rock and knocks her off her horse, she quickly recovers and is about to stab him when Wales intervenes. Lone Watie says to him, "Lucky you stopped me when you did. I might have killed her." As in *Little Big Man*, Chief Dan George brings an endearing humor to his character. Another example occurs when Lone Watie and Wales are talking about the shootout and Wales, assuming that Little Moonlight has been killed by the soldiers, says, "Whenever I get to liking someone, they aren't around long." Lone

Watie responds, "I noticed that when you get to disliking someone, they aren't around long either."

Just as the humorous character of Lone Watie plays against the image of the stoical Noble Red Man, so the character of the Comanche chief, Ten Bears, plays against the image of the Savage. A minor character in the film describes Ten Bears: "He is the greatest Comanche war chief. Each year he is pushed farther across the plains. But Ten Bears will move no more." Like Wales, he is a warrior who has been mistreated by corrupt politicians and soldiers, and when the two men meet they become blood brothers. Seen in close shots that emphasize their equality, Ten Bears eloquently accepts the offer of Wales to live in peace: "It is good that warriors such as we meet in the struggle of life or death. It shall be life." Though he is a fierce adversary to evil whites who are after his land, Ten Bears responds with honor to an equally honorable character.

Ten Bears, Little Moonlight and Lone Watie are among the most rounded, least stereotypical Native American characters in the Westerns. The same is true for the character of Wales, who doesn't ride off into the sunset like the typical lonely hero but returns to live with his extended, multi-racial family after he and the man pursuing him make their peace. As in his recent *Unforgiven* (1993), Eastwood questions the formulas of the Western in *The Outlaw Josey Wales* and portrays outsiders like Lone Watie with a new sense of empathy. As such the film is an appropriate transition to *I Heard the Owl Call My Name* and *When the Legends Die,* both of which depict contemporary Native American characters who transcend the images of the Westerns.

In the Canadian film, *I Heard the Owl Call My Name* (1973), a tribe from a remote village in British Columbia deeply affects the life of a young clergyman and finally teaches him how to die. As the young Anglican minister, Mark, travels to his new parish, he asks the boatman from the tribe, Jim Wallace (Paul Stanley), about the size of his village, and Jim responds, "Everything is my village, all of nature, all the history of the tribe and me. I am the village and the village is me." This organic view of life is at the core of what Mark learns from the tribe, especially when he finds out that he has only a short time to live. At the village, he immediately encounters the death of a child and his Christian prayer at the burial site pales in comparison to the death song of George Hudson (George Clutesi), the chief of the tribe. Later, when the tribe sees that he is a man dedicated to their welfare, they forgive him for his Christmas sermon in which he tells them to prepare their children to leave the village. At this point, George Hudson teaches him more about the ways of the tribe. He tells him the Story of the Raven and the Owl, the bird that calls a person about to die, and concludes, "Most of our legends have death in them. It is something we know about."

As Mark absorbs the life of the tribe, he comments in a voice-over, "In ten months the Indians have given me a lifetime of learning. They all have touched my life." One who especially touches him is Keetah (Marianne Jones), a young woman who is struggling to find her identity within the life of the village, even though she loves a young man who has moved to the city. After visiting him there, she returns to the village because she finds out that it is the only place she can know herself. Even when she tells Mark that she became pregnant so something of the young man would be left in the village, he accepts her and supports her in her decision to marry Jim Wallace. In his sermon on the second Christmas, Mark acknowledges the power of the village. He admits that he was wrong in his first Christmas sermon when he used a boat analogy to suggest that the children should leave, and then says, "I learned of the strength of your life here. Your children are building a bridge so they and all people can go back and forth, learning from each other without fear." Shortly after this sermon, he must face his own death and George Hudson and Marta (Margaret Atleo), the old woman who has cared for him, tell him, "We ask you to stay with us to the end. This village is your home, your place." After Mark dies out on the boat that originally brought him to the village, Keetah and Jim look at his grave and then walk off hand in hand, a symbol of the new life that will come to the village.

The film leaves the audience with a respect for the strength and wisdom of this Canadian tribe, a feeling that is the first step towards empathy for their way of life. The native actors who play all the characters in the tribe and the setting of an actual village on the coast of British Columbia also strengthen the empathetic view of a truly distinct culture. The last of the representative films, *When the Legends Die* (1972) tries for such empathy in its portrayal of a contemporary Native American, but finally provokes more sympathy than empathy.

A *Time* critic notes that *"When the Legends Die* is one of the rare movies that seem genuinely to express, even in a small way, the strangled rage and uncertainty of the modern Indian" (6 Nov., 86). Based on the Hal Borland novel of the same name, the film highlights the exploitation of Thomas Black Bull (Frederick Forrest) by white society. In its attempt to expose the effects of prejudice on the main character, the script of the film leaves out major parts of the novel which detail Thomas Black Bull's family life, his education in the old ways of the Ute tribe and his final catharsis of hatred in a hunt for a bear. These details from the novel give the reader a sense of empathy for Ute culture and are part of the reason it became a classic of adolescent literature. The film focuses on the rodeo career of Thomas Black Bull and thus fails to depict a very complete picture of the traditions he loses in the white world.

At the beginning of the film an old Ute, Blue Elk (John War Eagle), comes for young Thomas (Tillman Box), who, after the death of his parents, is living the traditional life of the Utes in a wilderness lodge. Blue Elk forces Thomas and his pet bear to accompany him to a school for young Native Americans. Like Keetah in *I Heard the Owl Call My Name,* who finds life in the city unbearable, Thomas cannot stand the civilized life at the school and tries to escape with his bear. However, Blue Elk tricks him and forces him to go back to the school, saying to him, "I have done this for your own good. You must learn the new ways." Thomas Black Bull's years at the school introduce him to the new ways and also start the destruction of his identity.

This process continues when he leaves the school and

becomes the ward of a white man, who, like Blue Elk, sees a way to exploit the young man. Just as Blue Elk had taken Thomas to the institution for money, Red Dillon becomes his guardian because he recognizes that Thomas's skills with horses will allow him to use Thomas to make money on the rodeo circuit. Thomas arrives at Red's ranch house and undergoes gruelling training for the saddle bronco event. In the training sequences, Red is seen on the top of the corral from low-angles, dominating his student, and Thomas is seen from a high-angle as a victim even in this early stage of his rodeo career. When Meo, the old Mexican companion of Red who had been a great bronco rider (and also exploited by Red), tells Thomas that he is a good rider, the young man just says, "I like horses." At the rodeos, however, when Red starts to make him cheat so they can con more money out of local bettors, and white cowboys sneer and refer to him as "chief," "Geronimo," and "Crazy Horse," Thomas finally confronts Red and says, "The old days are gone. I feel like a thief; I'm sick and ashamed." Red responds by telling Thomas he owns him and then beats him up. After this incident, Thomas can only express his frustration and anger by hurting the horses he once loved, so badly that he becomes known as (horse) Killer Tom Black.

After Thomas leaves Red, he joins the major rodeo circuit, makes a great deal of money and becomes an empty, depressed man. After a serious injury and an attempt to live with a white nurse, he finally decides to go back to Red's ranch. In their final scene together, Thomas stands above Red who is dying of alcoholism in a hotel bed, and the high-angle and low-angle perspectives of their early scenes together are reversed. Figuratively, Thomas is finally free from the one who gave him such a bitter lesson in the new ways of greed and exploitation. Thomas completes his separation by burning Red's ranch house before returning to his reservation. Entering a room with black and white posters of famous chiefs like Dull Knife, Thomas tells members of the tribal council gathered there—the types who had forced him as a young man to give up his old ways—"Listen to me. I have learned the new ways." After

he tells them he will work with the horses on the reservation, a close up of his face freezes to black and white,
making him look like the other traditional leaders in the
posters.

The implication at the end of *When the Legends Die* is that
Thomas Black Bull will renew his identity on the reservation by living a new version of the traditional ways, though
the film never makes the nature of these ways very clear.
This change of emphasis from the novel and the choice of a
white actor to play the central character diminish the
empathy of the film, at least in comparison to *I Heard the
Owl Call My Name*. However, like Keetah in that film,
Thomas Black Bull finds new strength in a return to his
home land and ancient tribal traditions. This theme of tribal
identity manifests itself in a growing number of films about
contemporary Native Americans during the next decade.

IMAGES OF THE SAVAGE

During this period, the typically Savage characters come
close to disappearing. Also, because of the decline in the
number of Westerns, the more detailed categories of attacks
by hostile warriors used for the earlier periods will be
combined under one heading.

Attacks on Representatives of Progress

El Condor (National General, 1970). John Guillermin
Renegade Apaches led by Santana (Iron Eyes Cody) help
the villain accomplish his evil designs. At the end, he kills
Santana.

The Red, White and Black (Hirschman-Northern, 1970). John
Cardos
Soldiers kill a warrior from the tribe of Chief Walking
Horse (Robert Dix) and Kayitah (Bobby Clark), who have
been stealing horses. Though a black leader of the soldiers

and Walking Horse are friends, they are forced to fight against each other.

The Deserter (Paramount, 1971). Burt Kennedy
After the Apaches of Chief Durango (Mimmo Palmara) and Natchai (Ricardo Montalban) attack and kill his wife, the hateful hero attacks and kills all the Apache warriors in a bloody battle.

Ulzana's Raid (Universal, 1972). Robert Aldrich
Discussed in the introduction (182–83), this film depicts a small Apache band that escapes from a reservation and attacks soldiers and settlers in a desperate attempt to survive. By the end, all of them are dead.

Alien Thunder (Onyx-Al, 1973). Claude Fournier
In the wilds of Saskatchewan, a Mountie pursues a cunning Cree (Chief Dan George) who lays traps for him.

Breakheart Pass (UA, 1976). Tom Gries
The Paiutes of White Hand (Eddie Little Sky) conspire with the villains and threaten people on a train.

Bridger (Universal, 1976). David Lowell Rich
As he blazes a trail across the Rockies to California, the hero encounters various tribes. The Native American characters are a Shoshone woman (Margarita Cordova), a Crow chief (X Brands), a Paiute chief (Skeeter Vaughn) and a Modoc chief (Robert Miano).

Mr. Horn (Lorimar, 1979). Jack Starrett
One of the exploits of the legendary bounty hunter is the capture of Geronimo (Enrique Lucero), the great enemy of progress.

Kidnapping

The Bravos (Universal, 1972). Ted Post
Hostile warriors led by Santana (Joaquin Martinez) kidnap the hero's son.

Against a Crooked Sky (Doty-Dayton, 1975) Earl Bellamy

After hostile warriors from the tribe of Temkai (Geoffrey Land) kidnap a young white woman, the hero struggles to rescue her. A *Variety* critic notes that the film "harks back to the not-so-good old days when Indians were depicted as lascivious villains bent on kidnapping white girls and murdering pet dogs. . . . It's amazing that this film was made in 1975" (24 Dec.).

Eagle's Wing (Rank, 1979). Anthony Harvey

A Comanche warrior, White Bull (Sam Waterston), struggles with a white man for the possession of a white horse called Eagle's Wing. In the process, White Bull captures a white woman whom he treats harshly at first but finally grows to love. At the end, he leaves the woman and rides off alone on Eagle's Wing. Other Native American characters are Red Sky (Jorge Luke) and Lame Wolf (Jose Carlos Ruis).

Vengeance

Cry Blood, Apache (Golden Eagle, 1970). Jack Starrett

When Apaches refuse to reveal the location of a gold mine, a group of whites kill everyone in the band except Jemme (Maria Gavha) and her brother, Vittorio (Don Kemp). After Vittorio hunts down and gets his revenge on most of the whites, Jemme kills him before he takes the life of the hero, whom she loves.

Land Raiders (Columbia, 1970). Nathan Juran

When a villain incites Apaches to war to decrease the value of their land and then frames them for the killing of an Indian agent, they retaliate by attacking a stagecoach. In what becomes a cycle of revenge, the whites attack the Apache village and the Apaches attack the town.

Chato's Land (UA, 1972). Michael Winner

When a posse pursuing Chato (Charles Bronson), an Apache leader who killed a sheriff, rapes and kills his wife (Sonia Ragan), he hunts them down and takes his revenge.

The White Buffalo (UA, 1977). J. Lee Thompson
Crazy Horse (Will Sampson), whose daughter has been killed by the white buffalo, struggles with Wild Bill Hickok to be the one who kills the mythical beast. At the end the two rivals become friends.

IMAGES OF THE NOBLE RED MAN

During this era, the varieties of this image continue to multiply, especially in the non-Western films dealing with contemporary characters.

Friendship and Loyalty

King of the Grizzlies (Buena Vista, 1970). Ron Kelly
Moki (John Yesno), a young Cree, protects his white boss from a grizzly which he had cared for as a cub and with which he still feels a mystical connection.

The McMasters (Chevron, 1970). Alf Kjellin
White Feather (David Carradine) gives his sister, Robin (Nancy Kwan), to a black man who had helped him. After some troubled times, she and the man are married. At the end, her brother's tribe rescues them in a time of distress.

Song of the Loon (Hollywood Cinema Assoc., 1970). Andrew Herbert
The tribe of Singing Heron (John Kaflas), Acomas (Martin Valez), Tsi-Nokah (Brad Dela Vale), Tiasholah (Michael Traxton) and Bear-Who-Dreams (Lucky Manning) teach their customs to a white homosexual man.

The Animals (Levitt-Pickman, 1971). Ron Joy
Chatto (Henry Silva) rescues a white woman who has been raped and helps her track down and kill the men. At the end, however, a posse mistakes him for the villain and kills him.

Captain Apache (Scotia Inter., 1971). Alexander Singer

Captain Apache (Lee Van Cleef), an Apache Union officer, investigates the murder of an Indian agent and stops a conflict with his tribe by discovering that the villain had incited them to war to get at gold and oil on tribal land.

Man in the Wilderness (Warner, 1971). Richard Sarafian

A friendly chief (Henry Wilcoxon) helps the hero get revenge on the villains.

Buck and the Preacher (Columbia, 1972). Sidney Poitier

With his sister Sinsie (Julie Robinson) as interpreter, the chief (Enrique Lucero) of a beleaguered tribe gives the black hero five days to bring his wagon train through their land. Later the tribe helps the heroes escape from the villains and rescues them during the final shootout.

Cancel My Reservation (Warner, 1972). Paul Bogart

Bob Hope tries to solve the murder of Mary Little Cloud (Betty Carr) with the help of her father, Joe Little Cloud (Henry Darrow), Crazy (Anne Archer) and Old Bear (Chief Dan George), a mystic. At the end, he finds out that a rancher killed the young woman.

Billy Two Hats (UA, 1973). Ted Kotcheff

Billy Two Hats (Desi Arnaz, Jr.), a mixed-blood Kiowa, protects his wounded outlaw white friend and falls in love with the wife of a white man killed by the Apache. At the end, he gives his friend a Kiowa burial and leaves with the white woman.

Cahill, U. S. Marshall (Warner, 1973). Andrew V. McLaglen

Lightfoot (Neville Brand), a mixed-blood Comanche, is the wise and loyal friend of the hero.

Charley One Eye (Paramount, 1973). Don Chaffey

A black man and a stoical, crippled Native American (Roy Thinnes) become friends as they try to escape from a bounty hunter.

I Heard the Owl Call My Name (Tomorrow Enter., 1973). Daryl Duke

Discussed on pps. 185–87, this film tells the story of a dying priest who is befriended by a tribe in remote British Columbia and learns how to accept death from them.

One Little Indian (Buena Vista, 1973). Bernard McEveety

In this Disney film, the hero gets in trouble for rescuing Native American women and children during a cavalry raid. However, a boy he befriends from the tribe of Jim Wolfe (Jay Silverheels) finally helps him prove his innocence.

Santee (Crown Inter., 1973). Gary Nelson

John Crow (Jay Silverheels) is the loyal friend of the hero.

Harry and Tonto (20th Century-Fox, 1974). Paul Mazursky

After meeting in jail, the hero (Art Carney) and humorous old Sam Two Feathers (Chief Dan George) become friends.

One Flew Over the Cuckoo's Nest (UA, 1975). Milos Forman

In this film based on Ken Kesey's novel, Chief Bromden (Will Sampson) befriends the hero and sticks with him during his final agony. A *New Yorker* critic comments: "The film has its climactic Indian-white love-death, and at the end Kesey's reversal of the American legend (now the white man is sacrificed for the Indian) is satisfying on the deepest pop-myth level" (1 Dec., 134).

Rancho Deluxe (UA, 1975). Frank Perry

The hero and his Native American friend, Cecil Colson (Sam Waterston), go on a joy ride that ends in prison.

The Great Scout and Cathouse Thursday (American Inter., 1976). Don Taylor

Joe Knox (Oliver Reed), the educated Native American friend of the hero, helps him to get revenge on a crooked partner. He also goes for personal revenge by infecting whites with syphilis.

Mustang County (Universal, 1976). Paul Krasny
The hero helps young Nika (Nika Mina) capture a mustang.

The Outlaw Josey Wales (Warner, 1976). Clint Eastwood
Discussed in the introduction (183–85), this film deals with the friendships between the hero and Lone Watie, Little Moonlight, and Ten Bears.

Return of a Man Called Horse (UA, 1976). Irvin Kershner
John Morgan returns from England to rescue his adopted Yellow Hand tribe of Chief Lame Wolf (Regino Herrara), his son, Standing Bear (Pedro Damlen), and Elk Woman (Gale Sondergaard), Raven (Enrique Lucero), Moonstar (Ana De Sade), Thin Dog (Humberto Lopey-Pineda), Grey Thorn (Patricia Reyes) and Owl (Rigoberto Rico). The Arikara of Running Bull (Jorge Luke), who work for evil French traders, have decimated the Yellow Hand tribe and taken their women to the fort of the French. After going through sweat and Sun Dance ceremonies, Morgan inspires the tribe to defeat the Arikara and the French. At the end, Morgan decides to spend the rest of his life with the Yellow Hand. A *Time* reviewer comments: "The movie is too glib about Indian spirituality to be good, too self-conscious about being on the Indians' side to be wholly convincing" (16 Aug., 87).

Guardian of the Wilderness (Sunn Classics, 1977). David O'Malley
Teneiya (Don Shanks) is the Native American friend of the hero who helps him build a cabin in the wilderness.

The Incredible Rocky Mountain Race (Schick Sunn, 1977). James L. Conway
In this TV movie, Eagle Feather (Larry Storch) helps the hero win the race. Eagle Feather and Crazy Horse (Mike Mazurki) are both rather wacky characters.

The Last of the Mohicans (Schick Sunn, 1977). James L. Conway

This TV movie retells Cooper's story of the conflict between the hero and his friends, Chingachgook (Ned Romero) and Uncas (Don Shanks), and the hostile Huron, Magua (Robert Tessier).

The Deerslayer (Schick Sunn, 1978). Dick Friedenberg

In this TV movie, the hero and his friend, Chingachgook (Ned Romero) fight the warlike Hurons of Chief Rivenoak (Victor Mohica).

Ishi: The Last of His Tribe (E. M. Lewis, 1978). Robert O. Miller

Based on *Ishi in Two Worlds* by Theodora Kroeber Quinn, this film tells the story of Ishi (Elroy Casados), the last survivor of the Yahi tribe. Befriended by a white anthropologist, Ishi succumbs to the modern world and dies young.

Night Wing (Columbia, 1979). Arthur Hiller

Youngman Duran (Nick Mancuso), a tribal policeman in love with a white woman, and Walker Chee (Stephen Macht) try to eradicate vampire bats turned deadly by tribal magic. Abner Tasupi (George Clutesi), a seer from the tribe, helps them deal with this threat to the whole area.

Fish Hawk (CFDC, 1979). Donald Shebib

Reared by whites after soldiers killed his family, Fish Hawk (Will Sampson) drinks heavily until his drunkenness leads to the death of his dog and threatens his friendship with a young white boy. After teaching the boy many good and sometimes painful lessons, Fish Hawk leaves to find his own people and learn their ways before he dies.

Prophecy (Paramount, 1979). John Frankenheimer

The hero helps the tribe of Hawks (Armand Assante) when pollution from a paper mill threatens their existence. M'Rai (George Clutesi) is a seer who finds out that animals have been turned into monsters because of mercury poisoning.

The Peace-loving Chief

Little Big Man (National General, 1970). Arthur Penn

Discussed on pps. 178–80, this film deals with the relationship of a white man, Little Big Man, and his surrogate father, Old Lodge Skins, the peace-loving chief of the Cheyenne who finally joins the Sioux for the Battle of Little Big Horn.

I Will Fight No More Forever (Wolper, 1975). Richard Heffron

The Nez Perce tribe of the peace-loving Chief Joseph (Ned Romero) and Wahletis (John Kaufman), Olloket (Emilio Delgato), Rainbow (Nick Ramus), Toma (Linda Redfearn), White Bird (Frank Salsedo) and Looking Glass (Vincent St. Cyr) want to stay on their own land. However, after being forced to go to a reservation, they fight the soldiers of General Howard and make a heroic attempt to flee into Canada, only to be stopped just before they make it over the border.

Winterhawk (Howco Inter., 1976). Charles B. Pierce

The heroes pursue and attack Winterhawk (Michael Dante), a Blackfeet chief who is only trying to find serum for the smallpox which is wiping out his tribe. He gets his revenge by kidnapping a white woman with whom he falls in love. Other members of his tribe are Red Calf (Ace Powell) and Pale Flower (Sacheen Littlefeather). A *Variety* critic notes that "Pierce can't get inside the Indians he is trying to ennoble. Title character Michael Dante is little more than a cigar store Indian, speaking pidgin English and gazing balefully at the horizon" (28 Jan.).

Romances between Native American Women and White Men

Dirty Dingus Magee (MGM, 1970). Burt Kennedy

In this comedy, the hero's lover is Anna Hotwater (Michele Carey), a nymphomaniac whom Chief Crazy Blanket (Paul Fix) wants for his woman. After escaping from a sheriff and the Chief with Anna's help, the hero finally leaves her because he can't keep up with her demands. This stereotype of the Native American female as insatiable is repeated with the sisters of Sunshine in *Little Big Man*.

A Man Called Horse (National General, 1970). Elliot Silverstein
Discussed on pps. 180–82, this film tells the story of John Morgan, an Englishman captured by the Yellow Hand Sioux. Finally, he is adopted by the tribe, becomes a warrior, and falls in love with Running Deer, who is killed in the final battle with the Shoshone.

Jeremiah Johnson (Warner, 1972). Sydney Pollack
The hero, his wife, Swan (Delle Bolton), the daughter of Blackfeet chief, Two Tongues Lebeau (Richard Angarola), and his adopted son become a devoted and happy family. However, when he violates a Crow burial ground by leading soldiers through it, the warriors of Paints His Shirt Red (Joaquin Martinez) kill Swan and the boy. After Johnson takes revenge by killing many Crow, Paints His Shirt Red finally makes peace with him. A *Variety* critic notes that the film provides "a newer look at Indian-white relations, without branding either as good or bad but of differing, yet clear-cut, cultures that could have existed side by side with some understanding" (10 May).

Journey Through Rosebud (GFS, 1972). Tom Gries
A hip draft dodger drifts onto the Rosebud Sioux Reservation, makes friends with Frank (Robert Forster), an alcoholic and rebellious Vietnam vet, and falls in love with Shirley (Victoria Racimo), the activist ex-wife of Frank. After learning of the problems on the reservation and witnessing the suicide of Frank, he moves on. A *Newsweek* critic notes that "these sentimentalized Indians seem no more real, arouse little more compassion than the ones who used to bite the dust in the B Westerns" (24 Apr., 89).

The White Dawn (Paramount, 1974). Philip Kaufman
In this film based on James Huston's *An Eskimo Saga*, the behavior of three white whalers stranded among the Eski-

mos, one of whom is in love with Neevee (Pitliak), leads to trouble. Other characters played by an all-native supporting cast are the Shaman (Sagiaktok), Sowniapik (Munamee Sake), and his wife (Pitseolala Kili).

Marie-Anne (Canadian, 1978). Martin Walters
The heroine appeases her husband and his hot-blooded native common-law wife (Tantoo Martin) by allowing herself to be adopted by the tribe of Chief Many Horses (Gordon Tootoosis).

See also *Little Big Man* (1970).

Romances between Native American Men and White Women

Run, Simon, Run (Aaron Spelling, 1970). George McGowan
A Papago released from prison, Simon Zuniga (Burt Reynolds) falls in love with a white woman as he searches for the killer of his brother. At the end, he gives her up in order to take vengeance on the killer, and, in the process, he is killed.

House Made of Dawn (Firebird, 1972). Richardson Morse
Discussed on pps. 253–55, this film tells the story of Abel who struggles with living in the city. While in Los Angeles he falls in love with a white social worker who finally convinces him to return to his reservation.

Grayeagle (Howco Inter., 1977). Charles B. Pierce
Grayeagle (Alex Cord), a noble Cheyenne warrior, captures the daughter of a white woman and her friend, Standing Bear (Iron Eyes Cody). Eventually, Grayeagle and the young woman fall in love, and, after he fights off hostile Shoshone, he returns to her. At the end, they are ready to live happily together in the wilderness.

See also *Flap* (1970), *Billy Jack* (1971), *Billy Two Hats* (1973), *Winterhawk* (1976) and *Eagle's Wing* (1979).

Native Americans as Victims

Soldier Blue (Avco-Embassy, 1970). Ralph Nelson

Just as *Little Big Man* establishes a parallel between the killing in Vietnam and the Battle of Washita, this film, based on Theodore Olson's *Arrow in the Sun*, finds Vietnam in the Sand Creek Massacre. After the Cheyenne of Spotted Wolf (Jorge Rivero) and Running Fox (Jorge Russek) kill a party of soldiers, a cavalry unit attacks the tribe despite efforts of a good soldier and a white woman. During the attack, the soldiers commit atrocities such as raping the women and mutilating the children.

The New Land (Swenskfilm, 1972). Jan Troell

This Swedish film about the trials of Scandinavian immigrants in the Midwest depicts the uprising of the Sioux as the result of mistreatment by the government and shows the hanging of almost forty warriors.

When the Legends Die (20th Century-Fox, 1972). Stuart Millar

Discussed on pps. 187–89, this film portrays the mistreatment of Thomas Black Bull, a Ute bronco rider, by his own people and white society. At the end, he returns to his reservation to find his identity.

Chino (Italian, 1973). John Sturges

Chino (Charles Bronson), a mixed-blood, suffers the prejudice of white society as he tries to protect his ranch. After being rejected by a white woman he loves, Chino and a white boy join a tribe which is barely surviving. Later, after being beaten by the villains, Chino burns his ranch house and rides off alone.

Cotter (Independent, 1973). Paul Stanley

Cotter (Don Murray), a Sioux rodeo clown with a drinking problem, returns to his homeland, only to be wrongly blamed for the murder of a rancher because of his reputation as a drinker.

Rooster Cogburn (Universal, 1975). Stuart Millar

After villains kill a minister and some of his young Native American wards, Wolf (Richard Romancito) and the minister's daughter help the hero bring the villains to justice.

Buffalo Bill and the Indians, or Sitting Bull's History Lesson (UA, 1976). Robert Altman

In this film based on Arthur Kopit's *Indians*, Buffalo Bill Cody hires Sitting Bull (Frank Kaquitts) and his interpreter, William Halsey (Will Sampson), to be in his Wild West Show. Sitting Bull remains impervious to the crazy outbursts of Buffalo Bill, who can only symbolically triumph over him in a fake battle at the end of the show.

The Villain (Columbia, 1979). Hal Needham

This spoof of B Westerns is difficult to categorize. Nervous Elk (Paul Lynde) is an effeminate chief of a tribe whose rituals, horsemanship, treatment of white women, and rights to their own land are all ridiculed. Though the film is a satire, the Native American characters are really victims of the filmmakers—though, of course, this is true of most Westerns.

Contemporary Native Americans

Flap or *The Last Warrior* (Warner, 1970). Carol Reed

In this film based on Clair Huffaker's novel, *Nobody Loves a Drunken Indian*, Flapping Eagle (Anthony Quinn) is a hard-drinking war hero who, along with his friends Lobo Jackson (Claude Akins) and Eleven Snowflake (Tony Bill), battles a construction company, steals a train and claims a town for his tribe. Loved by a white prostitute and given dubious help by a self-styled lawyer, Bear Smith (Victor Jory), Flapping Eagle is finally killed by his enemy, Rafferty, a brutal mixed-blood policeman. Other Native American characters are Ann Looking Deer (Susanna Miranda), Larry Standing Elk (Rudy Diaz), She'll-Be-Back-Pretty-Soon (Pedro Regas) and Luke Wolf (John War Eagle). A *Variety* critic notes that the film makes "no attempt to show any Indian as a responsible person . . ." (28 Oct.).

Geronimo Jones (Learning Corp., 1970). Bert Salzman
   In this short film, a young Native American gets caught between the values of the past and present when he trades an old medallion for a TV.

Billy Jack (Warner, 1971). T. C. Frank (Tom Laughlin)
   Billy Jack, a mixed-blood Vietnam veteran who does tribal rattlesnake dances and rides a Triumph cycle, defends Native American children and their white female teacher from villains in the nearby town. When the villains kill a boy from the reservation school, Martin (Stan Rice), and rape the teacher he loves, Billy Jack uses his judo skills to punish them and then gives himself up to avoid more violence. A *NYT* critic comments that in Billy Jack there is "something of both Tonto and the Lone Ranger. . . . He is a comic strip character with delusions of grandeur" (11 Mar., 1973).

Climb an Angry Mountain (Warner, 1972). Leonard Horn
   Lawmen pursue a Native American, Joey Chilko (Joe Kapp), in the wilderness of Mount Shasta.

The Loners (Fanfare, 1972). Sutton Roley
   Stein (Dean Stockwell), a mixed-blood Navajo, joins two other young men, gets in trouble and escapes with them to the reservation, where his father (Hal Jon Norman) is saddened by his son's rejection of the Navajo ways. When the young men leave the reservation, they are killed.

Injun Fender (Duke U., 1973). Robert Cordier
   In this student film, a Native American rock musician named Fender (Dennis Campbell) kills several whites.

Nakia (Screen Gems, 1974). Leonard Horn
   Nakia Parker (Robert Forster), a Navajo deputy sheriff, gets in trouble when members of his tribe, two of whom are

Naiche (George Clutesi) and Diane Little Eagle (Maria Eleva Cordero), try to save a mission from white developers.

Trial of Billy Jack (Taylor-Laughlin, 1974). Tom Laughlin
Billy Jack (Tom Laughlin) returns from prison to deal with whites who are mistreating students from the reservation school by trying to stop their use of TV for political action. Other Native American characters are Blue Elk (Guy Greymountain), Patsy Littlejohn (Sacheen Littlefeather), Thunder Mountain (Rolling Thunder), Little Bear (Buffalo Horse), Sunshine (Susan Sosa), and Oshannah (Oshannah Fastwolf).

Joe Panther (Artist's Creation, 1976). Paul Krasny
Joe Panther (Ray Tracey), a Seminole who fights alligators, his friend, Billy Tiger (A. Martinez), and Turtle George (Ricardo Montalban), a wise man who gives the two young men advice, try to find their place in society. Other Native American characters are Tommy Panther (Gem Thorp Osceola), Jenny Rainbow (Monika Ramirey), and Joe's Mother (Lois Red Elk). A *Variety* critic notes that "where the film fudges is in the simplistic treatment of Indians' struggles with white society. . . . The problem is much more complex than the film's rosy resolution makes it seem . . ." (3 Nov.).

Shadow of the Hawk (Columbia, 1976). George McCowan
Old Man Hawk (Chief Dan George), a medicine man, summons his Grandson (Jan-Michael Vincent) from the city and teaches him the arts of magic so he can fight the evil spirits loosed by an evil tribal witch, Dsonoqua (Marianne Jones).

Billy Jack Goes to Washington (Taylor-Laughlin, 1977). Tom Laughlin
This time Billy Jack (Tom Laughlin) takes on the whole U.S. Government in his fight for justice for his people.

Orca (Paramount, 1977). Michael Anderson
Umliak (Will Sampson), a Native American knowledge-

able of his tribal lore, pursues Orca, the killer whale, and finally is killed.

Three Warriors (Fantasy Films, 1977). Keith Merrill
Discussed on pps. 257–59, this film tells the story of Michael, a teenage Native American from the city who visits his grandfather on the reservation and finds a new pride in his heritage.

The Manitou (Avco Embassy, 1978). William Girdler
Standing Rock (Michael Ansara), a contemporary Sioux medicine man, exorcises a 400-year-old demon spirit which has attached itself to the back of a white woman.

Dreamspeaker (CBC, 1979). Claude Jutra
An emotionally disturbed white boy escapes from an institution and is taken in by an old shaman (George Clutesi) and his companion, a mute Native American man. In contrast to the scientific methods of the whites, the shaman's ancient way of healing brings some joy and health to the boy. When the old man dies, the boy, who has been taken back to the institution, and the mute commit suicide and rejoin the shaman in the afterlife.

Spirit of the Wind (Doyon Ltd., 1979). Ralph Liddle
Discussed on pps. 255–57, this film tells the story of George Attla, Jr., the Athabaskan dog sled racer who overcame tuberculosis to become a champion for many years.

* * *

The depiction of the Sand Creek massacre in *Soldier Blue* (1970) and the Washita massacre in *Little Big Man* (1970) reveal the excesses of the politically motivated anti-Westerns in the first part of this decade. In each of these examples, the filmmakers parallel the Cheyenne victims of the evil soldiers, especially the women and children, with the civilian victims of the Vietnam war in order to make the rather obvious point that the victimization of native peoples in the westward expansion is being recapitulated in Vietnam. Later in the period, several years after the Vietnam war, *Three Warriors* (1977) and *Spirit of the Wind* (1979) herald a new type of film in which central Native American characters become significant in and of themselves. Such films dealing with the lives of contemporary characters become more common in the next decade.

CHAPTER SEVEN

FILMS OF THE 1980S

In this decade, variations of the Savage and Noble Red Man images persist in the Western, even though the genre itself is near extinction. In *Windwalker* (1980), a film that portrays Native American life before contact with whites, a noble Cheyenne family struggles to survive the attacks of savage Crow enemies. A more traditional Western, *The Mountain Men* (1980), while focusing on a typical romance between the white hero and a Native American woman, portrays the Crow as Noble Red Men and the Blackfeet as the Savages led by a villainous chief. A Canadian film, *Ikwe* (1986), on the other hand, treats a marriage between an Ojibway woman and a white trader from a historical perspective which resists the traditional images. The three other representative films continue the trend of depicting Native American characters in contemporary settings. In *Emerald Forest* (1985), Noble Red Men from the Amazonian jungles adopt a white boy who then leads them in a fight against a savage tribe and whites who are exploiting their rain forest. In *War Party* (1989), three young Native Americans get caught up in a vicious battle with their white neighbors in which the whites become the savages and the young men noble warriors. And, finally, *Running Brave* (1983) tells the story of Billy Mills, the mixed-blood Lakota runner who must overcome the prejudice of white society and his own identity problems before he can become an Olympic champion runner.

The first of the representative Westerns is *Windwalker* (1980), a film based on a novel by Blaine Yorgason, a

Mormon writer known for his children's stories, and produced by Mormon filmmakers for the family market. Through a series of flashbacks, it follows two generations of a Cheyenne family and uses the motif of the lost son reunited with his family. This complicated narrative structure gives the film the feeling of a folk tale. Beginning in the present with an ailing, old Windwalker (Trevor Howard), surrounded by the family of his son, Smiling Wolf (Nick Ramus), the film flashes back as Windwalker tells his story to the children. In this extended flashback, the young Windwalker (James Remar) falls in love with the beautiful Tashina (Serene Hedin). After stealing horses from the Crow to give to her parents, he marries her and they have twin boys. With occasional cuts back to old Windwalker, the story continues with the idyllic life of young Windwalker until it is destroyed when a disgruntled suitor of Tashina and the evil Crow Eyes (Rudy Diaz) kill the young mother and kidnap one of their sons. After telling his story, old Windwalker is ready to die, and his son, Smiling Wolf, puts him on a platform grave. Then, riding a white stallion, the warrior leads his family into the wilderness.

At this point, Crow warriors, Crow Hair (Harold Goss-Coyote), Wounded Crow (Roy Cohoe) and Crow Eyes, whose face is covered with eerie black and white war paint, begin to stalk Smiling Wolf and the Cheyenne women and children. In a sequence that makes effective use of camera angles and cross-cutting, the savage Crow finally attack and seriously injure Smiling Wolf before the family manages to hide from them. While the audience is in suspense about when the Crow will find the family, the film cuts back to the platform grave where Windwalker, in a scene similar to the one at the end of *Little Big Man*, realizes that he is not dead and says in a voice-over, "My feet are cold. Grandfather [the Great spirit], this is a good joke. Free my spirit or free my limbs, but do not leave me in this cold." Apparently the Great Spirit has more work for Windwalker to do, because he lets him escape from a wolf attack and kill a giant bear, after which the old warrior says, with characteristic humor, "Grandfather, such a long life is not healthy for an old man." After these adventures, he finds his son's family and realizes he has been sent back to save them from the Crow warriors.

In this last part of the film, the Cheyenne children, though a key part of the family structure from the beginning, are central to its survival. The two boys (both played by Native American actors) save one of the women during the first Crow attack, and then, tutored by Windwalker, they set traps which sabotage the final assault by the Crow and allow for the capture of a warrior (the Lost One, Nick Ramus) who turns out to be the other son of Windwalker. The little girl in the family also shows her spunk and kindness in a scene where she chews a piece of meat and then puts it in the mouth of the captured Lost One. Throughout the film, these children have an honored place in the family and their actions at the end prove their worth. The Crow, on the other hand, are portrayed as lone warriors who kidnap children and, in the case of the Lost One, treat them very harshly.

In fact, throughout the film, the Crow are the savage enemies who must be defeated by the noble Cheyenne, with their strong family and religious values. At the end, before Windwalker rejoins Tashina in the cloud spirit world, his lost son defeats Crow Eyes in hand-to-hand combat and makes him leave in shame. Though the film follows the Savage versus the Noble Red Man formula, it does offer a unique perspective on Native American cultures. A *Variety* critic, noting the use of the Cheyenne and Crow languages and subtitles, comments: "Coupled with the absence of non-Indian characters in the film, which takes place in the 18th Century, this gives the Indians on the screen a dignity they have been denied previously, even in the most sympathetic westerns" (10 Dec.). This film, which deals exclusively with Native American life, a type very popular in the silent films, does portray the culture of "Indians" positively, unless, of course, the viewer happens to be of Crow heritage.

Given the vagaries of the traditional images, in *The Mountain Men* (1980) the Crow are the roguish but Noble Red Men who are friendly to the hero and the Blackfeet woman he loves, Running Moon (Victoria Racimo). At the beginning, Cross Otter (Cal Bellini), whose Crow band takes turns with the hero in stealing each other's horses, helps the hero rebuff an attack by the Blackfeet during which the warriors from each side moon each other. Later, at the rendezvous of the trappers, the hero meets Iron Belly (Victor Jory), the chief of another Crow band, known for his Spanish breastplate. Iron Belly shows his friendship by telling him of a valley in Blackfeet country where he can find many beaver to trap. Another Crow at the rendezvous is Medicine Wolf (David Ackroyd), a trick rider and old friend of the hero. Both of these characters suffer for their friendship: when Heavy Eagle (Stephen Macht) and his warriors seek vengeance on the hero, they kill everyone in Iron Belly's camp and torture Medicine Wolf.

These Blackfeet characters, and especially their chief, Heavy Eagle, are depicted as deadly Savages. From the beginning, Heavy Eagle, seen in a close-up with black war paint on his face and flames flickering in front of him, is portrayed as a vengeful, diabolical character. Heavy Eagle lives up to his image, not only by his vicious treatment of the Crow mentioned above, but also by scalping the hero's friend, torturing the hero, raping the beautiful and devoted Running Moon, and cutting off the head of a man who comes to parley with him. In the climactic scene when the hero comes to rescue his beloved Running Moon, Heavy Eagle, whose face is then completely painted black, engages him in hand-to-hand combat, and, after gaining an advantage by biting, is about to kill him when Running Moon shoots the evil warrior. Thus ends the career of a Savage character so extreme that his presence in a 1980s film is quite surprising.

Played against the background of the savage Blackfeet and the noble Crow is the romance between the hero and Running Moon. Their first two meetings are something less than romantic: in the first, he knocks her out with a musket, and in the second, she pushes him into a river after finding him with a woman at the rendezvous. After that, she stays with him because, as she says, "I could never go back to Heavy Eagle" (not surprisingly) and "it is the custom that I go with you." After the hero is separated from his trapper friend, Running Moon comforts him. Then, in a softly focused sequence with equally soft music in the background, they hunt and work together, make love, and exchange gifts that reveal their devotion to each other. Their peaceful time together is short-lived, however, because Heavy Eagle captures them and they are separated until the end when Running Moon saves her lover's life. At the very end, seen from a high angle that emphasizes their vulnerability, they ride off to the high country, the only sort of remote place where, in the Westerns, the few happy romances between whites and Native Americans can be lived out.

In the Canadian film, *Ikwe* (1986), the liaison between a young Ojibway woman, Ikwe (Hazel King), and a Scottish trader is much less romanticized. This film, which focuses on the female characters, begins with a dream of Ikwe's in which she sees a hairy man spirit and flashes of sick children on the ground. She asks her grandmother, N'okom (Gladys Taylor), to interpret the dream, but the old woman tells her that she will have to find the meaning on her own. Part of her answer seems to appear when a bearded white trader and his Cree guide arrive at the village. When these two men make a trade agreement with the Ojibway chief, the guide decides to show good faith by arranging a marriage between Ikwe, the chief's daughter, and the Scot, who has no desire to marry a "savage" but accepts the arrangement to cement the trade agreement. Ikwe also reluctantly agrees to the match because the Scot appears to be the man spirit of her dream. After building a wigwam and comforting her husband during the rigors of the first winter at the remote location of his new trading post, she has several children over the next seven years. Although Ikwe and her husband love their children and even show some affection for each other, the Scot never accepts her as an Ojibway and insists on calling her "Mary."

Finally, despite a warning from Ikwe's father, the family moves to the big trading post, where there not only is Ikwe exposed to smallpox, but also loses her oldest son when her husband sends him away to a white school. After asking her husband, "What will he learn? To be like you!", she spits in his face. In the night, she takes her children back to her village. Not knowing that she is already infected with smallpox, she gives a necklace to a friend in order to acknowledge the warm welcome she receives from her tribe. After a brief happy time during which she reeducates her daughter in the tribal ways, a smallpox epidemic begins with the death of the woman wearing the necklace. As a hand-held camera moves among the sick and dying people and emphasizes the devastation, Ikwe, who finally understands the meaning of her dream, sends her daughter away. The film ends with a close-up of the terrified girl looking back at her dying village and a freeze-frame as she runs down the rocky shore.

Ikwe is a unique film in that it tells this tragic and often-repeated historical story from the perspective of the Ojibway characters. In the early scenes, the tribe's sense of humor comes out while they go about their daily lives. Using their native language (with subtitles), the women joke about their lazy men while preparing food and working hides. And the men have a good laugh about the Scot, speculating that his beard was the result of his mother being a dog. Such dialogue and scenes of children playing underscore the happy, traditional life of the tribe before the advent of the white traders, who ultimately destroy their traditional culture. As a whole, the film avoids the Noble Red Man image in its harsh but true-seeming reenactment of historical cultural conflicts, much like the more recent Canadian film, *Black Robe* (1991).

A similar exploitation of a primitive tribal culture occurs in *The Emerald Forest* (1985) when a noble tribe of Native South Americans are threatened by whites building a dam in the Amazon wilderness. This tribe, known as the Invisible People, captures and raises a white boy whose father is one of the builders, whom the tribe calls Termite People because they are "eating up" the forest. The chief, Wanadi (Rui Polonah), a wise and good-natured man, becomes the surrogate father of the boy, whom he calls Tomme. This character stands out because the native actor who plays him has a strong screen presence, similar to that of Chief Dan

George. For example, when Tomme aims his arrow at a sloth, Wanadi, seen in a close-up, tells him not to shoot the animal and then, with a sly smile, says, "he is old and slow like me." As with Chief Dan George in *Little Big Man*, Wanadi's charming character enhances the noble image of his tribe.

On the other hand, the antagonists of Wanadi's tribe, the Fierce People, are Savages, displaced from their traditional land by whites building a dam. Supplied with guns by evil whites, the Fierce People prey on the peaceful tribes to capture young women to sell as prostitutes to the whites. These Savage characters, led by a vicious, evil-looking chief, move through the forest looking for the women of the Invisible People.

The most beautiful young woman in Tomme's adopted tribe is Kachiri (Dira Pass), and when Tomme becomes a young man he falls in love with her. When Wanadi sees this happen, he knows the time has come for Tomme's initiation into manhood. In a harsh ritual, reminiscent of *A Man Called Horse* (1970), Tomme is covered with large ants and must survive the agony of their bites. At the end of his ordeal, Wanadi pulls him out of the water and says, "The boy is dead and the man is born." In the second stage of his initiation, the chief blows a powder through a long pipe into Tomme's nose and this powerful hallucinogen transports his consciousness to his spirit-being and he sees through the eyes of an eagle. After gaining this vision and knowledge about himself, he becomes a warrior and is free to marry Kachiri after he gives gifts to her parents.

Tomme's marriage to Kachiri marks the end of tranquillity for his adopted tribe. Shortly thereafter, when Tomme and Wanadi are away from the tribe, the Fierce People attack, burn their village, and kidnap Kachiri and the other young women. In the last part of the film, Tomme, Wanadi and his warriors attempt to rescue them, the life blood of the tribe, from these evil characters. Because the compound where the captured women are being forced to be prostitutes is surrounded by a high fence and guarded by men with automatic weapons, Tomme and the warriors not only fail in their first rescue attempt but Wanadi is fatally wounded. After giving the old man the traditional funeral of burning his bones and consuming part of the ashes in a liquid, Tomme becomes the leader of the tribe.

Like the hero of *A Man Called Horse,* Tomme becomes the savior of his adopted people. To do this, Tomme calls upon his eagle spirit, travels to the city where his family lives and elicits the help of his father, who had earlier found his son in the jungle and finally decided he belonged with Kachiri and the Invisible People. With the help of his father, Tomme and his warriors rescue the women and return to the jungle. However, to save his people, Tomme must also destroy the dam so that the land of the Invisible People will not be inundated. Again taking the form of his eagle spirit, Tomme makes the frogs sing, which in turn brings torrential rains that cause a flood which becomes "the great anaconda" that breaks up the dam. With a shot of Tomme, Kachiri and other young men and women who will be the new life of the tribe, the film ends with statistics about the destruction of native peoples, and a note about the few tribes who have never had contact with the outside world and who "still know what we have forgotten." Though this sympathy for the people and the land and of the Amazon region is laudable, the film's subtext about the white savior isn't much different from that of *A Man Called Horse,* and the contemporary Native South Americans become a version of the Noble Red Man.

A similar concern for the exploitation of contemporary Native Americans appears in *War Party* (1989), a film with the message that as long as racism exists, the massacres of the past will be replayed in the present. Though such a message is also laudable, though rather obvious, the tone of the film is irresponsible. As a *New York Times* critic notes, *War Party* is a movie that "pretends to be high-minded in its concern for the plight of Indians while exploiting existing tensions in order to portray a bloodbath" (29 Sept.). What leads to the bloodbath is a decision by Mr. Crowkiller (Dennis Banks), the head of the tribal council, and the mayor to draw tourists by reenacting a historic battle between the U.S. Cavalry and the Blackfeet during the town's "Bonanza Days." When the simulated battle turns

into a real one, the whites take on the traditional characteristics of the Savage, and the three young heroes, Sonny
Crowkiller (Billy Wirth), Skitty Harris (Kevin Dillon) and
Warren Cutfoot (Tim Sampson) become Noble, but
doomed, Red Men.

From the beginning the white men are driven by hatred
and vengeance. The violence begins when a hateful young
white man starts a fight with a young Blackfeet after a pool
game and gets cut on the face. The next day, in the
reenactment of the battle, the young thug from the pool
game, using real bullets, kills the Blackfeet man who cut
him, and Sonny, in turn, kills him with a war axe from the
original battle which he had stolen from the local museum.
After more killing on each side, the three heroes escape and
the savagery of the townspeople starts to reveal itself as the
rest of the film becomes a pursuit drama. The first instance
of this savagery occurs when they surround one of the
companions of the heroes with their pickups and finally
shoot and then scalp him. As the three young men continue
to elude their pursuers, the governor brings in the troops, a
move resisted by Sonny's father, the usually conciliatory
Mr. Crowkiller. When he realizes that the whites are out for
total revenge, he exclaims, "All my life I've tried to understand the white man and I've never learned a goddamned
thing." At this point, however, he is powerless to stop the
deadly pursuit of his son.

As the troops and a professional tracker and his Crow
companion (Rodney Grant), close in on the three young
men, Skitty, exhibiting the same frustration as Mr. Crowkiller, says, "Same old shit! Nothing has changed in 100
years." When he and Sonny are finally trapped, however,
they ask to see not Mr. Crowkiller but Freddy Man Wolf
(Saginaw Grant), the rebellious and drunken old medicine
man. After singing the proper songs, this traditional member of the tribe tells the young men that those negotiating
with them are telling lies. He finally advises them to die like
warriors. Shortly thereafter, baring their chests and putting
on war paint, they ride their horses into the deadly fire of
automatic weapons. As the camera looks at their bodies
from a high angle, it focuses in on the war axe Sonny had

been carrying, the same axe seen in close-up at the beginning of the film which depicts the aftermath of the original battle. The recurring use of this symbolic object is typical of the heavy-handed way this film reinforces its message about racism, certainly a good message but one expressed in a quite hateful way.

The last of the representative films, *Running Brave* (1983), is also rather obvious in its attempt to reveal the prejudice of white society towards Native Americans. Produced by the Canadian Ermineskin tribe, this film is based on the life of Billy Mills, the Olympic champion and potential role model for young Native Americans. The title character is played by Robbie Benson, an actor who looks the part of a runner and somewhat resembles Mills. Some Native Americans objected to the choice of a white actor and to the fact that Native American actors only play the minor characters of Billy's reservation family. In fact, a critic from *Variety* finds the portrayal of the family to be a problem: "Billy's Indian relatives come and go throughout the movie as stereotypical Indians. One is bitter and hateful of white men [Eddie], the other is a crushed alcoholic with unrealized talent [Frank]" (5 Oct.). Billy's father (August Schellenberg) and traditional grandfather (George Clutesi) are seen rather briefly in flashbacks, and his half-brother, Frank (Denis Lacrois), sister, Catherine (Margo Kane), and friend, Eddie (Graham Greene), appear in only a few parts of the film.

The real center of the film is the story of Billy's struggle to prove himself as a runner. His coach at the University of Kansas reveals the stereotypes Billy must overcome in a comment to a colleague: "You know as well as I do what happens to these Indian boys. They are gifted natural runners, but they have no discipline. They can't take orders and they're quitters. Sooner or later they all end up back on the reservation pumping gas or dead drunk on skid row." Billy, however, feels confident that he will be different: in a letter/voice-over to his sister (a recurring device), Billy says, "I want to prove that this is one Indian who can make it in the white world." At first he has great success and does whatever his coach wants, including leading the races from the beginning and crushing his opponents, both of which feel unnatural to him. However, as time goes on he lets the coach use him up to the degree that he tells his sister, "I've lost my love for running. I'm just a running machine." Despite the love and encouragement of a white woman and the friendship of his roommate, Billy finally feels he must quit school and return to the reservation.

While at the reservation, Billy rekindles his relationship with Frank and his friendship with Eddie, whose anger and distaste for whites had earlier disrupted a party at the home of Billy's fiancée. During this happy time in his homeland he also rediscovers his love of running. Then Frank commits suicide and Billy decides to leave the reservation, marry his beloved Pat and join the armed forces so he can train for running in his own way. As he trains for the Olympics, he says that he "feels his family running with him" and that his competing is "his chance to give something back to his people." However, the rest of the film focuses on the big race at the Olympics and the only other allusion to his "people" occurs at the end of the film while the crowds are cheering him. Billy sees an old Native American man in the crowd and they exchange a mysteriously knowing glance.

This ending makes the audience feel as though they missed something. And in a way they have because this film is more about a sports hero than about contemporary Native American life. In fact, the director insisted on a pseudonym because he was so unhappy with this emphasis. Though the film suggests that Billy's triumph is connected with his return to the reservation and tribal values, it doesn't illustrate this theme with the detail or empathy of films released later in the decade, like *Journey to Spirit Island* (1988) or *Powwow Highway* (1988), both of which will be discussed in the last chapter.

IMAGES OF THE SAVAGE

The Mountain Men (Columbia, 1980). Richard Lang

Discussed on pps. 208–10, this film portrays Blackfeet led by Heavy Eagle, their diabolical chief, as vicious adversaries of the hero and the Blackfeet woman he loves.

The Wolfen (Orion, 1981). Michael Wadleigh

In this thriller, wolf-like spirits of Native Americans inhabit the South Bronx and prey on humans. Native American characters are a steel worker (Edward J. Olmos) and an old man (Dehl Berti). A *Newsweek* critic notes that "though the movie pretends to be championing the Indians, it defames them" (3 Aug., 51).

The Ghost Dance (Ahremess, 1982). Peter F. Buffa

In this horror movie, archeologists find the mummified body of Nahalla, a revengeful Ghost Dance leader, who takes over the body of Aranjo (Henry Bal) and starts killing people. Despite the efforts of Ocacio (Frank Sontonoma Salsedo) to do away with the evil spirit, Nahalla takes over the psyche of the white female anthropologist and, at the end, they kill Ocacio and Tom Eagle (Victor Mohica), the man she had loved.

Fleshburn (Crown Inter., 1984). George Gage

Calvin Duggai (Sonny Landham), a Navajo, escapes from a mental institution and takes revenge on those who had him committed.

Sacred Ground (Pacific Inter., 1984). Charles B. Pierce

When a white man and his family build their cabin on sacred burial grounds, the tribes of Wannetta (Mindi Miller), Little Doc (Serene Hedin), Prairie Fox (Elroy P. Casados), Wounded Leg (Vernon Foster) and Brave Beaver (Larry Kenoras) attack.

Stagecoach (Heritage Enter., 1986). Ted Post

The hero, Doc Holliday, expounds on the evils of manifest destiny and the rights of the Apache to their ancestral lands. Near the end of the film, the warriors of Geronimo stage a perfunctory attack, which the cavalry stops almost immediately. A *Variety* critic comments: "Those who recall the wonders of *Stagecoach* [Ford's version] and the race against Apaches can only hope, in this instance, the Indians will win" (21 May).

IMAGES OF THE NOBLE RED MAN

Friendship and Loyalty

Bronco Billy (Warner, 1980. Clint Eastwood
   In this off-beat film, the hero befriends two down-on-their-luck snake dancers, Chief Big Eagle (Dan Vadis) and his wife, Lorraine Running Water (Sierra Pecheur). They become part of his contemporary traveling Wild West show.

The Legend of the Lone Ranger (Universal, 1981). William A. Fraker
   After villains kill his mother, the Lone Ranger grows up with Tonto's (Michael Horse) tribe, and the two young friends become blood brothers. Later the hero rejoins Tonto and they rescue President Grant from the evil Cavendish gang. A *Variety* critic notes that the "Indians are presented in a more modernist, revisionist light . . ." (20 May).

Never Cry Wolf (Buena Vista, 1984). Carroll Ballard
   The Innuit wiseman, Ootek (Zachary Litimangnag), befriends the hero and teaches him the wolf myths. Another Innuit character is Mike (Samson Jorah), a man who hunts wolves for a living.

Revolution (Warner, 1985). Hugh Hudson
   When the hero kills two Iroquois, the Huron tribe of Tosti (Skeeter Vaughn), Honehwah (Larry Sellers) and Ongwata (Graham Greene) make friends with him because the Iroquois are their enemies. They take the hero and his son to their camp and save the boy's life by cauterizing his wounded feet.

The Return of Josey Wales (Reel Movies Inter., 1987). Michael Parks
   When Mexican villains kill the hero's friend, Chato (Raphael Campos), he goes to Mexico, takes revenge, and

rescues an Apache girl who is about to be raped and hanged by an evil Mexican policeman.

Noble Natives of South America

The Emerald Forest (Embassy, 1985). John Boorman
Discussed on pps. 211–13, this film tells the story of a white boy who is adopted by an Amazonian tribe called the Invisible People. After marrying a young woman from the tribe, he becomes the savior of his people.

The Mission (Warner, 1986). Roland Joffe
A Catholic priest and a slave trader who is converted and joins the religious order grow to respect and love the local Guarani tribe led by a kind and peaceful chief (Asuncion Ontiveros). At the end, evil whites provoke the tribe and the two heroes die in the fighting.

Where the River Runs Black (MGM-UA, 1986). Christopher Cain
The son (Allesandro Rabelo) of a woman from an Amazonian tribe and a white priest grows up with the tribe. When villains kill his mother, he lives with dolphins until he is found and brought to an orphanage.

White Slave (Italian, 1986). Roy Garret
Captured by an Amazonian tribe, the heroine becomes friends with a young warrior, Umu Kai (Alvaro Gonzales), and is finally accepted by the tribe. At the end she leaves the tribe to revenge the murder of her parents.

Romances between Native American Women and White Men

Scalps (Italian, 1983). Werner Knox
A villain captures a Comanche woman, Yarin, and she escapes with the help of a farmer, with whom she falls in love. After the farmer wins a fight with a warrior betrothed

to Yarin, together they take revenge on the villain and then return to his farm.

Ikwe (National Film Board of Canada, 1986). Norma Bailey
Discussed on pps. 210–11, this film tells the story of Ikwe, an Ojibway woman who marries a white man and eventually leaves him and brings smallpox back to her tribe.

Hawken's Breed (MLG Properties, 1987). Charles B. Pierce
The hero falls in love with Spirit (Serene Hedin) and they fight hostile Shawnee warriors. After they are separated, the hero rescues her from an evil white man, and they live a long and happy life together.

See also *The Mountain Men* (1980) and *Emerald Forest* (1985).

Romances between Native American Men and White Women

Running Brave (Buena Vista, 1983). D. S. Everett (Donald Shebib)
Discussed on pps. 215–16, this film tells the story of Billy Mills, the mixed-blood Sioux who became an Olympic champion distance runner. While at the University of Kansas, Billy falls in love with a white woman and, after a period of separation, they marry before he wins the Olympic medal.

Second Thoughts (Independent, 1983). Lawrence Turman
The hippie hero, a mixed-blood named William Littlehorse (Craig Wasson), falls in love with a female lawyer and takes her captive when she tries to abort their child.

Romances between Native Americans

Windwalker (Pacific Inter., 1980). Keith Merrill
Discussed on pps. 206–8, this film tells the love story of Windwalker and Tashina, who are finally reunited in the

cloud spirit world after Windwalker rescues the family of his son.

Legend of Walks Far Woman (NBC, 1982). Mel Adamski

In this TV movie, Walks Far (Raquel Welch), daughter of a Blackfeet father and Sioux mother, joins a band of Sioux led by Left Hand Bull (Nick Ramus). After being captured by Grandfather (George Clutesi), she finally wins the respect of his family. Eventually, she marries Horses Ghost (Nick Mancuso), who loses his mental balance after being wounded in the Battle of Little Big Horn. Finally forced to kill him, Walks Far leaves the Sioux and lives with a mixed-blood trader. Other Native American characters are Big Lake (Branscome Richmond), Elk Hollering (Alex Kubis), Feather Earrings (Elroy Phil Casados), Many Scalps (Frank Salsedo) and Red Hoop (Hortensia Colorado).

Triumph of a Man Called Horse (Classic, 1983). John Hough

John Morgan's mixed-blood Sioux son, Koda (Michael Beck), falls in love with a Crow woman, Redwing (Ana de Sade), and together they fight villains who are after gold in the Black Hills and finally drive them from Sioux land.

The Mystic Warrior (Wolper, 1984). Richard Heffron

In this TV mini-series based on Ruth Beebe Hill's *Hanta Yo*, a young Sioux warrior, Ahbleza (Robert Beltran), falls in love with a beautiful woman from the tribe (Devon Erickson) and becomes the leader of the Sioux. A *Newsweek* critic quotes a comment by a Native American anthropologist on the script of the series: " 'It's still a bunch of Hollywood pap. They're still having us speak Hiawatha English, as if we really walked around saying "Many horses have I" ' " (21 May, 76).

Contemporary Native Americans

In this growing category, fewer of the films portray the Native American characters as complete victims of white society. Many of the positive characters struggle with the dominant society but finally discover their identities by a return to tribal values.

48 Hours (Paramount, 1983). Walter Hill
Billy Bear (Sonny Landham) and his white friend, a psychopathic killer, are the antagonists of the heroes.

Harold of Orange (Film in the Cities, 1984). Richard Wiese
Discussed on pps. 261–63, this film tells the story of Harold Sinseer and his merry trickster warriors who con grants for bizarre schemes from institutions.

Return of the Country (Independent, 1984). Bob Hicks
In this satire of traditional Hollywood images, a newly appointed female commissioner of the BIA is transported to a world where a Native American Bureau of White Affairs watches over white society.

Cold Journey (National Film Board of Canada, 1985). Martin Delfaco
This film tells the sad story of Buckley (Buckley Peta-wabano), a Canadian Cree teenager who doesn't fit in with his family or at a boarding school. An Ojibway, young John (John Yesno), befriends him and the Elder, old John (Chief Dan George), gives him advice, but in the end he can't find an identity that he can live with, and he freezes to death, alone.

Thunder Warrior (Trans World Enter., 1986). Larry Ludman (Frabrizio De Angelo)
Thunder (Mark Gregory), a Navajo, fights lawmen and owners of a construction company to stop them from destroying a tribal burial ground protected by a treaty signed by his grandfather.

Thunder Warrior 2 (Trans World Enter., 1987). Larry Ludman
Thunder (Mark Gregory) returns from prison to his Navajo homeland to investigate the murder of a local chief. Again he and his wife, Sheena (Karen Reel) must fight the corrupt police.

Finding Mary March (Malo Film Group, 1988). Ken Pittman
Micmac guide Ted Buchans (Rick Boland) searches for his wife, Bernadette (Tara Manual), who lost her way looking for the last of the Beothuk tribe, Mary March (Jacinta Cormier). Nancy George (Audrée Pelletier), a native photographer searching for her cultural roots, also is looking for the graves of the Beothuk.

Journey to Spirit Island (Seven Wonders Enter., 1988). Laszlo Pal
Discussed on pps. 259–61, this film tells the story of Maria, a teenage Native American who, along with two white friends, stops the development of the sacred island into a resort. With the special help of her grandmother, Maria finds her true tribal identity.

Powwow Highway (Hand Made Films, 1988). Jan Wieringa
Discussed on pps. 263–67, this film tells the story of Philbert Bono and Buddy Red Bow as they ride in an old Buick to rescue Buddy's sister. In the process, they both gain a new awareness of their Cheyenne traditional values.

War Party (Helmdale-Tri Star, 1989). Franc Roddam
Discussed on pps. 213–15, this film tells the story of three Blackfeet teenagers who get caught up in a deadly battle with the townspeople and the National Guard when a staged re-creation of a historical battle for a town festival turns into a bloody fight. At the end the three young warriors are hunted down and killed.

* * *

The few Westerns of this era continue the traditional images, while films like *Harold of Orange* (1984), *Journey to Spirit Island* (1988) and *Powwow Highway* (1988) create more empathetic images of contemporary Native American characters. However, with the release of *Dances With Wolves* in the first year of the next decade, the revisionist Western stages a comeback.

CHAPTER EIGHT

FILMS OF THE 1990S

A testimony to the persistence of the formulas, *Dances with Wolves* (1990), the most notable film of this decade, is very similar to *Broken Arrow*, the film which established Native Americans as viable central characters in Westerns at the beginning of the 1950s. In each a hero, who speaks to the audience in voice-overs, becomes friends with noble leaders of hostile tribes and falls in love with a woman from the tribe. In addition, not only are the Noble Red Man characters set against hostile members of their own tribe (Geronimo) or other more savage tribes (the Pawnee), but also their languages are either acknowledged or used in the film with subtitles.

Such echoes of earlier films are common in the self-conscious Hollywood Westerns of this decade. *Son of the Morning Star* (1991) parallels *They Died with Their Boots On* (1942) by establishing Crazy Horse as the antagonist of Custer, but it goes far beyond the original in its attention to historical detail and its focus on battles with the Plains tribes. *The Last of the Mohicans* (1992), a Western set in the East, follows the script of the 1936 version (see above, 65–67) but portrays Chingachgook, Uncas and Magua as more believable screen presences. The Canadian film, *Black Robe* (1991), also depicts life among the Eastern tribes but avoids the traditional Savage and Noble Red Man images of *The Last of the Mohicans* in its detached view of Algonquin, Iroquois and Huron cultures. Another Canadian film, *Clearcut* (1992), takes an equally detached and harsh look at a contemporary tribe struggling for its rights with a lumber company. Finally, the last of the representative films, *Thun-*

derheart (1992), deals with a similar, and equally violent, struggle on a contemporary Sioux reservation in South Dakota.

The noble ancestors of the characters in *Thunderheart* appear in *Dances With Wolves* (1990), the surprisingly popular Western that re-established national interest in Native Americans. A *Variety* critic comments on the film's characterizations: "the script by Michael Blake portrays the Sioux culture with appreciation, establishing within it characters of winning individuality and humor" (12 Nov.). Often seen in medium and close-up shots and given a significant amount of dialogue in their native language, the major Lakota characters do become memorable presences. The handsome and well-dressed Kicking Bird (Graham Greene) is a spiritual leader and philosopher who tries to learn about the hero, John Dunbar, so he can figure out the best course for his tribe in a world he knows is changing. And yet he is also a man who can be startled by the antics of Dunbar and is chided by his wife, Black Shawl (Tantoo Cardinal), when he is slow to tell Stands-with-a-Fist (Mary McDonnell) that her mourning period is over. The brash warrior, Wind-in-His-Hair (Rodney Grant) can unwittingly reveal fear or affection for Dunbar by speaking a little too loudly, and yet later calmly stand up for him in a conflict with another warrior. Chief Ten Bears (Floyd Red Crow Westerman) shows his quiet leadership as he cleverly handles conflicts between members of his tribe. And Stands-with-a-Fist, the white woman rescued from the Pawnee, is devoted to the ways of her adopted tribe and must struggle to translate Dunbar's English words into her now native Lakota tongue. Despite such distinguishing touches to the characters, the film as a whole portrays their tribe as Noble Red Men, especially as they are described in the Dunbar's journal/voice-over.

The voice-over narration of the hero highlights the nobility of the Sioux tribe (just in case the audience didn't get the point). For example, as he begins his journal, he tells that in his first contact with "wild Indians," the man he encountered (Kicking Bird) was "a magnificent looking fellow." Later, after the tribe accepts him, he notes that "the Indians" are not what he had heard, but noble and courteous. After the buffalo hunt while he lives with the tribe, he observes how dedicated the "Indians" are to each other. He says, "the only word that came to me was *harmony*." Finally, after the battle with the Pawnee, he praises the warriors of the tribe because they fight only to protect their families, not for motives of greed or conquest like the whites. This running commentary reduces the tribe to Noble Red Men, and finally, even the individualized main characters blend into this image.

The Pawnee antagonists of Dunbar's adopted tribe, on the other hand, have few distinguishing traits, other than the bloodthirsty ways which establish them as stock Savages. Their nameless leader (Wes Studi), a bare-chested warrior with mohawk-type hair and a sinister, fierce visage, leads his warriors against the muleskinner, whom they riddle with arrows, scalp and mutilate. Seen from low-angle and close-up shots that emphasize their fierceness, these warriors appear later as they prepare to attack the Lakota camp. Before that attack, suspense builds with shots of the Pawnee warriors stalking towards the camp, killing a dog, and going for the Lakota horses. However, the Lakota warriors, warned and armed by Dunbar, are ready for their savage enemies and quickly rout the main force. Then, in the climactic scene of the battle, they surround the leader of the Pawnee in a river and, though he resists with the fury of a wild animal, they close the circle, shoot him and smash his body with rifle butts. After the defeat of the savage Pawnee, their new antagonists are the soldiers who eventually capture the hero. As is typical in recent revisionist Westerns, these soldiers have the same evil traits as the traditional Savages, and, like the Pawnee, are routed when Dunbar's noble adopted tribe rescues him.

Though this rescue now means the tribe will be hunted by the soldiers, it is a typical gesture of gratitude and friendship that Noble Red Men make toward heroes such as Dunbar. Like John Morgan in *A Man Called Horse* (1970), Dunbar is both the savior of his adopted tribe and the reason for its vulnerability at the end. Also like Morgan and Tom Jeffords in *Broken Arrow* (1950), he and Stands-with-a-

Fist must ride off alone (the other two heroes had typically seen their Native American wives die, while Dunbar can leave with his white wife). Though *Dances with Wolves* never really transcends the images of the Savage and Noble Red Man, it does depart from earlier Westerns in the degree of its respect for the native languages. All of the dialogue of the native characters is in Lakota (with subtitles) and the hero learns the language of the people he grows to respect and love. The amount of time that the cast of whites and Native Americans of various tribes spent learning Lakota (from Doris Leader Charge and Albert White Hat of Sinte Gleska College) clearly imbued them with a feeling for Lakota life, a feeling most clearly expressed in the warmly lit teepee scenes. Like *Broken Arrow* forty years earlier, *Dances with Wolves* certainly does mark a step forward in the portrayal of Native American characters, unless, of course, the viewer happens to be of Pawnee heritage.

Son of the Morning Star (1991), a TV film that appeared a year after *Dances with Wolves*, also attempts to portray in even more detail the unique cultures of the Plains tribes. A *Newsweek* critic notes that "All their cultural trappings—costumes, makeup, weaponry, village life, even the glass beads they bartered—emerge from history through meticulously exact research" (4 Feb., 73). Based on the massively detailed biography of George A. Custer by Evan S. Connell, this film is the latest entry in a very long line of Custer movies, the most notable of which is *They Died with Their Boots On* (1942) (see above, 69–71). That film from the patriotic era of World War Two paid little attention to history as it glorified Custer; *Son of the Morning Star*, on the other hand, uses the research of its source and other contemporary accounts to tell not only Custer's story but also the parallel story of the Plains tribes. The same *Newsweek* critic comments on the depiction of these tribes: "As for the film's treatment of Native Americans, it's nothing if not politically correct" (4 Feb., 73). The film does strive to be "correct," not only in the portrayal of the Plains tribes but also in representing a female perspective, something lacking in most Westerns.

The primary technique used to accomplish these two

purposes is the voice-over. Though common in films sympathetic to Native American characters, the voice-overs of Libby Custer and a Cheyenne woman, Kate Big Head, are major structural elements in this film. For example, after the depiction of the Fetterman Massacre, the two narrators comment on the growing hostilities between the whites and the Plains tribes. Libby says, "The Indian war had begun. The war would end for me ten years later on that hill they call Custer's Last Stand." And then Kate says, "They call it Custer's Last Stand, but it was not his; it would be our last stand." Throughout the rest of the film, the contrasting voice-overs interpret from the white and Native American perspectives the wars between the cavalry and Plains tribes which ended for Libby Custer at Little Big Horn and for Kate Big Head at Wounded Knee.

Kate Big Head's narration and the accompanying dramatizations establish the main Lakota characters, Crazy Horse (Rodney Grant) and Chief Sitting Bull (Floyd Red Crow Westerman). Though these characters have no dialogue, the narrator provides sharp little historical vignettes. Kate Big Head tells the story of Crazy Horse from his youth to his death: as a boy named Curly before his warrior vision, as the strategist in the Fetterman battle, as a Lakota leader shot in the face for taking another man's wife, as a grieving father, as the warrior who joins Sitting Bull and leads the fatal attack on Custer, and, finally, as the fatally wounded victim of Little Big Man. As Crazy Horse dies, he is seen from a high angle with a circle of soldiers around him, a perspective very similar to that of Custer as he lies dead at Little Big Horn. As in *They Died with Their Boots On*, this film parallels the characters of Custer and Crazy Horse, but it also brings in other Native American leaders such as Sitting Bull, whom the narrator depicts within the details of his culture. After doing a sweat ceremony, Sitting Bull participates in the three-day Sun Dance, and only after these demanding and spiritually powerful rituals does he have a vision of success at Little Big Horn. After emphasizing the spirituality of both Sitting Bull and Crazy Horse in their preparation for battle, the narrator concludes: "We were strong; we were ready; we had to fight."

The Cheyenne narrator pictures even minor characters with individualizing details. For example, when Chief Red Cloud (Nick Ramus), known as a peace chief, visits Washington, he befuddles the politicians by sitting on the floor and speaking in his native tongue. Another example is Bloody Knife (Sheldon Peters Wolf Child), Custer's scout. Though Custer teases and bullies his Crow friend, he shows his true admiration when he gives Bloody Knife a medal. Two other instances occur during the Battle of Little Big Horn. In the heat of the fighting, the camera lingers on a young warrior who reluctantly takes his first scalp and then gets sick as he looks at it. And after the battle, two old Cheyenne women protect the body of Custer and then, as a gesture of friendship, put long needles in his ears and push them through his head so he will be able to hear the truth in the afterlife. Such details give a very different view of the battle and humanize the Native American characters in ways not even dreamed of in earlier versions of the Custer story such as *They Died with Their Boots On*.

The fact that *Son of the Morning Star* is a four-hour TV historical drama allows for considerable historical detail in its depiction of the Native American characters. The hectic pace of the new *The Last of the Mohicans* (1992) gives little chance for the development of even its major characters, Chingachgook (Russell Means), Uncas (Eric Schweig) and Magua (Wes Studi). At the beginning, the hero, Nathaniel/ Hawkeye, Chingachgook and Uncas, referred to as the "last of a vanishing people," run wildly through the forest as they hunt down an elk. When the hero shoots the animal, they converge on it and Chingachgook says in his native tongue (with subtitles), "We are sorry to kill you, brother. We do honor to your courage, speed and strength." This statement gives the audience a sense of the Mohican's tribal beliefs, and the use of the native languages throughout the film highlights that part of the culture in a positive way similar to that of *Dances with Wolves*. By contrast, in the 1936 *The Last of the Mohicans*, from which this film is adapted, the primary Native American characters, played by white actors, speak in the clipped "Movie Indian" version of English. In the new version, the two Mohicans and Magua, played by Native American actors, not only converse in their native tongues, but also in English and French. Despite this significant change, and other revisions in pace and historical setting, however,these characters in the new version are ultimately just more believable variations of the Noble Red Man and Savage images.

Chingachgook, played by former AIM activist Russell Means, is the most developed character in the new version in that he has some dialogue and is often seen in close-up shots. Dressed in a nice outfit and wearing nice long hair (the hero and his Mohican friends all have fine hairdos), he is a noble father figure and a skillful warrior, whose weapon is a large blade which can cut, chop or be thrown. In the first Huron ambush, he throws the blade with deadly accuracy, and at the end of the film he again uses it to hack apart Magua after the evil warrior kills Uncas. Though his character has some new trappings of historical accuracy and a vivid screen presence, it is basically as flat as the one in the 1936 version of the film. At the end of the film, when he stands next to Hawkeye and Cora and gives his little speech about being the last of the Mohicans, the audience doesn't have much reason to care about his words.

The character of Uncas is even more flat, given that he has almost no dialogue and little importance in the plot. In the novel and the 1936 film version, Uncas falls in love with Cora Monro and their relationship is a significant subplot. In the new version, whether to keep the focus on the romance of Hawkeye or to avoid the issue of miscegenation, this relationship is just hinted at. Uncas becomes just an attractive part of the setting, often seen in lingering close-up shots. Like his father, Chingachgook, he is a powerful screen presence, but little is ever revealed about his past or about the unique culture of his tribe. When he dies at the hand of Magua, the audience has little reason for grief or sense of what is lost in his passing.

Magua, on the other hand, is more developed and sympathetic than the evil character of the 1936 version. The first view of Magua is a long shot in the shadows at the back of a room, followed by a close-up as he speaks in his native tongue and then in English. Though he looks the part of a fierce warrior with his mostly bare chest and Mohawk type hair, he also proves to be an intelligent and skilled manipulator of his enemies. Portrayed as a character eloquent in his native language as well as in those of his white enemies and allies, he is considerably more eloquent than the Magua character in the 1936 version. The new version also builds more sympathy for his character by giving him a stronger motive for his vengeance on Colonel Monro, whose allies, the Mohawk, destroyed Magua's village, killed his children and took him as a slave. Though this motivation makes his desire for vengeance more believable, his overreaching revenge itself is that of a Savage: he cuts out Colonel Monro's heart, forces Alice to jump off a cliff, and finally slits the throat of Uncas. When Chingachgook takes revenge on him, the audience knows that another Savage character has received his just deserts.

Because both *The Last of the Mohicans* and *Dances with Wolves* follow the Hollywood pattern of the historical romance which subordinates all characterization to the development of the white hero and his love affair, their Native American characters still need to be variations of the Noble Red Man or Savage images associated with this formula. Such is not the case with *Son of the Morning Star* or the recent Canadian film, *Black Robe* (1991), which focuses on Eastern tribes in a way very different from Hollywood films like *The Last of the Mohicans*.

Black Robe establishes the profound differences between the culture of the whites and that of the Algonquins, Iroquois and Huron tribes. A *New Yorker* critic notes that "the movie's portrayal of the Indians' mysticism is straightforward, unromanticized; it has an anthropological detachment" (18 Nov., 120). In fact, the portrayal of the religious beliefs is just part of a generally detached view of both cultures as radically different. From the beginning, the Australian director of the film cross-cuts between the cultures with matching shots of a Native American and a white man dressing themselves to the sounds of their contrasting music. Then he juxtaposes similar high-angle shots of a wigwam and a European church. Played against this Old World versus New World visual background are the central conflicts of the Jesuit missionaries and the tribes and the struggle among the tribes themselves for supremacy. The action begins when the missionary, Laforgue, and his young friend, Daniel, accompany their guides, a small group of Algonquin led by Chomina (August Schellenberg), to find the Huron. When the rigid Laforgue refuses to give the Algonquins any of the goods he is bringing to trade with the Huron, and Daniel falls in love with Chomina's daughter, Annuka (Sandrine Holt), the differences between the cultures and the uniqueness of Annuka emerge.

From her first appearance in the film, the camera singles out Annuka with a series of close-ups that establish her as a significant presence, and, indeed, her character is very different from the traditional noble or savage female image. She has a completely unromantic and honest view of the physical and spiritual realities of life in the wilderness. When she notices that Daniel is watching her (many shots of her are from his perspective) and realizes her attraction to him, she accepts his furtive kiss, kisses him back and makes love with him simply because they both feel the urge. The naturalness of their act is punctuated by the reaction of Laforgue, who sees them and then flogs himself to drive away his feelings of lust. In fact, Annuka sees the chastity of missionaries as unnatural and evil; she says, "Black Robes are demons; they never have sex." Not only does she accept the physical realities of life, but she also lives by the spiritual realities of her tribal beliefs, which include an afterlife very different from that of the missionaries. She shows the power of her beliefs in the last moments she spends with her father as he prepares to die. Because she knows that he will die in the place he dreamed of earlier and thus enter the afterlife, she accepts his death quietly. Throughout the film, Annuka is a unique, unpredictable character who reveals the "otherness" of her Algonquin tribe.

Like his daughter, Chomina is a strong character who sees life in a very different way from the white men he has pledged to guide to the Huron tribe. He, however, as a leader of his tribe and an ally of the French, has more difficult decisions than his daughter. After having a dream that he will die at the end of his journey, he decides to consult the holy man, Mestigoit (Yvan Labelle), who tells him to leave the company of the demon missionary. This advice, plus his disapproval of his daughter's romance and the anger of his people at Laforgue, convince him to leave the Black Robe. Not long afterwards, however, Chomina's sense of honor and his political alliance to the French move him to return with his family to find Laforgue. This decision turns out to be a tragic one because, upon his return, the fierce Iroquois ambush his family, killing his wife (Tantoo Cardinal) and capturing him, his children and the two white men. After the captives suffer a cruel beating as the Iroquois make them run the gauntlet, Chomina must also watch the murder of his son.

During the night before the Iroquois will torture and kill their captives, Annuka again displays her practical strength of character by offering herself to the Iroquois guard and then knocking him out after he mounts her. Though this courageous act of his daughter enables them to escape from the Iroquois, Chomina, weakened by the ordeal, contracts pneumonia and dies as predicted in his dream of a Raven (death) and a snow-covered island. Thus, though Chomina's decision to return to Laforgue is honorable on one level, it does lead to the death of everyone in his family except Annuka. After the death of her father, she and Daniel know they must escape the influence of the missionary so that they can have a chance to make a new life in the wilderness.

The destructive influence of the Black Robe on the Algonquin family is recapitulated for a whole tribe when Laforgue finally reaches the Huron village. These people, who are decimated by the fever, are willing to go against their religion and be baptized in order to drive away the evil spirits of their disease. Though the tormented Laforgue knows that baptism will not help them, he goes through with the ceremony. On that ironic note, the film ends with an epilogue, which explains that after the Jesuits left, the Christianized Huron were eventually conquered by the fierce Iroquois.

Another Canadian film, *Clearcut* (1991), takes an equally

hard look at a similar conflict between white and Native American cultural values in a contemporary setting. A critic from the Canadian magazine, *Maclean's*, compares the two films: "Neither *Black Robe* nor *Clearcut* is a movie in the Hollywood mould: they are too dark, too disturbing and painfully lacking in redemption. They are adventures in Canadian masochism" (7 Oct., 1991, 72). Whether or not their view is masochistic, these two films—and *Ikwe* (1986) and *Cold Journey* (1985)—reveal a grim, unromantic attitude toward the conflicts between white and Native American cultures quite unlike that of American films. Of all these Canadian films, *Clearcut* (1991) pushes audiences farthest into the real and potential violence of such conflicts. The central character of the film is an avenging spirit named Arthur (Graham Greene), who represents the other danger-ously excessive side of traditional trickster spirits. Though Arthur has the same verbal sense of humor as the trickster-type characters of Philbert Bono in *Powwow Highway* (1988) or Harold Sinseer in *Harold of Orange* (1984), he has come for revenge and blood, not to trick and befuddle the white man. Wilf (Floyd Red Crow Westerman), the Elder of the Ojibway tribe whose land is being destroyed by the clearcutting, tells a story to the tribe's white lawyer which explains the origin and danger of Arthur. In the old days an avenging spirit "stained the ground with the blood" of the tribe's enemies until he had to be stopped. Wilf tells the story to the lawyer because he realizes that Arthur is not only the ancient spirit but also the personification of the lawyer's own frustration and anger, which only he can ultimately stop.

The film begins with the lawyer witnessing the police beating up members of the tribe at the site of the clearcut-ting. A classic liberal who has failed in all his lawsuits against the lumber company, the lawyer can only seethe with ineffectual anger as he watches the violence. Wilf senses his problem and invites him to participate in a traditional sweat ceremony, to "purify yourself and to find out what you really want." After having a vision of blood and seeing the face of Arthur during the sweat, the lawyer realizes that "someone has to pay" for what is happening to the tribal land. Shortly thereafter, he meets the mysterious Arthur and suggests, tongue-in-cheek, that they could solve the problem of the clearcutting by blowing up the lumber mill and skinning the manager alive. The lawyer can only joke about his outrage and desire for revenge because at his core he abhors violence and believes in the sanctity of the law. Arthur, however, has come to act out the feelings of the lawyer. For example, at his apartment, he is burning with frustration because he cannot stop the people next door from making noise; then Arthur arrives and solves the problem by threatening them with a large commando knife and then wrapping duct tape around their arms and mouths. When he's finished, Arthur, who, unlike his name-sake, believes not in chivalry but in vengeance, smiles at the shocked lawyer and says, "Now let's do some real work."

The "real work" is vengeance on the owner of the lumber mill. After Arthur kidnaps the lumberman and takes him into the wilderness, the lawyer, who is now also his pris-oner, becomes horrified when he realizes that Arthur is going to take his earlier joke seriously and torture and kill the man. Arthur, whose dialogue takes on a crazy humor which plays on the movie stereotypes, says, "I could scalp him and be a real Indian. I should be a real Indian." Later, when the lawyer confronts him as he skins the lumberman's leg, Arthur says, "I am your friendly neighborhood cruel Indian," and then reminds the lawyer of white cruelty towards his people such as that of soldiers who cut off the breasts of Navajo women and played catch with them. When two policemen come and Arthur kills one and wounds the other, he says to the wounded man, "It's the Indian guy that's supposed to be dead, that's what you think," before he kills him with a wooden war club. As Arthur's actions become more and more violent, Wilf must remind the lawyer that his anger is real and "someone must pay." He must also must warn the lawyer that, like the ancient avenging spirit, Arthur has be stopped.

After the three men arrive at a sacred place with ancient pictographs, Arthur, who is becoming more and more troubled, forces the men to do a sweat ceremony, "to purify ourselves for what is coming next," and then finally provokes the lawyer into a violent fight during which he loses his glasses (the last emblem of his civilized self) and shoots Arthur. Last seen in an extreme close-up before he sinks into the water from which he came, Arthur gives the lawyer a look that says, "now you understand that I am the dark part of your own anger." After the disappearance of Arthur, the lawyer finally understands the identity of an Ojibway girl, Polly (Tia Smith), whom he saw at the beginning smoking a cigarette and now sees, upon his return to the village, wearing the medallion of Arthur. He knows the ancient spirit can change shapes and be an innocent child or come back as a bloody adversary whenever his tribe or mother earth is threatened.

The violence in *Clearcut* is excessive in parts, but it is only a small part of the film's passionate and somewhat heavy-handed commitment to expressing the uniqueness of the tribe's ceremonies and its feeling for the land. Like the lawyer, the audience learns a new mythology of the environment, a new sense of the evil forces released by violence to the environment. This environmental theme, in fact, is common in such recent films dealing with native people as *Emerald Forest* (1985), *Journey to Spirit Island* (1988), *Powwow Highway* (1988) and *Medicine Man* (1992). The last of the representative films, *Thunderheart* (1992) continues this environmental theme.

Though a more glossy Hollywood production than *Clearcut*, *Thunderheart* also focuses on the struggle of a tribe to preserve both its traditional values and the resources of its land. The film is directed by an Englishman, Michael Apted, who a year before had made the documentary, *Incident at Oglala* (1991), an in-depth (90-min.) exploration of AIM, the killing of two FBI agents at Pine Ridge Sioux Reservation, and the trial of Leonard Peltier. This experience obviously taught Apted not only about the conflicts between traditional and modern values on contemporary reservations, but also about the beauties and mysteries of the South Dakota landscape. A *Variety* critic comments that *Thunderheart* "takes a poignant, witty and often deeply moving journey into the Indian community to reveal the secrets of the Badland landscapes, the messages carried by animals and the magic of the ancient beliefs and ceremonies, all against the backdrop of historical oppression" (30 Mar., 77). The audience makes this "journey" into Lakota culture with Ray Lavoi, an FBI agent of mixed-blood Sioux heritage, as he finds his native identity through interaction with tribal policeman Walter Crow Horse (Graham Greene), traditional Elder Grandpa Sam Reaches (Chief Ted Thin Elk), and radical leaders Maggie Eagle Bear (Sheila Tousey) and Jimmy Looks Twice (John Trudell).

When Ray Lavoi first meets Walter Crow Horse they are almost a complete study in opposites. Ray is dressed in the classic FBI uniform, a dark suit, white shirt, striped tie and expensive dark glasses, while Crow Horse, the tribal policeman, wears faded jeans, denim jacket, cowboy hat and cheap sunglasses. Ray Lavoi responds with the trained intensity of the FBI agent as he fails to recognize Crow Horse as a law officer and subdues him violently. As he is being held to the ground, Crow Horse, on the other hand, reacts with his typical laid back humor when he says, "You guys got off on the wrong exit. You looking for Mount Rushmore?" He also tells Ray that he has to "make the journey." The differences between these characters start to disappear, however, when Ray Lavoi begins to take the same "journey" towards his Lakota identity that Crow Horse took earlier.

Later, when Crow Horse meets Ray at a powwow, they are still at odds, even though they are beginning to respect each other as investigators. Crow Horse tells Ray about his childhood, during which he, like Ray, was ashamed of his Native American heritage: "When we played cowboys and Indians, I was always Gary Cooper." He then explains that the ARM (Aboriginal Rights Movement—a fictional AIM) radical warriors and their spiritual leader, Grandpa Sam, helped him to take pride in his Lakota heritage. After this exchange, the two men go to Grandpa Sam's trailer and have one more fight before the old man comes out and berates them for "acting like a couple of old women," and then invites them in to watch TV. This breaks the tension, cements their friendship and marks the beginning of their fight against the evil forces of the FBI and the goons of the tribal council chairman. A sign of their connection to Grandpa Sam is the fact that Crow Horse now wears the Ray Ban sunglasses which Ray traded to Grandpa Sam, who then traded them to Crow Horse.

As with Crow Horse, Ray and Jimmy Looks Twice (played by former AIM spokesman John Trudell) are at first antagonists who meet when the FBI agents interrupt the sweat ceremony to apprehend Jimmy. Again, after Ray accepts Grandpa Sam as his Elder, he begins to understand that Jimmy is a new kind of warrior who uses the old beliefs to protect the environment and heritage of their people. Later, when Ray sees Jimmy at Grandpa Sam's trailer, Jimmy explains his fight against the evil government forces: "They have to kill us because they can't break our spirit. . . . Its in our DNA, you have to do what the old man (Grandpa) says . . . there is a way to live with the earth—and a way not to live with the earth; we choose the way of earth—it's about power, Ray!" Just before this scene, Ray receives the same message from the other ARM leader, Maggie Little Bear, a character to whom he is also drawn as he accepts his Lakota identity.

As with Crow Horse and Jimmy Looks Twice, Ray has several angry exchanges with Maggie before he gains her respect. Their relationship changes when Ray, who is visiting Maggie's grandmother, risks his life during an attack on Maggie's house by reservation goons to take her wounded son to the hospital. Later, when they meet for the last time, they share an intimate conversation in which Ray admits he knew his Native American father and says, "I was ashamed of him so I buried him, but my own people dug him up, my own people." Then, after refusing to help him identify the killer (though she later does), she explains to him that the real power is the river, which she knows is being poisoned, and the other natural resources of the reservation. As she and Ray part, with the hint of romantic feelings, she calmly tells him she is going to "the source" and that he will have to do the same. The "source" turns out to be Red Rock Table where the forces of evil are preparing to mine uranium. In that lonely place, Ray and Crow Horse find her body. (The mystery of her murder parallels that of AIM member Anna

Mae Aquash, and is only one of numerous parallels between the characters of the film and historical figures.)

With the death of Maggie and the imprisonment of Jimmy, the responsibility to carry on their fight falls on Ray and Crow Horse. By this time, Ray has been prepared by several dream-visions of his ancestors, one of whom Grandpa Sam tells him is Thunderheart, a warrior who fought at the Wounded Knee Battle. With this realization of his warrior spirit, Ray joins his friend, Crow Horse, to take on the FBI and the reservation goons, whom they lead on a wild chase until cornered at an area called "the stronghold." However, just as they are about to be killed, Grandpa Sam and other traditional people, seen on the bluff behind the heroes in sweeping low-angle shots, rescue them and stop the government's evil plan to destroy the reservation with the uranium mines. Though quite stirring, this rescue is pure Hollywood and quite a contrast to the more ambiguous and realistic ending of *Clearcut*.

Despite this, *Thunderheart* is certainly the strongest of the Hollywood films at giving an empathetic view of the sense of humor and respect for tribal rituals and traditions that help Native Americans survive on contemporary reservations. Grandpa Sam, wonderfully acted by Ted Thin Elk in the tradition of Chief Dan George, has a trickster sense of humor in his appreciation of Mr. Magoo on TV and in his trading of objects with Ray, which is humorous at first and then significant at the end when Ray gives him his Rolex and, with a laugh, he gives Ray the sacred pipe, a symbol of his new warrior identity. The other character who has a distinctive sense of humor throughout the film is Walter Crow Horse. For example, when Ray tells him about his dream, Crow Horse teases his new friend: "You had yourself a vision. Most people wait a lifetime, but along comes an instant Indian, with a fucking Rolex and new pair of shoes, and a goddamned FBI man to top it all off, and he has a vision!" Even Ray, after he sheds his FBI demeanor, shows some humor when he calls the stray dog he acquires Jimmy, as a joke on that character's reputation as a shape changer. In addition to the humor, the valuing of tribal tradition can be seen in Ray's learning of his new identity through an acceptance of visions and the rituals of the warrior, a theme that is central to the independent films discussed in the final chapter.

IMAGES OF THE NOBLE RED MAN

The following films, with a few exceptions among the revisionist Westerns, all employ variations of the Noble Red Man image. Though Savage character types appear as foils to the noble characters, the stereotypical Savage character type has disappeared in this politically correct early part of the period.

Friendship and Loyalty

Dances with Wolves (Orion, 1990). Kevin Costner
   Discussed on pps. 225–27, this immensely popular film tells the story of the friendship between the hero and the noble tribe of Ten Bears, Kicking Bird and Wind-in-His Hair. The opposing savage tribe are the Pawnee.

Showdown at Williams Creek (Kootenai Productions, 1991). Allan Kroeker
   While the Metis, Canadian mixed-bloods, nurse the hero back to health, he falls in love with one of their women and marries her. Meanwhile, villains sell liquor to more hostile tribes who then massacre white settlers. In this way, the film establishes the contrast between the noble Metis and other savage tribes.

Last of His Tribe (HBO Pictures, 1992). Harry Hook
   Ishi (Graham Greene), the last member of the Yahi tribe of California, is taken into the home of an anthropology professor who eventually wrote a well-known book about him. Though the professor learns Ishi's language and helps

him adapt to white society, he acts as though he owns Ishi as an object for study and never appreciates him or the story of his tribe on a human level, as Ishi tells him in the film: "You put Ishi in a book, not in your heart." Only after Ishi's death does the professor realize how he had failed him as a friend and how deeply he had cared for him.

The Last of the Mohicans (20th Century-Fox, 1992). Michael Mann
    Discussed on pps. 229–31, this film follows the script of the 1936 version in which the romance of the hero and the daughter of the British Colonel is the center of the plot. The hero's friends and only family are the noble Mohicans, Chingachgook and Uncas. The opposing savage character is Magua, the leader of hostile Hurons.

Legend of Wolf Mountain (Majestic Entertainment, 1992). Craig Clyde
    In this children's movie, the ancient spirit of the wolf who lives on the mountain takes the form of a Native American (Don Shanks) and protects some children who are being pursued by escaped convicts. Near the end of the film, the Native American spirit man gives one of the kids a histori-cal sketch of his people and their attitudes towards the environment.

Miracle in the Wilderness (Turner Pictures, 1992). Kevin James Dobson
    In this TV Christmas movie, the hostile Blackfeet of Chief Many Horses (Sheldon Peters Wolf Child) capture a white family living in the wilderness. After being taken to the Blackfeet village, the young mother tells the Nativity story to the chief and his tribe, complete with cuts to visuals of a Native American family acting out the story. The Nativity story pacifies the chief to the point that he banishes his hostile son Grey Eye (Steve Reevis) and decides not to fight the cavalry who are prepared to attack his tribe. This film must be seen to be believed—and most likely even that won't help.

Call of the Wild (Kraft Premier TV, 1993). Alan Smithee

Charlie (Gordon Tootoosis), a Tlingit, makes friends with the young hero and teaches him the values of his tribe. Their strong friendship continues to the end when hostile Yeehat warriors attack them and kill the hero.

Free Willy (Warner, 1993). Simon Wincer

Randolf (August Schellenberg), a Haida who cares for Willy, the killer whale, befriends the rebellious young hero. After teaching him the Haida myth of Orcas, the killer whale, Randolf encourages the boy's affection for Willy and eventually helps him free the whale.

Maverick (Warner, 1994). Richard Donner

Joseph (Graham Greene), who leads a rambling band of warriors, is a friend of the hero. A con-man (or trickster) himself, Joseph helps Maverick to hoodwink his adversaries by having his men pretend to be hostile warriors. In the process of this trick, and another one in which he lets a Russian nobleman shoot at an "Indian," he manages to out-do his friend in the business of conning. Joseph also offers some snide comments about the film-inspired stereotypes of his people.

Savage Land (Savage Land Productions, 1994). Dean Hamilton

In this children's film, a small group of Cherokee, led by Skyano (Graham Greene), protects two youngsters from villains posing as Native Americans. Skyano befriends the boy and tells him about Cherokee history and culture. At the end, the friendly and good-natured Cherokee return the children to their father.

Revisionist Histories of Native Americans

Though such revisionist films have appeared in the earlier periods, this type becomes more dominant in the 1990s.

Black Robe (Alliance Entertainment, 1991). Bruce Beresford

Discussed on pps. 231–33, this film is based on a Brian

Moore novel of the same name, which in turn is drawn from *The Jesuit Relations*. The missionary who strives to convert the native peoples really sets up the destruction of a friendly Algonquin family and the Huron tribe, who are eventually conquered by the fierce Iroquois. Neither the friendly nor the hostile tribes, however, conform to the Noble Red Man or Savage images.

Son of the Morning Star (Republic, 1991). Mike Robe
    Discussed on pps. 227–29, this TV movie, based on Evan S. Connell's historical study of the same name, tells the story of Custer and the Plains tribes he fought. Custer's story is narrated by his wife, Libby, while the story of Crazy Horse, the central Lakota character, is paralleled to that of Custer by a female Cheyenne voice-over narrator, Kate Big Head.

The Broken Chain (Turner Pictures, 1993). Lamont Johnson
    Second in the series of Turner Network movies about Native Americans, this film tells the story of the Iroquois Confederacy and focuses on the life of Thayendanegea or Joseph Brant (Eric Schweig), a Mohawk warrior and the voice-over narrator throughout the film. The foil to Joseph Brant is Lohaheo (J. C. Whiteshirt), his more traditional brother who has visions of the Peace Maker of the Iroquois (Graham Greene) and refuses to fight other tribes in the Confederacy. Offering guidance to these young warriors are the traditional Mohawk chiefs (played by Floyd Red Crow Westerman and Wes Studi) and the council of clan women led by Mother Goshina (Buffy St. Marie). As the young men mature and gain stature in the tribe, they both find devoted wives and become fathers. Then, after the death of Lohaheo at the hands of the American revolutionaries, Joseph joins the British and thus contributes to the disintegration of the Confederacy. At the end, an epilogue explains that the Iroquois Confederacy still exists in a new contemporary form.

Geronimo (Turner Pictures, 1993). Roger Young
    The first in the series of Turner Network movies and

documentaries about Native Americans, this film chronicles the life of Geronimo (Joseph Runningfox) to show that his rebelliousness was fully justified. As an old man visiting Washington, Geronimo tells his story to a young Apache and becomes a voice-over narrator while the film fades back to his youth. After he wins the hand of the woman he loves, the Mexicans attack his village and kill his wife, child and mother. Then his chief, Mangas (Nick Ramus), chooses him to convince Cochise (August Schellenberg) to join his band and punish the Mexicans. Later, Geronimo marries the daughter of Cochise, and, even though U.S. soldiers kill his new wife, he agrees to honor the treaty Cochise makes with General Howard. After the death of Cochise, the Apaches are forced onto the San Carlos Reservation, and Geronimo finally escapes to the mountains. After he finishes his story, the old Geronimo meets the President, who comments at the end, "I would have done exactly as he."

Geronimo: An American Legend (Columbia, 1993). Walter Hill
In this film narrated by a sympathetic young soldier, Geronimo (Wes Studi) is a fierce but dignified warrior. After some of the older Apache such as Nano (Rino Thunder) opt for peace, Geronimo decides to fight and eludes the soldiers of both Generals Crook and Miles. Accompanied by Apache scout Chato (Steve Reevis), the young voice-over narrator and an honorable lieutenant pursue Geronimo, Mangas (Rodney Grant) and his small band into Mexico. Finally the lieutenant finds them and Geronimo decides on surrender as a way of saving his people from more suffering. In the scenes where the Apaches are together, such as in the train car at the end, they speak their native language (with subtitles). Throughout the film, Geronimo is an eloquent character whose presence is enhanced by a series of low-angle and close-up shots.

Noble Native South Americans

Amazon (Villeafa Films Production, 1991). Mika Kaurismaki
In another film about the destruction of the rain forests,

the hero, Kari, a Finn, falls in love with Paola (Rae Dawn Chong), a teacher in a remote Amazon village who tries to instill a strong sense of ecology in her students. After being nursed back to health by a noble native tribe, Kari returns to the village of Paola.

At Play in the Fields of the Lord (Universal, 1992). Hector Babeno

Louis Moon (Tom Berenger), a mixed-blood Cheyenne pilot, leaves the group of whites he is guiding and joins an Amazonian tribe who at first thinks he is Kisu, an evil sky god. After learning their language (the native tongue with subtitles) and being adopted by the tribe, he infects them with a deadly flu when he comes upon a beautiful woman from the tribe bathing and kisses her. Unlike the adopted heroes in *The Emerald Forest* (1985) or *A Man Called Horse* (1970), the hero, and the missionaries he brings, destroy rather than save the tribe.

Medicine Man (Hollywood Pictures, 1992). John McTiernan

A doctor living with a noble Amazonian tribe, whose language he knows and with whom he has a good-natured friendship, finds a flower and insects which promise a cure for cancer. Near the end, however, road builders burn the village and destroy his research. Despite this outrage to the environment, the doctor follows the Medicine Man (Angelo Barra Moreira) and the tribe deeper into the jungle to continue his research and enjoy the company of his female colleague.

Romances between Native American Women and White or Black Men

Spirit of the Eagle (Queens Cross Productions, 1990). Boon Collins

Villains capture the son of the hero and sell him to the tribe of Running Wolf (Don Shanks) and the beautiful Watana (Jeri Arredondo). Aided by his pet eagle, the hero finds his son and is wounded in his attempt to rescue him. Then Watana comes to his rescue, nurses him back to health, and falls in love with him. Finally, the hero, his boy, Watana and the eagle (who also had been wounded) live happily ever after.

Shadow Hunter (Republic, 1992). J. S. Cardone

A burnt-out Los Angeles policeman goes to the Navajo Reservation to pursue a violent witch-skinwalker named Two Bear (Benjamin Bratt). As he searches for the killer, he falls in love with Ray Whitesinger (Angela Alvarado), a beautiful Navajo tracker who accompanies him, along with tribal policeman, Frank Tosoni (Robert Beltran). When Two Bear captures Ray, the hero almost loses his life before he finally kills the bloodthirsty skinwalker and rescues Ray. At the end, he agrees to live on the reservation with Ray. Other Native American characters are the tribal doctor (Geraldine Keams), Begay (Tim Sampson) and Nez (George Agular).

Silent Tongue (A Belo/Alive Production, 1992). Sam Shepard

In this twisted tale of exploitation and revenge, a white man rapes a Kiowa woman named Silent Tongue (Tantoo Cardinal) and they eventually have two daughters. The greedy, drunken white man trades his oldest daughter, Awbonnie (Sheila Tousey) to another man and she dies while giving birth. Then the ghost of Awbonnie haunts all her tormentors, including her younger sister, Velada (Jeri Arredondo). At the end, the man who bought her burns her body and her agonized spirit is freed. Finally, Silent Tongue gains her revenge when her tribe captures the man who raped her.

Posse (Polygram, 1993). Mario Van Peebles

In this film which varies the typical subject matter of the Western by focusing on the history of African Americans in the West, the black hero falls in love with his older black friend's mixed-blood daughter, Lana (Salli Richardson).

Where the Rivers Flow North (Caledonia Pictures, 1993). Jay Craven

In remote Vermont, a rugged, fiercely proud old lumberman and his female Native American companion, Bangor (Tantoo Cardinal), fight developers who want to build a dam that will flood the area. After the old man drowns, Bangor survives as best she can. With superb acting, Tantoo Cardinal infuses in the character a quiet mixture of humor, vulnerability, strength, and dignity.

White Fang 2: Myth of the White Wolf (Walt Disney Pictures, 1994). Ken Olin

After being rescued by Lily Joseph (Charmaine Craig), the niece of the Haida chief, Moses Joseph (Al Harrington), the hero is seen by the tribe as the spirit of the White Wolf. With the help of Lily, he saves the tribe from starvation by overcoming villains who have blocked the migration of the caribou. By the end, the hero and Lily are deeply in love and will live together with the tribe. Other members of the tribe are Katrin Joseph (Victoria Racimo) and Peter Joseph (Anthony Michael Ruivar). In a comment that could apply to a number of 1990s films, a *Variety* critic notes that the film's "screenplay keeps the narrative simple and politically correct. The Haida are depicted as noble, compassionate and intelligent, while just about every white man. . .is a rotten, duplicitous exploiter." (18 Apr.)

See also *Amazon* (1991), *Black Robe* (1991) and *Showdown at Williams Creek* (1991).

Romances between Native American Men and White Women

Cheyenne Warrior (New Horizons, 1994). Mark Griffiths

After villains kill a white woman's husband and wound Soars Like a Hawk (Pato Hoffmann), the woman finds Hawk and nurses him back to health. To show his gratitude, Hawk brings the tribal midwife, who helps the woman through a difficult delivery. He also protects her from hostile members of his tribe led by his brother, Crazy Buffalo (Frankie Avina). By the end, Hawk and the woman have fallen in love, but, finally, they decide to separate and live with their own people.

See also *The Last of the Mohicans* (1992).

Romances between Native Peoples

Map of the Human Heart (Miramax Films, 1993). Vincent Ward
   In a film concerned with the suffering and displacement of native Canadian peoples, an Innuit named Arvik (Jason Scott) falls in love with a Metis (mixed-blood), Albertine (Anne Parillaud). After an intense relationship as teenagers, they are separated for years. Finally, they meet again during World War II and have a child together, only to be separated again forever. Their whole story is seen in a flashback from the perspective of an aged and sick Arvik.

See also *At Play in the Fields of the Lord* (1992), *Spirit Rider* (1992), *Geronimo* (1993), *The Broken Chain* (1993) and *Lakota Woman* (1994)

Contemporary Native Americans

The Lightning Incident (USA Movie, 1991). Michael Switzer
   Years after her mother and Native American father had conducted an experiment in South America which left all the women of a tribe barren, the remaining members of the tribe, who have become a voodoo cult, take the baby of the couple's daughter (Nancy McKeon). Aided by a Native American doctor (Tantoo Cardinal), the young mother interprets her voodoo-inspired dreams, goes to South America and rescues her baby.

Clearcut (Northern Arts, 1992). Richard Bugajsky
   Discussed on pps. 233–36, this film tells the story of Arthur, the personification of an ancient Ojibway avenging spirit and the dark side of a liberal white lawyer. While

lumbermen destroy the forests of the Ojibway, Arthur takes his revenge on the owner of the lumber mill.

Salmonberries (Independent, 1991). Percy Adlon
   In a remote Eskimo village, Kotzebue (k. d. lang), a troubled mixed-blood Eskimo searches for her identity. In the process, she falls in love with a German librarian in the village and together they find the truth of their pasts.

Shadow of the Wolf (Trans Film, 1992). Jacques Dorfmann
   In this story of conflict between whites and the Innuit tribe, a Canadian policeman searches for Agaguk (Lou Diamond Phillips), an angry young Innuit who has murdered an evil trader, rebelled against his father, Kroomak (Toshiro Mifune), and escaped into the frozen wilderness with his beloved Igyook (Jennifer Tilly). After his father kills the policeman, Agaguk returns to his village. At the end, Kroomak gives himself up to the Mounties to save his son. Then, as he flies away with the authorities in a plane, he turns into a hawk and escapes. This Canadian film is not quite up to the quality of *Clearcut* or *Black Robe*.

Spirit Rider (Owl TV and Credo Group, 1992). Michael Scott
   In this Canadian film, a rebellious young Ojibway, Jesse Threebears (Herbie Barnes) struggles with his identity after being forced to return to his Reserve and live with his grandfather, Joe Moon (Gordon Tootoosis). After falling in love with Camilla (Michelle St. John), he takes up horseback riding and suffers the insults of Paul (Adam Beach), his rival for her affection. In a climactic horse race, he and Paul become friends, and he finds strength in his tribal identity. Other people at the Reserve, Albert (Tom Jackson), Marilyn (Tantoo Cardinal) and Vern (Graham Greene), also support Jesse in his struggles.

Thunderheart (Tri Star, 1992). Michael Apted
   Discussed on pps. 236–40, this film tells the story of a mixed-blood FBI agent who goes to a reservation in South Dakota to solve a murder and ends up finding his Lakota identity. When he discovers the government is involved in

the murder and a plot to mine uranium on the reservation, he joins tribal policeman Walter Crow Horse and traditional Elder Grandpa Sam Reaches to stop the plot and preserve the environment of the reservation.

Cooperstown (Turner Pictures, 1993). Charles Haid

This TV movie tells the story of two professional baseball players, Harry, a white man, and Raymond Maracle (Graham Greene), a Mohawk. Harry, now an old man, finds out that Raymond, who died many years ago, has been chosen for the Baseball Hall of Fame. Though he has resented Raymond for years, the two men relive and reaffirm their friendship when the ghost of Raymond appears and the two of them take the trip to Cooperstown.

The Dark Wind (Seven Arts, 1992). Errol Morris

This is the first film adaptation of the popular Tony Hillerman mystery novels in which Navajo policemen, Jimmy Chee and Joe Leaphorn, are the heroes. Aided by his mentor, Lt. Joe Leaphorn (Fred Ward), and his friend, Hopi policeman Cowboy Albert Dashee (Gary Farmer), an inexperienced Jimmy Chee (Lou Diamond Phillips) brings to justice evil federal agents and a serial killer. At the end, Jimmy Chee, who also serves as voice-over narrator, is accepted as a policeman and as a traditional Navajo singer and healer. Shot on the Navajo Reservation, the film gives a sense of the area and the tribe, especially when minor characters (played by Navajo actors) speak their native language (with English subtitles).

Lakota Woman (Turner Pictures, 1994). Frank Pierson

Subtitled "Siege at Wounded Knee," this film tells the story of Mary Crow Dog (Irene Bedard) from the early days of her Christian schooling to her activities as an AIM member. Torn between the traditional views of her grandfather, Fool Bull (Floyd Red Crow Westerman), and her assimilated mother, Emily Moore (Tantoo Cardinal), she runs away from home, finally overcomes her drinking problems, and falls in love with an Apache AIM member, Spencer (Pato Hoffmann). After he leaves, the now pregnant Mary joins Leonard Crow Dog (Joseph Runningfox), Russell Means (Lawrence Bayne), Dennis Banks (Michael Horse), and Gladys Bissonnette (Lois Red Elk) in the battle with evil tribal council leader, Dick Wilson (August Schellenberg), and the takeover of Wounded Knee. At the end, after giving birth to her child and finding a new identity as a woman and Native American, Mary says in a voice-over (throughout the film, she is the voice-over narrator): "We reached out and touched our history. I was there; I saw it; it happened to me, so that our people may live."

Windigo (Allegro Films, 1994). Robert Morin
   In a remote area of Quebec, an obsessed Eddy Laroche (Donald Morin), the leader of the Aki, takes on the government and declares the traditional land of his tribe an independent state.

* * *

Clearly, the contemporary revisionist Western has become more self-conscious about using positive, and in some cases, more complex characterizations of Native Americans, though even these more carefully drawn characters are still mainly significant as contrasts to the white heroes. However, a new more empathetic view of Native American characters is emerging in Canadian films such as *Black Robe* (1991) and *Spirit Rider* (1992), and in the Turner Network movies such as *The Broken Chain* (1993) and *Lakota Woman* (1994). In the last chapter, we will look at recent independent films which are the harbingers of this new empathy for tribal cultures.

CHAPTER NINE

TRIBAL IDENTITIES: NEW IMAGES OF NATIVE AMERICANS

Recently a member of the Stockbridge Munsee Tribe in Wisconsin, the descendants of the Mohicans, reminded his audience that Cooper's novel and the 1992 *The Last of the Mohicans* had nothing to do with his tribe. We all know that in the fictions of literature and narrative films, any correspondence to real life is "purely coincidental." However, we must keep reminding ourselves that seeing Native American characters in a film is not seeing real Native American people of the past or present. Even for those of us who know Native American people and their history, this is not easy because we have witnessed the images of the Noble Red Man and Savage so many times that they simply feel comfortable. Despite knowing that the images are fantasies from the fictional past of the Westerns, we often can't completely stop ourselves from being encoded by them. For example, in *The Last of the Mohicans* (1992), the treacherous Magua (Wes Studi with a "mohawk" and bare chest), who brutally kills Uncas, is such a fine contrast to the noble and loyal Chingachgook (a well-dressed Russell Means with nice long hair), who is like a father to the hero. Or in *Dances with Wolves* (1990), the fierce leader of the Pawnee (again Wes Studi with a "mohawk" and bare chest), who riddles a mule skinner with arrows and mutilates him, balances so nicely against the noble and handsome Lakota holy man, Kicking Bird (Graham Greene with pretty hair and fancy dress), who befriends the hero. And the violent deaths of the Savage characters in these films, especially the killing of Magua by Chingachgook, seem so right. On the other hand, we resonate (we males, at least) to the deep, enduring feelings shared by the white heroes and their noble Native American friends. And, in spite of our knowledge that the characters are designed to please white audiences, we may respond to the Hollywood formula and feel a tender sympathy for these honorable Native Americans and whites as they face a sad and threatening future at the ends of the films.

However, starting in the 1970s, a few independent films broke from these comfortable images of the hostile Savage and the friendly Noble Red Man and portrayed contemporary Native Americans as fictional characters significant in and of themselves, not only as contrasts to the white heroes, as is always the case in the Westerns. In *House Made of Dawn* (1972), *Three Warriors* (1977), *Spirit of the Wind* (1979), *Harold of Orange* (1984), *Journey to Spirit Island* (1988) and *Powwow Highway* (1988), principal Native American characters, played by Native American actors, find strength and identity in a return to traditional tribal values and rituals. Although these characters are also fictional, and sometimes sanitized versions of their counterparts in the novels, they allow the films to explore contemporary themes of life on reservations as contrasted to that in the cities, Elders as teachers in extended Indian families, and the power of dreams, trickster stories and traditional warrior rituals. Such themes drawn from the real world build toward an understanding of Native American tribal traditions as distinct and worthy of respect. This understanding is a step away from the comfortable images of the Western, and a step towards the sometimes uncomfortable knowledge that can lead to empathy for Native American cultures.

House Made of Dawn (1972), with a screenplay written by N. Scott Momaday from his novel, is the most complicated and disturbing of these films. Like the novel, the film has a circular structure in that it starts and finishes with the main character, Abel (Larry Littlebird), running a ceremonial course which his Grandfather (Mesa Bird) had run many years before. The remainder of the film is a fabric of flashbacks and voice-overs which tell the story of Abel's growing up with his Grandfather, his fighting in Vietnam, his killing of an evil albino and serving a prison term, and his attempt to survive in Los Angeles. This central part of the film dramatizes Abel's struggle before he returns to his reservation for the ceremonial run. His two choices are the traditional ways of his Grandfather or life in the city as represented by his Navajo friend, Ben Bennally (Jay Varela), Millie, a white social worker, and John Tosomah (John Saxon), a priest of an urban Native American church.

At the beginning of the film, Abel is with his dying Grandfather, who had been his teacher and his only family. After the old man's death, Abel, seen from a high-angle perspective, prepares for the ritual of the run by taking off his shirt, removing the bandages from his hands (the result of a severe beating by a city policeman), and rubbing himself with ashes. This perspective, which emphasizes his vulnerability at the beginning of the ceremony, will be reversed at the end of the film when he completes the run. As Abel takes his first steps, a voice-over translation of his Grandfather's Pueblo language describes how the old man had run the race many years ago and concludes with, "Those who run are the life that flows in our people." While Abel runs ever more vigorously, the audience finds out through flashbacks why Abel decided to return to his Grandfather's land for this healing run.

In the main flashback to his life in Los Angeles, Abel encounters Tosomah, Millie and Ben. Tosomah, because of his intensely verbal, intellectual and cynical approach to life, has little effect on Abel: in a peyote ceremony led by the priest, Abel is the only one who cannot express his feelings in words. This suggests that, unlike the rituals of his grandfather, the non-traditional ceremonies of Tosomah have no power for him. Millie, the white social worker, has a stronger effect because she and Abel fall in love. However, this romance is very low key and when Millie sees that the city has literally and figuratively beaten up Abel, she advises him to go home. He accepts separation from her with little emotional strain. Abel's main struggle is the decision to separate from the only true friend he's ever had, Ben Bennally.

Ben Bennally has learned how to survive in the city by

accepting the new ways of Tosomah and giving in to the dominance of his foreman and an evil policeman. After a meeting with the policeman during which Ben's hands shake with fear and Abel's remain still, Abel asks Ben, "What happened? Don't you ever want to go home?" Ben answers, "Ain't nothing back there. Just old people dying." In addition to cutting himself off from his relatives and compromising his self-respect, Ben has lost contact with his basic Navajo traditions. When he tries to sing one of his tribal songs, he cannot remember it and needs Abel to sing it for him. Later, after Abel stands up to the evil policeman and takes a terrible beating, he finally realizes that he is too different from his friend to survive in the city. With Ben's encouragement, he decides to go home. At a bus depot, Abel and Ben say good-bye in a scene that brings the contrasts between them to a touching climax. Seen in two shots and individual close-ups, the two characters, skilfully underplayed by the actors, barely hold back their tears as they speak to each other slowly and quietly. Abel asks, "What's it going to be like?" Ben replies, "Sometime we'll meet out there and get drunk. We'll go out real early; we'll just see how it is out on the mesa. We'll sing the old songs and we'll get drunk and it will be the last time and it will be beautiful, the way it used to be, the way it always was." The scene ends with a close-up of Abel, whose eyes show the realization that he will never see his friend again.

The film makes the transition from this somber farewell back to the frame of the ceremonial run. At this point Abel, who has run a long way, falls and lies on the ground, panting with exhaustion until he again hears the words, "those who run are the life that flows in the people." This reminder of the run's spiritual and symbolic meaning gives him the courage to get up and run on. Soon Abel finds his wind and, seen from a low angle which emphasizes his new strength, runs up the ridges and changes into the traditional runner with long hair and a breechclout. Then, bathed in golden light, he runs freely towards the sun and a new identity based on the old values, an ending more unequivocally positive than that of the novel.

Though a less intense and literate film, *Spirit of the Wind*

(1979) also focuses on the relationship between identity and a return to the land and traditional values. Based on the life of George Attla, an Athabascan who overcame tuberculosis to become a champion dog sled racer, this film portrays the dynamics of a Native American family living in the back country of Alaska. Unlike Abel, George Attla, Jr. (Pius Savage) is surrounded by a loving family. His father, George Attla, Sr. (George Clutesi) has the patience to let his son make his own decisions. When George Jr. leaves his family because of his identity crisis, he eventually has the help of an extended family in the person of Moses Paul (Chief Dan George), who becomes a kind of grandfather for the young man. Without the traditional wisdom of these two Elders, George would never have found the strength and identity to become a champion.

When George is a young man, his father teaches him by example the skills of trapping and negotiating for the best possible prices for the finished pelts. A calm and dignified man, he shows his wisdom even when he has a trapping accident. After he catches his hand in a trap and George looks at the deep cut across his fingers, he says to his son, "I've been catching animals all my life; it's only fair that I catch myself once." Another example of his father's concern and humor occurs later, after George has spent years in the city recuperating from the tuberculosis that permanently crippled his leg. When George is about to make a deal for a lead sled dog with crafty old Moses Paul, his father says to the old man, "You've got to go easy on George; he's been around white men too long." George, however, has learned to deal from his father, and makes a clever bargain to get Jarvy, the dog that will lead his championship teams. A last example of his father's wisdom is some advice he gives George. Referring to the fighting and drinking the young men of the tribe do in the cities, he tells George, "If a man wants to prove himself, the land is the place for it." This, however, is a lesson George will not learn until he decides to leave his family.

Despite the patient support of his family, beautifully portrayed in a summer fishing camp sequence with the chanting of Buffy St. Marie in the background, George finally decides he doesn't fit with them. After he injures one of his father's dogs in a race and his father reacts with typical patience, George yells, "I'm not you! . . . I feel like two different people and I don't know what to do." George leaves for the city and ends up washing dishes at an oriental restaurant where he sees Moses Paul one evening. Moses insists that George come with him for the winter trapping season (he thinks George can cook Chinese food), and during this time, acting as a grandfather in an extended family, convinces George that if he wants to be a dog sled racer he must learn from his father. George heeds the advice of Moses and returns to his home, where he can find the traditional knowledge he needs.

After his return to his family, George and his father train Jarvy and the rest of the team in the old ways, and he wins his first big race in Anchorage. When George celebrates his victory by hugging Jarvy and the announcer praises the dog, the film cuts to his father and Moses listening on the radio, and Moses, with a twinkle in his eye, says, "I knew I should have kept that dog." Only Chief Dan George could read that line so perfectly, just as only George Clutesi, a noted Canadian Native actor, could respond with just the right sly smile. Their acting, along with that of the rest of the Native cast, and the singing of Buffy St. Marie in the background, provide the audience with a picture of a very different culture, one that is worthy of respect.

Native American actors infuse the same quality into *Three Warriors* (1977), another film in which a young Native American finds a new identity by a return to his reservation and the values of his Grandfather (Charles White Eagle). Sensing that his grandson, Michael (McKee Redwing), a teenager who is ashamed to be a Native American, needs help, the old man summons his daughter-in-law (Lois Red Elk) and her family to the reservation. Michael, of course, doesn't want to be there and not only does a lot of sulking, but also is rude to his Grandfather. Like George Attla, Sr., however, the old man has the patience of one who knows how to teach by example. Seen in a low-angle shot (the camera establishes his significance with a pattern of low-angle and close-up shots), he assures his daughter-in-law that "Michael will find peace." However, before the Grandfather teaches Michael the pride of the traditional warrior, he decides to educate a young U.S. Ranger who is assigned to protecting the wild horses on federal land near the reservation.

As the Ranger berates the people of the village for not helping to protect the mustangs (with Michael watching), Grandfather reminds him that "they're your horses," and then teaches him a lesson in politeness. When the Ranger asks him why he cooperated with the former Ranger, Grandfather replies that the other Ranger had learned how to be polite in the Native American way by always saying when he met him, "Hey, Uncle, how's your bones?" Then Grandfather, displaying the shrewdness of the trickster, manipulates the Ranger into giving him and Michael a ride to a rodeo, where he buys, for a very low price, a fine Palomino. Though the horse appears to be broken down, the old man, a very knowledgeable horseman, can see that it is just temporarily lame. Later, he cons the Ranger into taking them and the horse back to the reservation. When the Ranger drops them off, he says to the old man, "Hey, Uncle, how's your bones," and Grandfather acknowledges his politeness by inviting him to supper.

Though Michael has witnessed all of this, he still doesn't understand the cleverness and wisdom of the old man; in fact he still thinks his Grandfather is "a stupid old man." However, he soon learns his lesson when he is forced to accompany his Grandfather into the mountains. With all the whining of a typical teenager, Michael still resists his Grandfather. For example, when he fails to secure their food in a tree as he had been told to do, a bear takes it and he and his Grandfather have a very sparse supper. Holding the only can left behind by the bear, Grandfather, with a sly smile, says to the boy, "Tomorrow I will tell you what our people did—*before* chicken gumbo soup." The next day he makes a bow and arrows for Michael, teaches him how to fish, and tells him about the strength the eagle feather gives to the warrior. Then he sends Michael and his horse to the secret springs of the warriors for their healing ritual. When the boy returns, he asks about his father, a man who had been a source of shame for him. His grandfather explains that his son was a warrior, a good man who sometimes drank because he couldn't take the pain of his times. After this painful revelation, Grandfather teaches Michael how to catch the eagle and pull a feather from its tail. After Michael succeeds, he gives the feather to his Grandfather in recognition of his new love for him and his father. As a final indication of his pride, he names his horse "Three Warriors" after his Grandfather, father and himself.

In the last part of the film, he shows his strength as a warrior by rescuing his horse from evil rustlers who are slaughtering mustangs for their meat. Though this part has a certain "kids' show" quality, it does lead to a strong, emotional ending. His Grandfather and Michael are seen in an intimate close-up of their heads as the old man shows his understanding of the challenges the young man will face: "You have learned the old ways, Michael, but they are not the only ways. Yours is a new song, the song of a proud warrior. This song will stay in your heart as you learn the new ways. You will come back."

In a more recent film, *Journey to Spirit Island* (1988), such a healing relationship between a grandparent and a teenage Native American is reversed to that of a young Nahkut woman, Maria (Bettina), and her Grandmother, Jimmy Jim (Marie Antoinette Rodgers). At the beginning of this film, which is beautifully photographed by Vilmos Zsigmond, Maria sits on the top of a jutting cliff by the sea, where she is seen first from a low-angle long shot and then in close-ups (a pattern of such shots throughout the film establishes her as a strong central character). As she writes in her journal, she asks herself in a voice-over, "Why is it so hard to be an Indian?" and "Did Raven really make the trees and paint the birds?" This setting and the journal are frames the film returns to at the end when she has found her strength and pride. Maria is not only struggling with her identity but also with recurring dreams about Spirit Island, where the spirit of her great grandfather, Tupshin, a shaman, still is trying to free the soul of his son who died on the island. Her

Grandmother, who has had the same dreams, understands what Maria is going through and becomes her teacher and protector.

Her Grandmother takes Maria to a tribal council meeting where a member of the tribe, Hawk (Tony Acierto), and his friend, a white businessman, are trying to persuade the council to develop and build on Spirit Island. Grandmother tells the council that protecting the island is not a matter of profit "but our spiritual life," and, as she concludes with "Respect the sacred place," a wind comes through the room. Later Maria writes in her journal that "something is going on," and then has a dream about Tupshin and herself on the island. When she tells her Grandmother about the dream, the old woman gives her an amulet to protect her and then blesses the cedar canoe that Maria and her brother, Klim (Tarek McCarthy), will use on a trip to the islands. Two white boys who are visiting from Chicago, the youngest of whom adds humor to the film with his wild misconceptions about Native Americans, join Maria and her brother on their trip. At this point, Maria must become a leader, determine the meaning of her dreams and prove herself without any direct help from her Grandmother.

After an accident with one of the boats, all the kids get in the cedar canoe, which is then drawn by a powerful force to Spirit Island. That night Maria tells the story of Tupshin to her white friends and then dreams of things that will happen to her on the island. The next day they search for the canoe, which has disappeared, and Maria tells her teenage friend, Michael, "I don't know what's going on. You think because I'm Indian I should know all the great mystical secrets. Those are two completely different worlds. I know just enough about the old ways to scare me." Shortly thereafter, they find the bones of Tupshin's son and an amulet that matches the one given her by Grandmother. Then Maria puts the bones in a cloth, buries them in the bow of his boat, and does a ceremonial dance she learned from her Grandmother.

Meanwhile, the evil Hawk and his tough-guy sidekick arrive at the island to get rid of the eagles there, the last legal obstacle to the planned development. After they chase the young people into a cave and seal them in with a boulder, Maria comes to the rescue. Strengthened by a vision of her Grandmother and using the knowledge gained from her dreams, Maria finds a way out by swimming through a tunnel to the shore of the island. Then they find the canoe and return to the mainland just in time to foil Hawk. As they rush into the tribal council meeting, the contract has just been signed despite the opposition of Grandmother. However, when Hawk's white friend hears about his machinations from the kids, he tears up the contract. As with *Three Warriors*, this last part of the film is standard family show adventure fare, but it also offers an ending with a strong image of a young Native American woman who understands the power of dreams in her culture and her own new identity. The camera zooms in on Maria as she again sits on the cliff seen at the beginning. She writes in her journal and says in a voice-over, "I feel so different since we buried the bones. Tupshin can rest now. I'm not afraid of my dreams anymore. Grandmother says we have Great Grandfather to thank for all this. Thank you!" Maria is now a proud member of her tribe and has a new sense of its history.

Though each of the above films has some nice touches of humor, they all focus on serious, and sometimes wrenching, changes in the central characters. Like these films, *Harold of Orange* (1984) deals with the power of tribal traditions, but in the humorous fashion of trickster stories. In fact, this short film (c. 30 min.), with a screenplay by Gerald Vizenor, is a contemporary trickster tale in which Harold Sinseer (Charlie Hill) and his merry band survive by conning grant foundations. At the beginning, Harold speaks to the audience in a monologue: "We are the warriors of Orange, tricksters in the new school of social acupuncture where a little pressure fills the pocket book. We keep a clean coffee house, tend to our miniature oranges and speak about mythic revolutions on the reservation. What more is there to tell?" He then joins his fellow warriors and hands out old ties which they put on as amulets before they board their orange bus and head for the city and a meeting with the grant foundation. Having already received a grant for growing miniature orange trees on a remote part of the reservation, they are now out for a new grant to fund the building of coffee houses on the reservation, where they will serve a unique new pinch bean brew. In the city, Harold, seen from a low angle that suggests his power over the grant foundation, gives a bogus presentation to foundation members. Then he invites them to join his warriors on the orange bus for a trip to a park where they will play an Anglos-vs-"Indians" softball game, one the warriors intentionally lose to butter up the members before they vote on the grant.

On this trip, a rather twitty little man, known to be very skeptical about the new grant request, finally gets the attention of the warrior of Orange sitting next to him and listening to tribal songs on his headphones. The little man tells him that he had just read an article in *National Geographic* about the population of Indians at the time of Columbus. The warrior responds, "Who?" and the white man asks again, "How many Indians were here then?" The warrior answers, "None. Not one. Columbus never discovered anything and when he never did, he invented us as Indians because we never heard the term before he dropped it by accident." Then the man says, "Let me rephrase the question. How many tribal people were here when Columbus invented Indians?" The warrior replies, "49,732,000,196 . . ." and the man, with a sheepish look, says, "Well, I see—that many." This is just one of numerous examples in which the warriors of Orange use the methods of the trickster to tease and manipulate the white characters.

After the softball game, in which Harold wears layers of red "Indian" tee shirts and white "Anglo" tee shirts so he can change sides at will (like the trickster), everyone goes back to the foundation for the vote on the grant. Ironically, at the meeting the little man who is opposed to the grant asks a racist question, a mistake that motivates the rest of the politically-correct group to award the grant. After his latest success, Harold plays one more trick by talking the head of the foundation out of $1000 for what will be his Grandmother's second $1000 traditional funeral. At the end, then, Harold and his warriors have survived and even prospered by understanding that the traditional spirit of the trickster will enable them to befuddle and ultimately control those who are in power.

In *Powwow Highway* (1988), the traditions of the warrior and the trickster are also the key to the survival and identity of the two central characters, Buddy Red Bow (A. Martinez) and Philbert Bono (Gary Farmer). Based on the zany and rather excessive novel by David Seals, the film makes the two main characters more noble than their counterparts in the novel and both cleans up and diminishes the main female character, Bonnie Red Bow (Joanelle Nadine). In the film, the pivotal character is Philbert, a hulking Cheyenne who, like the trickster, is always hungry for food and adventure. His transformation into a warrior progresses as he gathers power by drawing on the Cheyenne traditions of the war horse, the medicine bundle and the stories of the trickster, Wihio. Like the trickster, Philbert moves in strange and seemingly misguided ways to the warrior identity, but in the process makes a believer of the cynical Buddy.

Philbert's decision to acquire a war pony, one that turns out to be a dilapidated old car, is his first step towards becoming a warrior. He gets the idea from a TV ad in which a car salesman, wearing a war bonnet, sits on the hood of a car and says, "Come off the 'res' and pick up your war pony today." Like the vigilant trickster, Philbert finds the right course of action from a most unlikely electronic source, just as he does later when he watches a scene from a W. S. Hart western and gets the idea of pulling the bars off Bonnie Red Bow's jail cell. At the used car lot, when he looks out the window at an old brown Buick, he has a vision (enhanced with electronic music and golden lighting) of a pinto running in slow motion. Knowing that this car, a castoff of white society, will become a magic pony if infused with the warrior spirit, he trades a lid of marijuana for it and names it Protector. His willingness to give up the marijuana for his war pony is significant because it marks his rejection of a non-traditional drug to gain the power of the traditional warrior.

Now that Philbert has found his war pony, he is ready to continue his quest to become a warrior, a quest that takes shape when Buddy asks him for a ride to Sante Fe where his sister, Bonnie, has been framed by the local police, and put in jail. Philbert agrees and shares Buddy's joint (an action he never repeats after he becomes a warrior). As they drive away from the reservation, Buddy asks him if he can count on him, and Philbert, already showing his warrior pride, answers in their native tongue, "We are Cheyenne!" However, Philbert's growth as a warrior is not complete and another electronic device, this time a CD radio Buddy had installed in the car, speaks to the potential trickster and warrior in him. After being asked by a Native American truck driver for his warrior name, he tells him that he knows part of it is Whirlwind. The man tells him to visit Bear Butte, the most sacred place in South Dakota, and he turns the car directly away from their destination.

While Buddy sleeps through the whole event, Philbert arrives at Bear Butte, the place the legendary Cheyenne holy man, Sweet Medicine, performed the sacred ceremonies of the tribe (the film uses different names for the place and holy man). After he makes it half way to the top, he finds a frame of a sweatlodge and in it he sleeps and has a vision of Sweet Medicine, who offers him the sacred pipe. At the top, just as he is about to bite into his Hersey bar, he sees gifts for the spirits left in the trees by other Native Americans, and he leaves his candy bar, a tremendous sacrifice for him. Then he has a vision of being an eagle who sees for miles in every direction. His elation at finding his ancestral past and the rest of his warrior name, Dreamer, is so great that on his return he rolls down the last part of the butte. At the bottom, he meets Buddy, who has just found out that they are in South Dakota rather than Colorado. Buddy yells at him, but backs off when Philbert, now aware of his own strength, lifts him off the ground and lets him know he will never be pushed around again.

After they are on the road again, Philbert's new awareness that religious power is essential to the warrior prompts him to stop the car at a river so he can sing a song to the setting sun. Despite Buddy's complaints, he walks into the river and sings until Buddy joins him and haltingly starts to sing with him. After a touching silhouette shot of the two friends singing vigorously together, the two men return to the car, where Philbert finds a pebble in his boot that becomes the first token for his warrior's medicine bundle. He finds the second token after stopping in a snow storm in Nebraska to look at the historical marker for Fort Robinson. After he has a vision of Dull Knife and his Cheyenne people escaping from the fort, he finds a white stone of the ancestors for his bundle. He doesn't find the third token until he has proved himself as a warrior. At the end of the film, after his car has crashed down a steep hill and burst into flames, he miraculously escapes and walks up the hill holding the door handle, which will then protect him after the loss of his war pony, Protector. The traditional bundle, however, has four tokens, as Philbert tells Bonnie's son. So even after Philbert has completed his quest to rescue Bonnie (and thus after the end of the film), he still must be looking for a new token to continue his growth as a Cheyenne warrior.

In addition to the medicine bundle and war pony, Philbert also has the knowledge of the warrior because he has been taught the traditional stories of his people. With the large smoke stacks of a plant in the background, he tells a trickster story to Buddy and his friends Wolf Tooth (Wayne Waterman) and Imogene (Margo Kane). Seen from a low angle which emphasizes the authority of his words, he says, "Wihio the trickster is sometimes a man and sometimes an animal, but he mostly likes pulling antics and telling dirty jokes. One day he saw some plums floating down the creek. Now Wihio loves to eat so he reached for the plums, but they disappeared and he fell into the creek. He crawled out all soaking wet and saw the plums again shimmering in the water and he kept diving and they kept disappearing." Philbert then explains that three days later Wihio's wife found him and, after he told her what had happened, she says, "Stupid dog of a dog! The plums are still on the tree." Then she tells him that he is like those people "chasing shadows while the true thing is hanging right over their heads." After Philbert finishes his story by noting that Wihio's wife hit him over the head with a pan, Wolf Tooth and Imogene praise him for his knowledge, but Buddy sees the story as a fairy tale that has no relevance to modern reservations where white men are stealing natural resources. Philbert responds that the "trickster won't let this happen. Wihio is the creator of the universe. He will play a little trick on the white man. Wait, you will see."

Philbert's trickster story dramatizes the difference between Buddy and himself. Philbert has gained the power of the warrior by looking in the right places, inside himself and at the traditional values of his tribe. Buddy, on the other hand, like Wihio, is looking in the wrong places, outside of his tradition and only at the evils of white society. Filled with anger and righteousness, he thinks like the white liberal he hates, always considering the big issues and blaming others rather than himself. As these two unlikely buddies approach Sante Fe, another incident underscores the differences between them. While Buddy is reaching for his pistol under the dashboard, he finds a tarantula and is about to smash it when Philbert swerves the car to save the spider. When Buddy falls out of the car and sees that his gun is broken, he yells at his friend, who calmly reminds him that "the trickster takes many forms. We must keep our medicine good." Now Buddy, the Vietnam veteran and member of AIM, will not be able to solve his problems with the violence of the gun. On the other hand, Philbert recognizes that the spider is sacred to his people and may even be a trickster who will help them accomplish their quest. Also, Philbert is now so infused with the warrior spirit that he realizes he no longer needs marijuana and refuses the joint Buddy offers him.

In fact, Buddy never does rescue his sister, Bonnie. That feat belongs to Philbert, who has earned his warrior name, Whirlwind Dreamer, and has found two of the four tokens for his medicine bundle. With the help of his Buick war pony, only Philbert has the magic to pull the bars and part of the wall from Bonnie's cell, rescue her and Buddy, elude the police and government agents, escape a seemingly fatal car accident and walk off with his friends to a new and better life on the reservation. Though this ending might seem like a fairy tale to some viewers, it can also be read as the conclusion to a trickster story in which Philbert mixes the tricks of the cowboy hero (or even the knight in shining armor) with his own power of the Cheyenne warrior and beats them all. As he said earlier in the film, "the trickster will play a little trick on the white man." This is what Philbert has just done, and will probably do again as he searches for his fourth token in the process of growing into a new kind of Cheyenne warrior, one who can survive and prosper in the modern world.

Like the other films, *Powwow Highway* reveals the power of traditional tribal values for contemporary Native American characters. On the level of content and theme, all these independent films promote empathy by depicting the details of tribal cultures fully enough for white audiences to see that they are different from their own, but worthy of respect. To a much greater degree than even the most enlightened Westerns, they also reveal the flavor of Native American life in various parts of the country. Woven into their plots are the simple realities of life such as preparing meals, joking and arguing at the supper table, washing clothes, or struggling to get up in the morning. Such details humanize the Native American characters in a way largely nonexistent in the Hollywood films.

On the level of film technique, these independent films enhance their portrayals by the use of Native American actors whose film presence and acting skill give a strong impression of the characters as unique human beings. In fact, a character like Philbert in *Powwow Highway* is almost unimaginable without Gary Farmer playing him, as is Grandfather in *Three Warriors* without Charles White Eagle. As we have seen above, patterns of low-angle and close-up shots underscore the stature of the principal characters, as does their placement in the most prominent parts of the frame. Finally, the background music, especially that written and performed by Native Americans, also builds the unique ambiance of the films.

Though *House Made of Dawn, Spirit of the Wind, Three Warriors, Journey to Spirit Island, Harold of Orange* and *Powwow Highway* do not match the glossy production standards of Hollywood films, all are of high enough quality to entertain and move the general film audience in positive ways. However, what has given these films the freedom to avoid the formulas of Hollywood, that is, their status as independent productions, has also limited them to small audiences. Our challenge is to find a larger audience by using them in high school and college courses, by including them in university and public library film programs, and by requesting that they be shown on public and commercial TV.

If enough people can see these films, maybe the images of the Savage and Noble Red Man will fade into the sunset. In 1967, a Native American writer considered the effect of the Hollywood Indians on his children: "I think they wonder, when are we ever going to win? I remember seeing such a movie when one of my boys was a kid. We came out of the movies and he pulled my hand and said, 'Daddy, we pretty near won that one'." (Armstrong, 155). These independent films just might let Native American people of today finally win one.

WORKS CITED

Armstrong, Virginia I., ed. *I Have Spoken. American History Through the Voices of Indians*. Athens, OH: Swallow, 1971.

Biskind, Peter. *Seeing Is Believing: How Hollywood Taught Us to Stop Worrying and Love the Fifties*. New York: Pantheon, 1983.

Bogdanovich, Peter. *John Ford*. Berkeley: U. of California P., 1968.

Bowser, Eileen, comp. *Biograph Bulletins, 1908–1912*. New York: Farrar, 1973.

Brownlow, Kevin. *The War, the West and the Wilderness*. New York: Knopf, 1979.

Buscombe, Edward, ed. *The BFI Companion to the Western*. New York: Atheneum, 1988.

Calder, Jenni. *There Must Be a Lone Ranger: The American West in Film and in Reality*. New York: McGraw-Hill, 1977.

Cody, Iron Eyes. *Iron Eyes: My Life as a Hollywood Indian* (as told to Collin Perry). New York: Everest House, 1982.

Cooper, James F. *Last of the Mohicans. Works of Fenimore Cooper*, Vol. II. New York: Collier, 1892.

Friar, Ralph E. and Natasha A. *The Only Good Indian . . . : The Hollywood Gospel*. New York: Drama Book Specialists, 1972.

Jameson, Fredric. *Signatures of the Visible*. New York: Routledge, 1992.

Marsden, Michael, and Jack Nachbar. "Images of Native Americans in Popular Film," *Course File, AFI Education Newsletter*, Sept-Oct., 1980, 4–7.

The New York Times Film Reviews. Plus Supplements. New York: New York Times, 1970.

Niver, Kemp R., comp. *Biograph Bulletins, 1896–1908*. Los Angeles: Artisan P., 1971.

O'Connor, John E. *The Hollywood Indian : Stereotypes of Native Americans in Films*. Trenton, NJ: New Jersey State Museum, 1980.

Parish, James R., and Michael R. Pitts. *The Great Western Pictures*. Metuchen, NJ: Scarecrow, 1976.

Price, John A. "The Stereotyping of North American Indians in

Motion Pictures," *The Pretend Indian.* Eds. Gretchen M. Bataille and Charles L. Silet. Ames: Iowa State U. P., 1980.

Spears, Jack. "The Indian on the Screen," *Hollywood: The Golden Era.* New York: Barnes, 1971.

Spehr, Paul C. *The Movies Begin: Making Movies in New Jersey,1887–1920.* Newark, NJ: Newark Museum, 1977.

Stedman, Raymond W. *Shadows of the Indian.* Norman: U. of Oklahoma P., 1982.

Tuska, Jon. *The American Western in Film.* Lincoln: U. of Nebraska P., 1988.

———. *The Filming of the West.* New York: Doubleday, 1976.

Variety Film Reviews: 1907–1984. Plus Supplements. New York: Garland, 1983.

Weaver, John T. *Twenty Years of Silents.* Metuchen, NJ: Scarecrow, 1971.

WORKS CONSULTED

Adams, Les, and Buck Rainey. *Shoot-Em-Ups: A Complete Reference Guide to Westerns of the Sound Era*. Metuchen, NJ: Scarecrow, 1986.

Balshofer, Fred J., and Arthur C. Miller. *One Reel a Week*. Berkeley: U. of California P., 1967.

Bataille, Gretchen M., and Charles L.P. Silet, eds. "Annotated Checklist of Articles and Books on the Popular Images of the Indian in American Film," *The Pretend Indian*. Ames: Iowa State U. P., 1980.

Frayling, Christopher. *Spaghetti Westerns*. London: Routledge, 1981.

French, Philip. *Westerns: Aspects of a Movie Genre*. London: Secker and Warburg, 1973.

Garfield, Brian. *Western Films*. New York: Rawson Assoc., 1982.

Henderson, Robert M. *D.W. Griffith: The Years at Biograph*. New York: Farrar, 1970.

Krafsur, Richard P., ed. *The American Film Institute Catalogue: Feature Films, 1961–1970*. New York: Bowker, 1976.

Leonard, Harold, ed. *The Film Index: A Bibliography*. Vol. 1. *The Film as Art*. New York: Museum of Modern Art Film Library and H.W. Wilson, 1941.

Logsdon, Judith, "The Princess and the Squaw: Images of American Indian Women in Cinema Rouge." *Women's Studies Librarian*, Summer, 1992 (U. of Wisconsin System): 13–17.

Miller, Randall M., ed. *The Kaleidoscopic Lens: How Hollywood Views the Ethnic Groups*. Englewood, NJ: Jerome S. Ozer, 1980.

Munden, Kenneth W. *The American Film Institute Catalogue: Feature Films 1921–1930*. New York: Bowker, 1971.

Nachbar, Jack and Others. *Western Films 2. An Annotated Critical Bibliograhy from 1974–1987*. New York: Garland, 1988.

O'Connor, John E., and Martin A. Jackson, eds. *American History/American Film: Interpreting the Hollywood Image*. New York: Ungar, 1979.

Pilkington, William T., and Don Graham. *Western Movies*. Albuquerque: U. of New Mexico P., 1979.

Place, J.A. *The Western Films of John Ford*. New York: Citadel, 1974.

Rothel, David. *Who Was That Masked Man? The Story of the Lone Ranger*. New York: Barnes, 1976.

Sandoux, Jean Jacques. *Racism in Western Film from D. W. Griffith to John Ford: Indians and Blacks*. New York: Revisionist P., 1980.

Sarf, Wayne Michael. *God Bless You, Buffalo Bill: A Layman's Guide to History and the Western Film*. East Brunswick, NJ: Associated U. P., 1983.

Solomon, Stanley J. *Beyond Formulas: American Film Genres*. New York: Harcourt, 1976.

Tompkins, Jane. *West of Everything: The Inner Life of Westerns*. New York: Oxford U. P.,1992.

Weiss, Ken, and Ed Goodgold. *To Be Continued . . .* New York: Crown, 1972.

GENERAL INDEX

FILM TITLE INDEX

ABOUT THE AUTHOR

MICHAEL HILGER (B.A. College of St. Thomas; M.A. Creighton U.; Ph.D. University of Nebraska-Lincoln) is a Professor of English and Film at the University of Wisconsin-Eau Claire. In addition to teaching a course called The American Indian in Literature and Film, he has produced video documentaries on the oral history and folk stories of the Lac Court Oreilles Chippewa Band in Wisconsin. He has also published a filmography entitled *The American Indian In Film* (Scarecrow, 1986).